PolyBase Revealed

Data Virtualization with SQL Server, Hadoop, Apache Spark, and Beyond

Kevin Feasel

Apress®

PolyBase Revealed: Data Virtualization with SQL Server, Hadoop, Apache Spark, and Beyond

Kevin Feasel
Durham, NC, USA

ISBN-13 (pbk): 978-1-4842-5460-8   ISBN-13 (electronic): 978-1-4842-5461-5
https://doi.org/10.1007/978-1-4842-5461-5

Managing Director, Apress Media LLC: Welmoed Spahr
Acquisitions Editor: Jonathan Gennick
Development Editor: Laura Berendson
Coordinating Editor: Jill Balzano

Cover image designed by Freepik (www.freepik.com)

Distributed to the book trade worldwide by Springer Science+Business Media New York, 233 Spring Street, 6th Floor, New York, NY 10013. Phone 1-800-SPRINGER, fax (201) 348-4505, e-mail orders-ny@springer-sbm.com, or visit www.springeronline.com. Apress Media, LLC is a California LLC and the sole member (owner) is Springer Science + Business Media Finance Inc (SSBM Finance Inc). SSBM Finance Inc is a **Delaware** corporation.

For information on translations, please e-mail rights@apress.com, or visit http://www.apress.com/rights-permissions.

Apress titles may be purchased in bulk for academic, corporate, or promotional use. eBook versions and licenses are also available for most titles. For more information, reference our Print and eBook Bulk Sales web page at http://www.apress.com/bulk-sales.

Any source code or other supplementary material referenced by the author in this book is available to readers on GitHub via the book's product page, located at www.apress.com/9781484254608. For more detailed information, please visit http://www.apress.com/source-code.

Printed on acid-free paper

To my wife Jialin. It turns out I actually was doing something all those hours cooped up in the office.

Table of Contents

About the Author

Kevin Feasel is a Microsoft Data Platform MVP and CTO at Envizage, where he specializes in T-SQL and R development, forcing Spark clusters to do his bidding, fighting with Kafka, and pulling rabbits out of hats on demand. He is the lead curator at Curated SQL (`https://curatedsql.com`).

A resident of Durham, North Carolina, Kevin can be found cycling the trails along the Triangle whenever the weather is nice enough.

About the Technical Reviewer

 **Ike Ellis** has over 18 years of experience in data engineering. He's a current Microsoft MVP. He is the General Manager of Data & AI for Solliance. He is a partner in Crafting Bytes, a San Diego software studio and Data Engineering group. He is an author who has written several books on Microsoft data and Azure topics. Ike has spoken at conferences around the world including PASS Summit, SQLBits, DevIntersection, TechEd, TechEd Europe, and SQL in the City. He'll be speaking at Craft in Romania in 2020. For more information, see www.ikeellis.com or follow him on Twitter at @ike_ellis.

Acknowledgments

This book is the product of many hours of research, rants, and head-scratching moments. Most of the head-scratching was mine, and I could not have written this book without the help of some very smart people. First, I would like to thank several Microsoft employees. Murshed Zaman gets top billing here for starting me on my PolyBase journey and helping solve my initial problems. James Rowland-Jones is next—James patiently explained various PolyBase details to me over and over, until I finally got them. Eric Burgess, Nathan Schoenack, and Suresh Kandoth at Microsoft CSS helped me understand common pain points and shaped the direction of several chapters, particularly Chapter 5. Finally, Jasraj Dange and Weiyun Huang helped connect the dots on PolyBase V2 functionality and left me excited about the future of the technology beyond SQL Server 2019.

I am grateful to Bill Preachuk and Scott Shaw at Cloudera (and previously, when they were at Hortonworks) for helping me through several land mines early on when working with Hadoop. I'll never forget going back and forth between Murshed at CAT and Bill and Scott at the Hortonworks booth at PASS Summit trying to get PolyBase and the Hortonworks Data Platform sandbox working at the same time on my laptop.

In addition to these two companies, I am heavily indebted to several people in the community. Ike Ellis is the best technical editor I could have asked for, at least until he calls in the favor. Gerhard Brueckl was great to bounce ideas off of and provided me with insights I never would have discovered otherwise. Jason Horner helped me test things I thought I knew about the product and made this book better as a result. Hasan Savran taught me most of what I know about Cosmos DB, though don't hold my limitations against him. There are plenty of others who played a role in this book, and I thank you all for it.

As is natural in these works, any errors which remain are mine and mine alone, although I will probably try to blame gremlins.

Introduction

This is an exciting time to be a data platform professional. Over the past decade, we have seen a proliferation of data platform technologies, all trying to solve the critical problem of our era: collecting, storing, managing, and querying ever-increasing amounts of data. To solve this problem, we have seen the rise of technologies like Apache Hadoop, Apache Spark, Google BigTable, Amazon Redshift, Microsoft Azure Synapse Analytics, and plenty more. In the meantime, the hard core of the data platform space—relational databases—has not ossified. Each new edition of SQL Server, Oracle, and PostgreSQL has new features and the ability to handle even more data. As great as these relational database platform products are, however, they do not fit every use case. Where there are gaps, other products fill the void. This leaves data platform developers at most enterprises—even companies of moderate size—juggling data between several systems.

Historically, the way we managed this juggling act was to learn a separate language for each platform: T-SQL for SQL Server; PL/SQL for Oracle; HiveQL for Apache Hive; Spark SQL, Scala, or Python for Apache Spark; and so on. The common adoption of SQL as a general interface (sometimes in spite of product developers' wishes) has simplified the task, but each product has its own dialect of ANSI SQL, and it can be difficult to remember which operators and functions exist in one database vs. another.

Furthermore, the most common task I see in this space is some variant of Extract-Transform-Load (ETL): moving data from one system to another, sometimes reshaping it along the way, in order to combine the products of two separate systems. We spend so much time moving data within systems, going from write-heavy Online Transactional Processing (OLTP systems) into reporting-friendly Online Analytical Processing (OLAP) databases. Add different data platform technologies and the problem grows even further: now we need to combine that general ledger data from Oracle, device statuses from Spark, device metadata from SQL Server, customer data entry from Cosmos DB, and historical rollups from Teradata in order to build a neural network which will solve all of our problems. The traditional approach has been to use purpose-built ETL tools like SQL Server Integration Services or Informatica, or to write custom code in a programming language of choice. These techniques work, but they are relatively effort-heavy, particularly in maintaining this separate ETL process as the source systems evolve over time.

A modern take on the classic problem of ETL is *data virtualization*: making this data appear to come from one source system while under the covers defining links to where the data really lives. An end user or analyst can read this data using one SQL dialect and join together structured data sets from different systems without needing to know the provenance of each data set and without waiting for database developers to build in the plumbing needed to move data from one system to the next. This simplifies greatly the analyst's life and is one of the key selling points of Microsoft's PolyBase technology.

PolyBase has been around since 2010 but came to the general public in SQL Server 2016. Its purpose was to integrate SQL Server with Hadoop by allowing us to run MapReduce jobs against a remote Hadoop cluster, bringing the results back into SQL Server and thus reducing the computational burden on our relatively more expensive SQL Server instances. Now, with SQL Server 2019, PolyBase has grown and adapted to this era of data virtualization. As you will see throughout this book, PolyBase gives us the ability to integrate with a variety of source systems. In the book, we will connect to a Hadoop cluster, Azure Blob Storage, other SQL Server instances, an Oracle database, Cosmos DB, an Apache Spark cluster, Apache Hive tables, and even Microsoft Excel! This leaves out the wide variety of other data sources, such as Teradata, MongoDB, DB2, and much more. The best part of it is that our developers need only one language for all of this: T-SQL.

PolyBase is no panacea, and there are certainly trade-offs compared to storing all data natively in one source system, particularly around performance. If you do, however, have existing, disparate systems which need to interact, PolyBase has a few tricks up its sleeves to make those integrations easier.

This book is intended for database developers, database administrators, and architects looking to solve multisystem integration problems. My key assumption throughout this book is that you are already familiar with the T-SQL language but might be less familiar with different data platform technologies such as Hadoop, Spark, or Cosmos DB. Naturally, having more experience with these other data platform technologies will help considerably when dealing with the headaches which come when trying to interconnect disparate systems.

My intent in this book is as much narrative as reference, meaning that the best way to read the book is in chapter order. Even if you do not make use of a particular data platform technology, there can be key components in the chapter which apply to other technologies. In particularly important cases, I will note when this is the case so you do not miss out on critical information.

The first part of this book focuses primarily on installation and then PolyBase V1, that is, integration with Hadoop and Azure Blob Storage. Chapter 1 walks us through installation and basic configuration. Then, in Chapter 2, we connect to Azure Blob Storage and learn about the key concepts in PolyBase. Chapter 3 takes us to a Hadoop cluster and shows the requisite configuration for SQL Server as well as Hadoop. Chapter 4 dives into predicate pushdown, the most important performance feature PolyBase has to offer. Finally, in Chapter 5, we will cover common errors and issues around integration with Azure Blob Storage and Hadoop.

Chapter 6 shifts our focus to PolyBase V2 and integration with the broader data platform space. In this chapter, we will integrate with another SQL Server instance and understand how PolyBase differs from linked servers. Chapter 7 shows off integrations with Oracle followed by Cosmos DB. In Chapter 8, we take advantage of PolyBase's generic ODBC functionality and connect to Apache Spark, Apache Hive, and Microsoft Excel.

Chapter 9 looks at the version of PolyBase in Azure Synapse Analytics SQL Pools. As we will see, it is neither PolyBase V1 nor PolyBase V2, but is instead a different flavor of PolyBase.

Chapter 10 moves us to the final section of the book, where we look at performance and implementation tips. In Chapter 10, we will look at the Dynamic Management Views available in SQL Server to help us troubleshoot PolyBase issues. In Chapter 11, we will look at execution plans when PolyBase external tables come into play, as well as using statistics to help SQL Server's query optimizer make the right decisions. Finally, in Chapter 12, we will review several practical use cases for PolyBase, showing examples where you can fit this into your existing infrastructure.

CHAPTER 1

Installing and Configuring PolyBase

In this first chapter, we will install PolyBase for SQL Server 2019. The first part of this chapter will help you decide if you should install PolyBase as a standalone service or as part of a Scale-Out Group—that is, a cluster of machines working together to solve data problems in parallel. The second part of this chapter will walk you through installing PolyBase as a standalone service running on a single machine. Then we will look at the alternative: installing PolyBase as part of a PolyBase Scale-Out Group. Finally, we will cover initial PolyBase configuration, regardless of which installation method you chose. At the end of this chapter, you will have PolyBase installed on at least one machine.

Choose the Form of Your PolyBase

Before you begin installation, it is important to know whether you want to install PolyBase as a standalone service or as part of a Scale-Out Group because you will not be able to switch between the two afterward without uninstalling and reinstalling the PolyBase features. If you are using SQL Server on Linux, the only option available to you at this time is to install standalone; SQL Server on Windows allows for both installation methods. All other things equal, a Scale-Out Group is preferable to a standalone installation. The reason for this is that PolyBase is a Massively Parallel Processing (MPP) technology. This means we can scale PolyBase horizontally, improving performance by adding additional servers. But that only works if you incorporate your machine as part of a Scale-Out Group, however; as a standalone installation, your SQL Server instance will not be able to enlist the support of other SQL Server instances when using PolyBase to perform queries.

© Kevin Feasel 2020
K. Feasel, *PolyBase Revealed*, https://doi.org/10.1007/978-1-4842-5461-5_1

The preceding text makes sense when all other things are equal, but installing PolyBase as part of a Scale-Out Group has some requirements which standalone PolyBase does not. To wit, in order to install PolyBase as part of a Scale-Out Group, all of the following must be true:

- Each machine hosting SQL Server must be part of the same Active Directory domain.

- You must use the same Active Directory service account for each installation of the PolyBase Engine service.

- You must use the same Active Directory service account for each installation of the PolyBase Data Movement service.

- Each machine hosting SQL Server must be able to communicate with all other Scale-Out Group members. Because of this cross-communication requirement, you will likely want to keep your servers in close physical proximity and on the same network rather than geographically distributed and communicating through the Internet.

- Each SQL Server instance must be running the same major version of SQL Server, meaning SQL Server 2019, SQL Server 2017, or SQL Server 2016.

Another important thing to note is that the PolyBase services are machine-level rather than instance-level services, meaning you can install PolyBase once per physical or virtual machine. Even if you have multiple instances of SQL Server on the same machine, you only get one installation of PolyBase.

These are the major points to consider when choosing between standalone and Scale-Out Group. If you intend to use PolyBase in a production environment, you should probably install it as part of a Scale-Out Group. A Scale-Out Group can still be a cluster of one node, and this gives you the flexibility to expand out later. Beyond that, my general recommendation comes down to whether you have an Active Directory domain already set up. If you have one, install PolyBase as part of a Scale-Out Group to keep your options open.

If you do not have an Active Directory domain set up and cannot set one up for whatever reason, use PolyBase as a standalone service. All of the code in this book will run the same, regardless of whether you use PolyBase standalone or in a Scale-Out Group.

Your performance profile might change, but for most of the small data examples we work with in this book, standalone performance will be approximately as good as (and sometimes better than) the Scale-Out Group. The differences only become apparent as we work with some of the larger examples in this book and in your environments.

To understand why this is the case, let's take a quick diversion into the math behind scaling out. There are three major costs to consider when dealing with Massively Parallel Processing systems: fixed costs, data size, and overhead. The formula to keep in mind is

$$ProcessingTime \approx FixedCosts + \frac{1}{N}.DataSize + Overhead_N$$

The first component is fixed costs, which represents the resources needed to perform a scale-out query in the first place. It takes some amount of CPU, memory, and network bandwidth to coordinate resources on different machines, as well as the time needed for all of this work to happen. On modern MPP systems, this cost is (nearly) independent of data size.

The second component is a variable cost which we define as the number of nodes N multiplied by the data size. Each node in the cluster independently and concurrently handles some fraction of the total amount of data. For the sake of simplicity, we assume linearity here, where all nodes share the work equally; in reality, this will not always be the case and can complicate the equation. Regardless of how complex you want to make this part of the formula, here is where we see the benefits from scaling out: as the amount of data we need to process grows, this part of the formula begins to overwhelm the others. Being able to cut that part of the cost down by—for example—an order of magnitude leads to considerably better performance when dealing with enormous data sets.

But even this benefit comes with an additional variable cost, that of overhead. Overhead includes additional resource utilization like cross-network communication, as well as taking the work the individual nodes performed and finishing it up for the end user. Overhead costs start out much smaller than data processing costs, but they tend to grow faster than linear scale, typically scaling positively with respect to the number of nodes. In most real-world clusters, which tend to be under 10,000 nodes, data processing is a much bigger problem than overhead cost, but there are cases where this rule of thumb breaks down.

When analyzing all of these costs, we make the assumption that the second term is by far the most expensive and work on ways to minimize that term. When dealing with hundreds of millions or billions of rows, this assumption is generally reasonable. But when dealing with a few hundred thousand rows, that second term shrinks to the point where the fixed costs and overhead variable costs dominate. At that point, it becomes more efficient to run a standalone service and eliminate the fixed costs and overhead variable costs, leaving processing time as a function of data size. This also breaks down at extremely large numbers of nodes, where the time we spend coordinating between servers dominates.

Let's put numbers to this by using an overly simplistic example. Suppose we have a Hadoop cluster and we want to process a data set with 100 billion rows. To keep things simple, we will perform a lone Map operation which exhibits constant time per row: 0.0001 seconds per row. Inverting that, we can handle 10,000 rows per second on a single node. A naïve calculation indicates that it would take 100 billion/10,000 seconds to complete processing, or 10 million seconds. That adds up to approximately 115.75 days and forms our baseline for the non-MPP scenario.

For our MPP scenario, we need to consider three costs: fixed costs, data processing time, and overhead costs. Fixed costs are fixed, and we will estimate that at 30 seconds for this particular operation, which is a fair estimate of the spin-up costs of a simple YARN job.

Data costs scale linearly, as we will distribute the data across N nodes and each row is independent of all other rows. This does not change from our preceding single-node scenario, so we still process 10,000 rows per node per second.

Overhead costs are limited in this scenario because we do relatively little shuffling and sorting of data between servers, but we will assume that overhead costs are 5 seconds multiplied by 0.5 times number of nodes times the natural log of the number of nodes (i.e., approximately $n * \log(n)$ complexity). This is a very rough estimate, but will serve to get the point across.

Table 1-1 includes these factors and total processing time for four scenarios: one machine, a 100-node cluster, a 1000-node cluster, and a 100,000-node cluster.

Table 1-1. *Scale-out makes things faster until overhead costs dominate*

Estimated Time	Standalone	100 Nodes	1000 Nodes	100k Nodes
Fixed cost (s)	30	30	30	30
Data processing (s)	10m	100k	10k	100
Overhead cost (s)	0	1151	17,269	2.8m
Total	115.75 days	28.34 hours	7.58 hours	33 days

Although this is a stylized example with fictional numbers (especially for overhead cost), it shows that at extreme values, the complexity of wrangling an enormous number of machines can outweigh the benefit of linear scaling. There is such a thing as too much scale-out.

Pulling this discussion back to PolyBase, if you expect to deal solely with smaller data sets, then running PolyBase as a standalone service or as a Scale-Out Group with just one node can potentially be more efficient than stringing together a large Scale-Out Group with a few dozen nodes.

Now that you have an idea of which form of PolyBase you wish to install, let's cover installation techniques. Even if you want to install PolyBase as part of a Scale-Out Group, I recommend reading the standalone section as well.

Installing PolyBase Standalone—Windows

In this section, we will install PolyBase as a standalone service on Windows. If you are using PolyBase strictly for standalone work, you can install it on any edition of SQL Server 2017 or 2019—even Express Edition. This also applies to any edition of SQL Server 2016 with Service Pack 1 or later. PolyBase changed considerably between SQL Server 2017 and SQL Server 2019, and that includes changes in the installation process. To take the fullest advantage of PolyBase throughout this book, we will install SQL Server 2019. If you are installing SQL Server 2016 or 2017, some of the instructions will differ, primarily around Java installation, and you will not have the ability to connect to a large number of data sources.

After you have obtained your SQL Server 2019 media, you will want to add a new standalone installation or add features to an existing installation. I will assume for brevity's sake that you have installed SQL Server at some point in the past and will focus on the PolyBase-specific installation components, starting with Figure 1-1, which shows the initial setup dialog and the option to select.

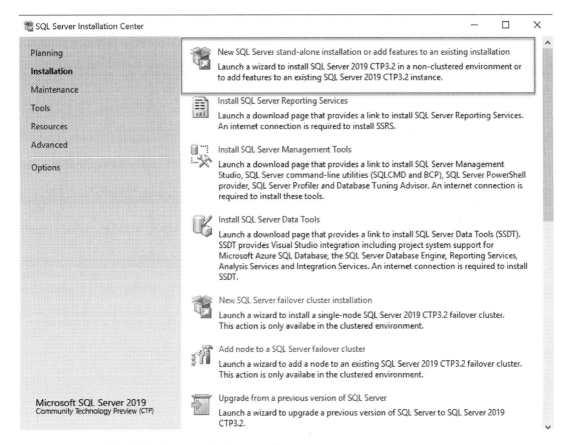

Figure 1-1. *The SQL Server 2019 installation screen*

Once you have clicked the "New SQL Server stand-alone installation or add features to an existing installation" link, continue the installation process. I will assume that you are installing PolyBase as part of a new SQL Server installation. If you are installing PolyBase as a new feature on an existing installation, choose any existing instance—PolyBase is a machine-level feature so the particular instance won't matter.

Regardless of whether you are installing new or atop an existing installation, continue through the installation wizard until you get to the feature selection section. At this point, we have a decision to make: we can install all PolyBase components or only the V2 components. Figure 1-2 shows this step with both sets of components selected.

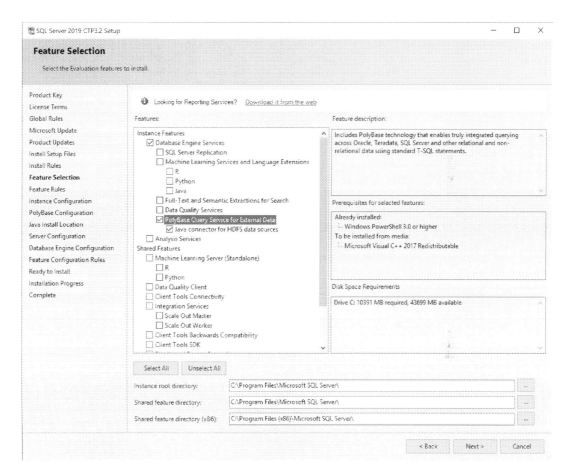

Figure 1-2. *We can install support for V2 sources independently of V1*

There are two components selected aside from Database Engine Services: the PolyBase Query Service for External Data and the Java connector for HDFS data sources.

The Java connector for HDFS data sources provides us support for connecting to Hadoop and Azure Blob Storage, which were the two endpoints available with PolyBase in SQL Server 2016 and SQL Server 2017; I refer to this throughout the book as PolyBase V1.

SQL Server 2019 also adds the PolyBase Query Service for External Data component, which includes support for services like Oracle, Teradata, MongoDB, Cosmos DB, and even other SQL Server instances. In order to install this component, SQL Server's installer will also install the Microsoft Visual C++ 2017 Redistributable.

Once you have selected your PolyBase components, continue along the installation process as you normally would until you get to the **PolyBase Configuration** section. Here is where we decide whether to use this SQL Server instance as a standalone PolyBase-enabled instance or as part of a Scale-Out Group. Figure 1-3 shows us our choice.

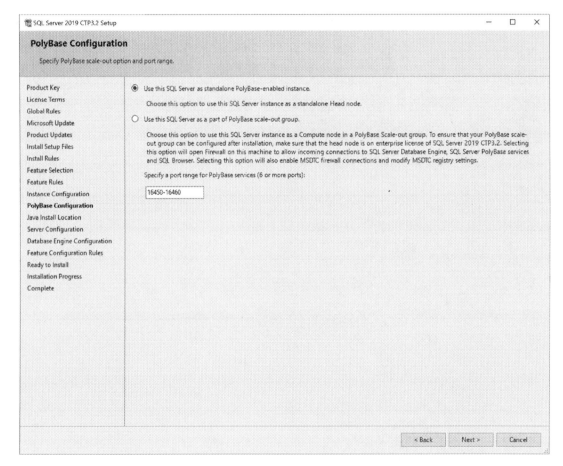

Figure 1-3. The moment of truth: making our installation choice

Because we want to install this as a standalone instance, we keep the first radio button selected and go on to the **Java Install Location** screen.

Java installation has changed considerably between SQL Server 2017 and SQL Server 2019. Prior to SQL Server 2019 CTP 3.2, SQL Server required that you install the Oracle Standard Edition Java Runtime Environment, version 7 update 51 or later. With Oracle changing the licensing model for Oracle Standard Edition (SE) Java, Microsoft has partnered with Azul Systems to give us three options for installation. Figure 1-4 shows the options available to us.

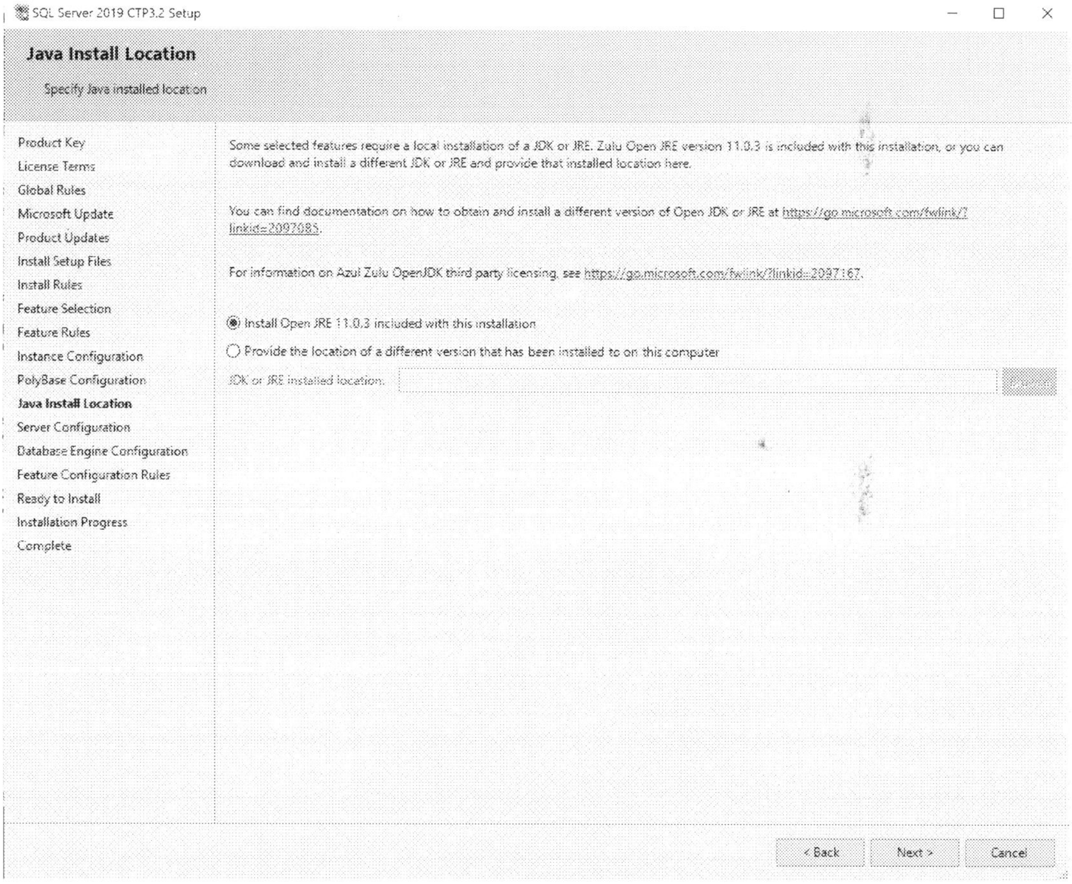

Figure 1-4. *If you installed the PolyBase V1 components, you will need to install some variety of the Java Runtime Environment*

The first option is to install the Azul Zulu Open JRE. This is a distribution of Oracle's Open Java Runtime Environment which Azul Systems supports. Your license for SQL Server includes support for this particular distribution of Open JRE, meaning that you could contact Microsoft support for issues related to the JRE. The link on the installation page includes more information on this licensing agreement.

If you are already a licensed Oracle Standard Edition (SE) customer, you can of course install the Oracle SE version of the Java Runtime Environment. To do so, select the "Provide the location of a different version that has been installed to on this computer" option and navigate to your already-installed version of the Java Runtime Environment. SQL Server 2016 and 2017 supported JRE version 7 update 51 and later, as well as JRE version 8. SQL Server 2019 supports later versions of the Java Runtime Environment, including version 11.

If you are not a licensed Oracle SE customer, you can also install Oracle's Open JRE. The downside to this is that your support options are limited to public forum access.

After taking care of your version of Java, we move to the next screen, which is **Server Configuration**. On this screen, we have the chance to fill out our service accounts. Figure 1-5 shows the default, which is to use the Network Service account.

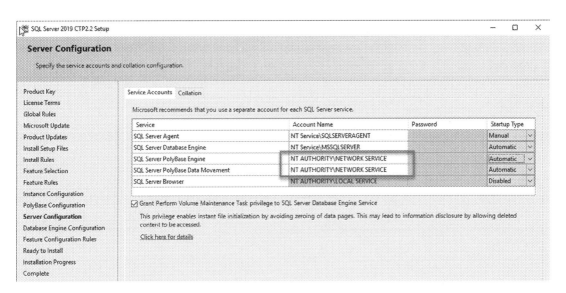

Figure 1-5. *Choosing the Network Service account to host PolyBase as part of a standalone installation*

You might already be familiar with *virtual accounts*, which are machine-specific pseudo-accounts intended to limit privileges. In Figure 1-5, you can see two virtual accounts, one used for the SQL Server Agent and one used for the SQL Server Database Engine. The easiest way to spot a virtual account is to look for the "NT Service\" prefix. In contrast to services like the SQL Server Agent or database engine, the two PolyBase services do not support the use of virtual accounts. For this demo, we will use the default of the local machine's Network Service account.

Note   You might also wish to use a Managed Service Account (MSA) here. These service accounts will allow you to run the PolyBase services using the lowest possible user rights. In a production environment, it is a good idea to use a specific, low-privilege user account or domain account unique to each PolyBase service. You also should avoid granting additional permissions to these service accounts or service groups; SQL Server's installation will take care of granting the rights necessary for PolyBase to work.

From this point on, you can complete the installation the way you normally would, setting up collations, configuring your data files, and so on. Once you have completed the installation, you should see a success message like in Figure 1-6, showing that we successfully installed the PolyBase Query Service for External Data and the Java connector for HDFS data sources.

Feature	Status
PolyBase Query Service for External Data	Succeeded
Database Engine Services	Succeeded
SQL Browser	Succeeded
SQL Writer	Succeeded
SQL Client Connectivity SDK	Succeeded
SQL Client Connectivity	Succeeded
Setup Support Files	Succeeded
Java connector for HDFS data sources	Succeeded

Figure 1-6. *Installation was successful, and we now have the PolyBase components we need*

If you would like to ensure that PolyBase did, in fact, install successfully, open up SQL Server Management Studio or Azure Data Studio, connect to your new SQL Server instance (or your current instance if you chose to install a new feature on an existing installation), and run the query in Listing 1-1.

Note   To connect to SQL Server 2019, you will need either a copy of SQL Server Management Studio 18 or later or Azure Data Studio. In this book, we will primarily use Azure Data Studio, but you can choose to run either.

Listing 1-1. Ensure that PolyBase is installed

```
SELECT
    @@SERVERNAME AS ServerName,
    SERVERPROPERTY('IsPolyBaseInstalled') AS IsPolyBaseInstalled;
```

Figure 1-7 shows us the results of this in Azure Data Studio. In this example, my server name is SQLWIN10; your machine's name will presumably be different from mine.

⊿ RESULTS	
(No column na...	IsPolyBaseInstalled
1 SQLWIN10	1

Figure 1-7. *PolyBase is installed on a machine named SQLWIN10*

At this point, we have installed PolyBase as a standalone service. We will continue to the next section to look at how this process differs if you are installing PolyBase as part of a Scale-Out Group, and then the section after that looks at standalone installation on Linux. Even though you have completed the installation process, I still recommend going through the next two sections because there are subtle differences between these installation techniques.

Installing PolyBase Scale-Out Group

For this section, I will install PolyBase on three separate VMs, each of which is part of the CSMORE domain which I have created. I have named these three VMs SQLControl, SQLCompute1, and SQLCompute2, respectively. Each VM is running Windows Server Core 2019, and the machines are not part of the same Windows Server Failover Cluster or otherwise connected together. SQLControl will be my *control node*, which is the node responsible for communicating with the outside world and coordinating with SQLCompute1 and SQLCompute2, the *compute nodes*.

Note   Licensing has changed a bit in SQL Server 2019. Prior to 2019, the control node needed to run Evaluation, Enterprise, or Developer Edition. With SQL Server 2019, we can also host a control node in Standard Edition.

We will need to install PolyBase independently on each machine hosting SQL Server. If you are installing SQL Server on Windows Server Core or wish to automate SQL Server installation across an environment, you can install entirely from the command line using a series of switches, but you might wish to create a configuration file to make installation a bit easier. Configuration files are optional, but I will demonstrate that route. The easiest way to create a configuration file is to step through the normal SQL Server installation process, so we will do this first on a machine running Windows 10 or Windows Server with Desktop Experience and with no prior installation of SQL Server. If you already have a configuration file or wish to install strictly from the command line, you can skip the "Building a Configuration File" section and continue with "Installing Without a GUI."

Building a Configuration File

In this optional section, we will simulate a normal installation process, ensuring that we select the PolyBase Query Service for External Data and the Java connector for HDFS data sources components. Eventually, we will reach the PolyBase Configuration section. Figure 1-8 shows the **PolyBase Configuration** screen and the two options available to us: either install as a standalone instance or install as part of a Scale-Out Group. We are going to choose the second option, installing as part of a Scale-Out Group.

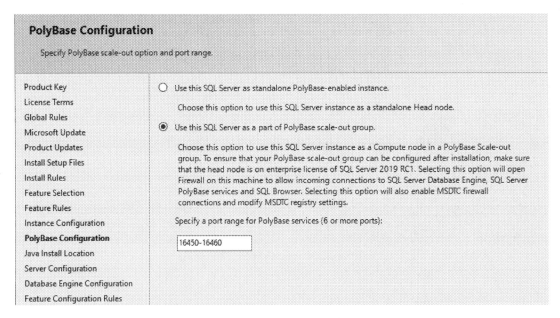

Figure 1-8. *Install SQL Server as part of a PolyBase Scale-Out Group*

Below the radio button, you will see a range of ports. By default, SQL Server runs PolyBase services between ports 16450 and 16460, but you can change that port range. If you have a reason to change from the defaults, pick a set of contiguous, open ports above 1024. After this screen, we have the same Java installation screen as in the standalone installation scenario, so choose the form of Java you wish to use and continue on.

The next section of the installation dialog is **Server Configuration**, where you define service accounts. In Figure 1-9, I have filled in an Active Directory domain account named PolyBaseService to host the SQL Server PolyBase Engine and the SQL Server PolyBase Data Movement services. This domain account does not need any special permissions; the SQL Server installer will grant the minimum rights necessary to this service account to run the PolyBase services.

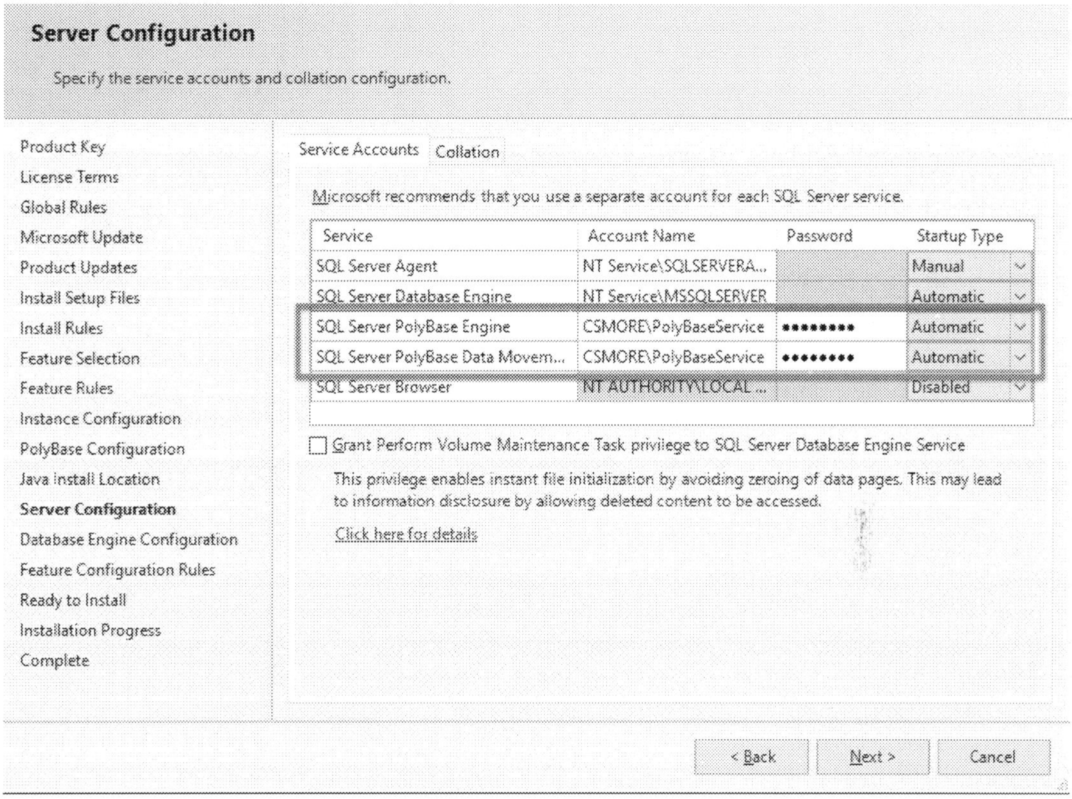

Figure 1-9. *Configure an Active Directory account to run the PolyBase services*

Note   You must use the same Active Directory account for each node of your Scale-Out Group.

Once you have reached the end of the installer but before installing SQL Server, you will see a summary page with the components to be installed, as well as a configuration file path. Figure 1-10 shows an example of this path.

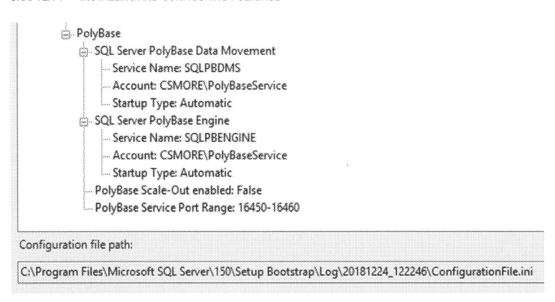

Figure 1-10. *We have done all of this work to get a configuration file, and here it is*

Before you go further, copy that configuration file off someplace safe, such as a GitHub repository or internal source control system. Then *cancel* the installation, as we only wanted to walk through this process in order to build out a configuration file; we will perform the actual installation on a real server through the command line.

Installing Without a GUI

With the configuration file you created earlier, you can see the configuration options relating to PolyBase. Listing 1-2 shows what my PolyBase configuration settings look like. Make sure that you have PBSCALEOUT="True"; if it is False, PolyBase will install as a standalone option, and the only way to fix this is to uninstall and reinstall the PolyBase components.

Listing 1-2. These are the PolyBase configuration settings which we need to set before installing on Windows Server Core or as part of any automated installation

```
PBENGSVCACCOUNT="CSMORE\PolyBaseService"
PBENGSVCSTARTUPTYPE="Automatic"
PBDMSSVCACCOUNT="CSMORE\PolyBaseService"
PBDMSSVCSTARTUPTYPE="Automatic"
```

```
PBSCALEOUT="True"
PBPORTRANGE="16450-16460"
```

Once you have modified the configuration file to your satisfaction, make it available to each machine you will include as part of your PolyBase Scale-Out Group. In my case, I put it in C:\Temp\ and named it ScaleOutConfigurationFile.ini, but it would also be good to make it available on a common UNC path and reference that single configuration for each installation. Then, attach or insert the SQL Server 2019 media for each machine, and run the following command in Listing 1-3 on each machine, being sure to set your sa account's password and use the correct Active Directory account password(s) for your PolyBase services.

Listing 1-3. Installing SQL Server on Windows Server Core via PowerShell. If you are running from the cmd shell, you do not need the preceding ".\" characters

```
.\Setup.exe /QS /IACCEPTSQLSERVERLICENSETERMS=1 /CONFIGURATIONFILE="C:\
Temp\ScaleOutConfigurationFile.ini" /PBENGSVCPASSWORD="<PWD>" /
PBDMSSVCPASSWORD="<PWD>" /SAPWD="<PWD>"
```

SQL Server will install and, assuming there were no errors, the installer will return control of the shell to you.

Installing PolyBase Standalone—Linux

PolyBase started out as a Windows-only feature, but as of SQL Server 2019, it is now available for Linux as well. SQL Server 2019 does have certain limitations for PolyBase on Linux. First, PolyBase on Linux does not support scale-out clusters, meaning that a Linux node can neither be the head node nor an additional data node for a scale-out cluster. In addition, PolyBase on Linux only supports PolyBase V2 sources, meaning that you cannot connect to Hadoop or Azure Blob Storage using PolyBase for SQL Server on Linux. If you are fine with these two limitations and want to try out PolyBase in a low-stress scenario, running SQL Server on Linux in a Docker container is great, as you can try it out, and when you are done, you can delete the container with no mess left over. In this section, we will spin up a Docker container running SQL Server on Linux and add PolyBase functionality to the container.

Note   If you are running SQL Server on Linux through a virtual machine or on bare metal, you can still follow along; simply ignore the Docker-specific commands. I do assume, however, that you already have SQL Server for Linux installed, and therefore I will not show SQL Server base installation instructions on Linux.

First, ensure that you have at least 4GB of RAM available for your SQL Server container. If you are running Docker on Windows, you can see this setting in Figure 1-11, where I have allocated 8GB of RAM to containers.

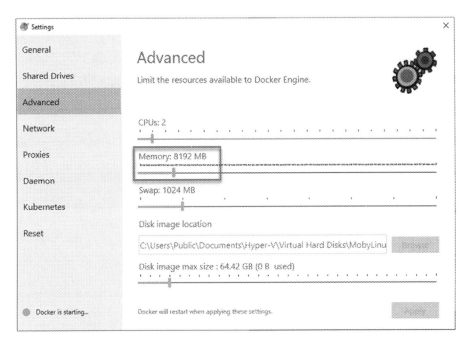

Figure 1-11. *Configuring Docker on Windows to allocate 8GB of RAM for containers*

Next, we will need to pull the SQL Server 2019 Docker image. To do this, run the command docker pull mcr.microsoft.com/mssql/server:2019-latest-ubuntu to obtain the latest version of SQL Server 2019. We can see this in action in Figure 1-12.

```
C:\WINDOWS\system32\cmd.exe - docker  pull mcr.microsoft.com/mssql/server:2019-RC1-ubuntu
Microsoft Windows [Version 10.0.18362.356]
(c) 2019 Microsoft Corporation. All rights reserved.

C:\Users\Kevin Feasel>docker pull mcr.microsoft.com/mssql/server:2019-RC1-ubuntu
2019-RC1-ubuntu: Pulling from mssql/server
59ab41dd721a: Already exists
57da90bec92c: Already exists
06fe57530625: Already exists
5a6315cba1ff: Already exists
739f58768b3f: Already exists
e39f945bda21: Pull complete
6689ce95f395: Pull complete
ec004dcfdfb5: Downloading [================================>                 ]   225.4MB/358.9MB
e44708601d04: Download complete
```

Figure 1-12. *Pulling the SQL Server on Linux Docker container. This can take a while*

Note   As of the time of writing, there is no `latest` tagged image for SQL Server 2019, so Figure 1-12 shows a specific version: Release Candidate 1. SQL Server 2017 has a `latest` tagged image, and I expect 2019 to follow suit. You can get a full list of tags from the Docker Hub at `https://hub.docker.com/_/ microsoft-mssql-server`.

After pulling down the Docker image, we should next spin up a container running SQL Server on Linux. To do so, run the command in Listing 1-4, changing the sa account password appropriately.

Listing 1-4. Create a new SQL Server container. This will run on one line without the backslashes for both Linux and Windows. If you are running this from a Linux shell like Bash, you can use backslashes to combine together multiple lines like in the following code. If you are running this command on Windows, use the caret (^) instead of a backslash to break things up onto multiple lines

```
docker run -e "ACCEPT_EULA=Y" -e "SA_PASSWORD=SqlPbPwd!10" \
-p 1433:1433 --name PolyBaseDemo \
-d mcr.microsoft.com/mssql/server:2019-latest-ubuntu
```

With this installed, we can connect to SQL Server using our sa account as in Figure 1-13. We can connect to this Linux-based instance using either SQL Server Management Studio or Azure Data Studio. From there, create a database called PolyBaseRevealed.

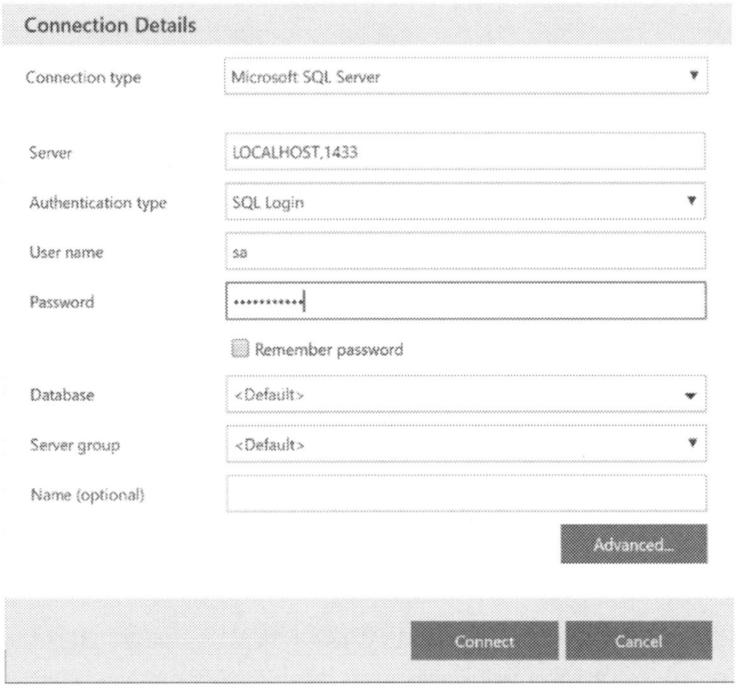

Figure 1-13. *Connecting to a SQL Server on Linux instance using Azure Data Studio. Note that you will need to use a comma to separate host and port rather than a colon. If your SQL Server instance runs on port 1433, specifying the port is optional*

Now that we have a SQL Server instance and a database set up, we can install the PolyBase components. To do this, we will need to open a shell on our Linux container. Listing 1-5 is the command we will need to run from a command prompt and will connect to our PolyBaseDemo container.

Listing 1-5. Connect to our SQL Server on Linux container and start a bash prompt

```
docker exec -it PolyBaseDemo /bin/bash
```

From here, there are several commands to run in order to retrieve Microsoft's apt key, connect to the appropriate SQL Server repository, and install the mssql-server-polybase package. You can find the full set of instructions in the accompanying code repository in a PowerShell script entitled SQL on Linux with PolyBase.ps1. After following these instructions, you will have an instance of SQL Server on Linux running PolyBase V2 and will be ready to continue on to the next step: configuration.

Configuring PolyBase

Now that you have the PolyBase service up and running, let's run through the steps for configuring PolyBase. In this section, we will install Azure Data Studio with SQL Server 2019 support, enable PolyBase, and connect together each node of our PolyBase Scale-Out Group, assuming you intend to create one.

Configuring a Client

There are two primary clients for accessing SQL Server 2019 instances: SQL Server Management Studio 18 (or later) and Azure Data Studio with the Data Virtualization extension installed. I use both on a daily basis, and you will see screenshots from both throughout the book, but my preference here is Azure Data Studio for a few reasons. First, Azure Data Studio tends to be faster than SQL Server Management Studio in terms of startup time. Second, it tends to be a bit simpler and more tightly focused than Management Studio. We only need a small subset of Management Studio's functionality for PolyBase, and Azure Data Studio does at least as well in this respect. In this section, we will download and configure Azure Data Studio. Third, Azure Data Studio is cross-platform, meaning that you can run it from Windows, MacOS, or Linux.

First, download Azure Data Studio, which is available for Windows, MacOS, and Linux. As of this writing, it is available at `https://docs.microsoft.com/en-us/sql/azure-data-studio/download`, or you can get it by searching for "Download Azure Data Studio" in your search engine of choice. Once you have downloaded the appropriate installer, install and run Azure Data Studio. Then, open the Extensions tab and type "Data Virtualization" into the search box to find the Data Virtualization extension. Figure 1-14 shows this.

Figure 1-14. *Searching for the Data Virtualization extension*

Click the Data Virtualization extension, and you will see an information panel like the one in Figure 1-15.

Figure 1-15. *Getting ready to install the Data Virtualization extension*

If the extension is not already installed, click the "Install" button, and this will install the extension for you without needing to do any additional work. After that, the extensions screen will show that you have the extension already installed and offer the opportunity to disable or uninstall, as shown in Figure 1-16.

Figure 1-16. *Confirm that the Data Virtualization extension is already installed*

Once it finishes, reload Azure Data Studio, and you now have full SQL Server 2019 support. Now we can continue to the next section, "Enable PolyBase."

Enable PolyBase

Now that we have installed PolyBase, we need to perform a bit of configuration to enable it. The first part of this section will walk you through installation regardless of the configuration option you chose earlier. Then, we will look at considerations specifically for Scale-Out Groups. Finally, we will perform a quick test to ensure that PolyBase is running correctly.

Mandatory Configuration

First, we will need to ensure that TCP/IP is enabled as a valid protocol for each SQL Server instance. This comes enabled by default if you install SQL Server Enterprise, Standard, or Evaluation Edition, but is disabled by default if you install Developer or Express Edition. If you are connected directly to the machine hosting SQL Server, you can run the SQL Server Configuration Manager application like in Figure 1-17.

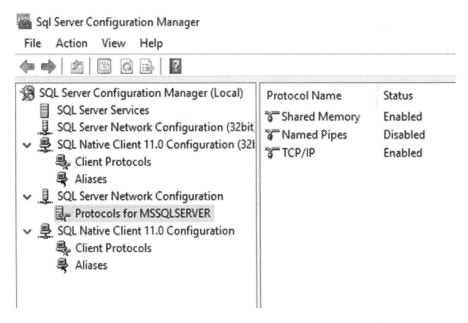

Figure 1-17. *Ensure that the TCP/IP is enabled*

If you would like to check a SQL Server install remotely, you can do so via the Computer Management tool in Windows 10. In this case, I will assume that your account does not have sufficient privileges to view and make changes to remote services, so we will run Computer Management as a different user.

The first step is to search for the Computer Management desktop app. Then, right-click the app and select "Open file location." As of Windows 10 1809 Update, you can also navigate to the Computer Management application with your keyboard, and the context menu will appear in a flyout panel to the right. Figure 1-18 shows an example of this in action.

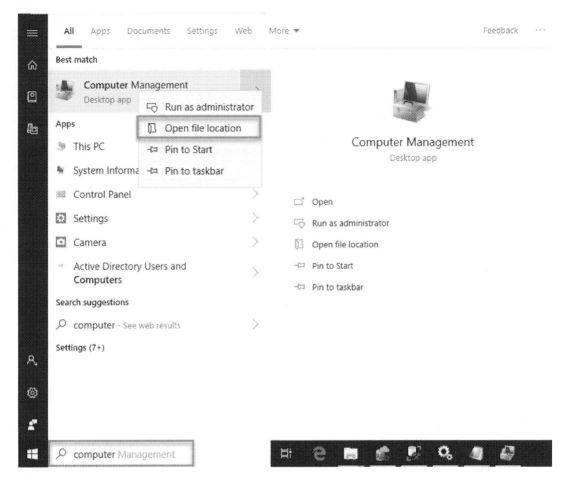

Figure 1-18. *Open the file location where the Computer Management shortcut lives*

Once inside that folder, hold down the right shift key and right-click the Computer Management shortcut. If you do this correctly, you will see a "Run as different user" option like in Figure 1-19.

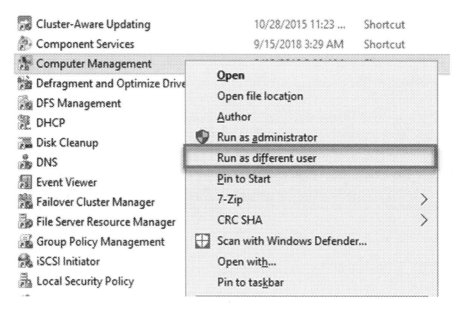

Figure 1-19. *Running Computer Management as a different user*

Once you enter your credentials, you will see the Computer Management application. In the Action drop-down menu, select "Connect to another computer …" and enter the name of the machine you wish to access. Figure 1-20 shows an example of connecting to the SQLControl machine.

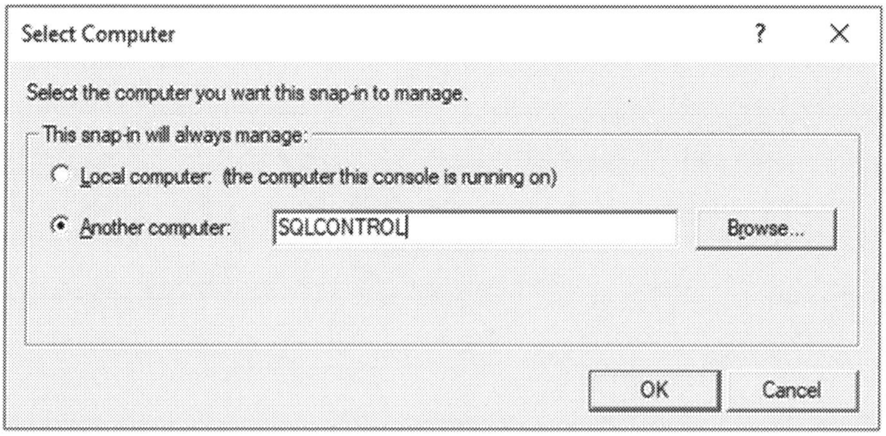

Figure 1-20. *Connecting to SQLControl from a remote machine*

Assuming your credentials are valid and you have the appropriate authorization, you can navigate the "Services and Applications" section for each of your SQL Server instances to ensure that TCP/IP is enabled. Figure 1-21 shows us the navigation tree.

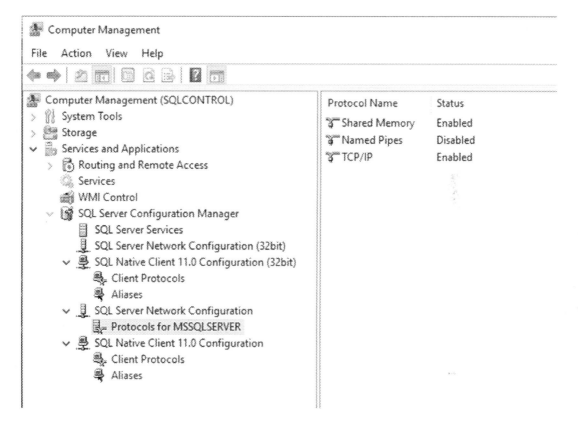

Figure 1-21. *Ensuring that TCP/IP is enabled for the SQL Server instance on SQLControl*

Next, we need to enable PolyBase in SQL Server by executing the `sp_configure` system stored procedure in our SQL client of choice. Listing 1-6 walks us through the process. Note that the first command is only necessary for SQL Server 2019; if you are installing PolyBase for SQL Server 2016 or SQL Server 2017, this option does not exist, and you will get an error.

Listing 1-6. Enable PolyBase. Run this against each SQL Server instance with PolyBase services installed, whether standalone or as part of a Scale-Out Group

```
EXEC sp_configure
    @configname = 'polybase enabled',
    @configvalue = 1;
GO
RECONFIGURE;
GO
EXEC sp_configure
    @configname = 'hadoop connectivity',
    @configvalue = 7;
GO
RECONFIGURE
GO
```

After executing these statements, you will need to restart the PolyBase and SQL Server Database Engine services.

Before moving on, I would like to explain the hadoop connectivity configuration option. This is a PolyBase V1 configuration setting and is required for Hadoop and Azure Blob Storage connectivity. If you are running on Linux, did not install the Java connector for HDFS data sources, or simply do not want to connect to Hadoop or Azure Blob Storage, set the value to 0 to disable Hadoop connectivity. If you want to connect to a Cloudera Distribution of Hadoop (CDH) cluster, use 6 as your configuration value. If you wish to connect to a Hortonworks Data Platform (HDP) cluster, use 7 as your configuration value. Azure Blob Storage support comes for free with either of the latter values. We will connect to Azure Blob Storage in Chapter 2 and both CDH and HDP clusters in Chapter 3.

Note   If you are interested in what historical options 1–5 represent, check out the <u>PolyBase Connectivity Configuration</u> page on Microsoft Docs. In short, these are obsolete versions of Hadoop, including an ill-fated attempt to bring Hadoop to Windows. Now let us never speak of Hadoop on Windows again.

If you have installed PolyBase standalone, you are now done with installation and configuration. If you have a Scale-Out Cluster, however, there are a couple more steps.

Scale-Out Group Configuration

In addition to enabling PolyBase and configuring Hadoop connectivity, you will need to perform two additional actions. First, ensure that firewall rules are set up on each of the machines you plan to enlist in the PolyBase cluster. All of the PolyBase ports should be open (16450–16460 by default), as well as the SQL Server Database Engine port (1433 by default).

Once you have confirmed that ports are open, review the code in Listing 1-7 on each compute node. Change the head node address, Data Movement Service channel port, and head node SQL Server instance name as needed and then execute.

Listing 1-7. Join a PolyBase Scale-Out Group. Run this from the individual compute nodes

```
EXEC sp_polybase_join_group
    @head_node_address = N'SQLControl',
    @dms_control_channel_port = 16450,
    @head_node_sql_server_instance_name = N'MSSQLSERVER';
```

Note   In the preceding example, my head node's name is SQLControl. Your name will likely differ from that, so make sure to review these settings before running the code and ensure that they comport to your setup.

After doing this, you will need to restart each compute node's PolyBase and SQL Server Database Engine services.

Troubleshooting Common Errors

You might run into errors when trying to add a compute node to a Scale-Out Group. If the PolyBase Engine service (SQLPBENGINE) fails to start on a compute node, make sure that your firewall configuration is correct and you have opened access on all relevant ports for the control node. In the extreme case, you might disable the Windows firewall for these servers if they are behind a hardware firewall on a corporate network or in a secure virtual network.

After you have opened up relevant ports, you will need to leave the Scale-Out Group by running EXEC sp_polybase_leave_group on the compute node. Then, try starting the SQL Server PolyBase Engine. If it starts successfully, rejoin the Scale-Out Group and restart your SQL Server services.

Testing for Success

Listing 1-8 shows you a quick and easy way to determine whether your PolyBase services are configured correctly by querying the sys.dm_exec_compute_nodes Dynamic Management View (DMV).

Listing 1-8. Check the dm_exec_compute_nodes DMV to make sure all of your compute and control nodes are configured correctly

```
SELECT
    n.compute_node_id,
    n.type,
    n.name,
    n.address
FROM sys.dm_exec_compute_nodes n;
GO
```

Figure 1-22 shows you what this result should look like for a Scale-Out Group. If you run this for a standalone installation, you will still see HEAD and COMPUTE results for compute_node_id = 1 representing your single standalone installation.

```
17    SELECT
18        n.compute_node_id,
19        n.type,
20        n.name,
21        n.address
22    FROM sys.dm_exec_compute_nodes n;
```

◢ RESULTS

	compute_node_id	type	name	address
1	1	HEAD	SQLCONTROL:1433	192.168.217.55
2	1	COMPUTE	SQLCONTROL:1433	192.168.217.55
3	2	COMPUTE	SQLCOMPUTE1:1433	192.168.217.57
4	3	COMPUTE	SQLCOMPUTE2:1433	192.168.217.56

Figure 1-22. *A successful PolyBase Scale-Out Group*

Because this DMV queries each compute node and does not simply look at configuration metadata, the query will run endlessly without returning a result set if at least one of the compute nodes is inaccessible. When everything is configured and all machines are on the same network and responsive, I can get a sub-second response. It is generally safe to assume that a long response for this DMV means cluster trouble, and the first place I would look is to ensure that each compute node's PolyBase Engine and Data Movement services are running.

Conclusion

In this first chapter, we reviewed the key decision to make with PolyBase: whether to install as a standalone service or as part of a Scale-Out Group. After that, we looked at installing standalone with the help of the SQL Server installer UI, and then as part of a Scale-Out Cluster using (mostly) the command line. After that, we enabled and configured PolyBase, including enlisting compute nodes in a Scale-Out Group. Finally, we looked at a couple common Scale-Out Group errors and a Dynamic Management View which helps us check the status of each node in our cluster.

In the next chapter, we will take our PolyBase cluster and access our first external resource: Azure Blob Storage.

CHAPTER 2

Connecting to Azure Blob Storage

In Chapter 1, we installed PolyBase for SQL Server 2019. Regardless of whether you chose to install PolyBase as a Scale-Out Group or standalone, we will use that cluster to connect to Azure Blob Storage. In the first part of this chapter, we will create an Azure storage account and upload our data to the account. Then, in the second part of this chapter, we will connect PolyBase to Azure Blob Storage, explaining the critical concepts of *external data sources*, *external file formats*, and *external tables* along the way. After that, we will test a number of queries, showing off the fluid integration between our native SQL Server tables and external data sources like Azure Blob Storage. We will retrieve data from and insert data into external tables. Finally, we will look at common issues when inserting data into external tables with PolyBase.

Making Preparations in Azure

In this chapter, I will assume that you already have a Microsoft Azure account. If you do not, you can sign up for a trial at `https://azure.microsoft.com/free/` if you wish to follow along with the instructions in this chapter. Even if you have to use a paid account, Azure Blob Storage is very cheap—we will not spend more than a few cents per month in this chapter. Following along here is important even if you will not use Azure Blob Storage in your production environment because we will introduce important concepts which pop up throughout the rest of the book.

© Kevin Feasel 2020
K. Feasel, *PolyBase Revealed*, https://doi.org/10.1007/978-1-4842-5461-5_2

Create a Storage Account

Once you have your account set up, go to `https://portal.azure.com` and sign in to Azure. From there, open up your storage accounts by clicking the "Storage accounts" link. Figure 2-1 shows two places where you can see the storage accounts link.

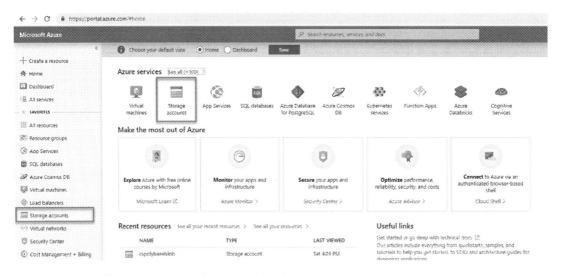

Figure 2-1. *There are several ways to find your storage accounts*

If you do not already have a storage account you would like to use, click the "Add" button on the storage accounts page to add a new storage account. Figure 2-2 shows the Basics tab, which takes us through the most important settings for this chapter.

First, you will need to choose a subscription and a resource group. If you are in a corporate environment, you may have multiple subscriptions from which to choose; if so, you will need to determine which is the best fit. Otherwise, if you have just one subscription, that choice is easy. Resource groups, meanwhile, are collections of different resources—storage accounts, virtual machines, and Azure services—which fit together. One nice thing about resource groups is that, when you are done, you can delete all of the resources in a resource group in a single operation. This is ideal for complex services like Azure HDInsight or Azure Synapse Analytics, but you should create a resource group specifically for each resource you use in this book so that you can delete them and avoid future charges after you have finished reading the book.

You will need to create a storage account name which is unique across all of Azure. I have already taken cspolybaseblob, but use your creativity and come up with something else—like cspolybaseblob1. After you have found a storage account name of your own, you may pick a location of your choice. I chose East US 2 for my location, and I recommend choosing a location relatively near you.

Create storage account

Basics   Advanced   Tags   Review + create

Azure Storage is a Microsoft-managed service providing cloud storage that is highly available, secure, durable, scalable, and redundant. Azure Storage includes Azure Blobs (objects), Azure Data Lake Storage Gen2, Azure Files, Azure Queues, and Azure Tables. The cost of your storage account depends on the usage and the options you choose below. Learn more

PROJECT DETAILS

Select the subscription to manage deployed resources and costs. Use resource groups like folders to organize and manage all your resources.

* Subscription	Visual Studio Enterprise
* Resource group	Screenshots
	Create new

INSTANCE DETAILS

The default deployment model is Resource Manager, which supports the latest Azure features. You may choose to deploy using the classic deployment model instead. Choose classic deployment model

* Storage account name ⓘ	cspolybaseblob
* Location	East US 2
Performance ⓘ	● Standard ○ Premium
Account kind ⓘ	StorageV2 (general purpose v2)
Replication ⓘ	Geo-redundant storage (GRS)
Access tier (default) ⓘ	○ Cool ● Hot

Review + create   Previous   Next : Advanced >

Figure 2-2. *Creating a new storage account*

As far as the performance settings go, for this chapter, I recommend Standard performance on the Hot access tier. In a production scenario, I would typically recommend Premium storage, but for learning about PolyBase, the Standard tier will do well enough. For account kind, choose StorageV2. PolyBase supports the general purpose v2 storage account type, which as of the time of writing is the latest generation of Azure storage. This kind of account also gives a few options for replication depending upon your region. I chose Zone Redundant Storage, but PolyBase also supports the Local Redundant and Global Redundant replication tiers.

Caution   The Azure portal changes frequently, so screenshots in this section are liable to change in the future as Microsoft introduces new features in Azure or changes the user interface. Be sure to review the page and any Azure documentation as you go through this chapter. In addition, offerings may change between the time when I wrote these words and the time you read them, so it may help to do a bit of research on the latest generation of Blob Storage and what it has to offer.

After you have completed storage account creation, you will need to obtain an access key. This access key will allow you to access your storage account remotely—such as from a SQL Server instance running PolyBase. In the storage accounts blade, click the storage account you want to use. Then, click the "Access keys" link, and you will see two keys for your account. Figure 2-3 shows a redacted version from my account.

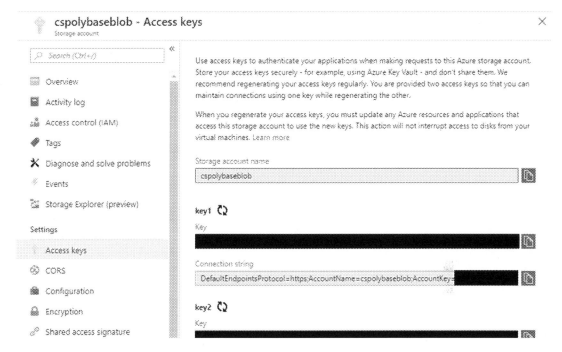

Figure 2-3. *Access keys for the cspolybaseblob Azure storage account*

We have two keys available, key1 and key2. You can use either key to access your Azure storage account, and clicking the refresh button next to the key name allows you to generate a new key—something you should do regularly as part of a key refresh process. Click the copy button next to either key1 or key2 to copy this key to your clipboard and save it someplace secure, as we will need it later. Copy and save the connection string as well.

Once you have the key and connection string copied, it is time to create Blob Containers and upload our data. To do this, I will use Microsoft Azure Storage Explorer, a free tool for managing Azure Storage available at https://azure.microsoft.com/en-us/features/storage-explorer/. Inside Azure Storage Explorer, click the plug icon to add a new account, like in Figure 2-4. This brings up a wizard which gives you several options for integrating with your Azure account.

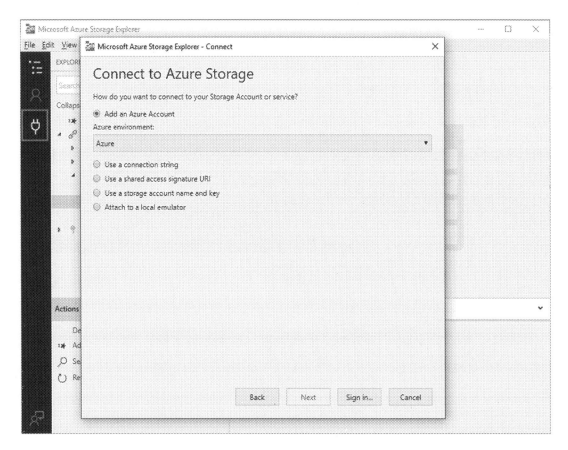

Figure 2-4. *Add a new account*

The first and simplest integration option is to add everything for an Azure account. This is a convenient option for individuals or smaller companies, but it might be overkill in larger corporate environments which make heavy use of Azure storage accounts. If you are in one of these corporate environments or if you do not have direct Azure storage account access, you can use one of the other methods: using a connection string, a shared access signature URI, or a storage account name and key.

In our case, the easiest of those options is to use a connection string because we already copied the connection string earlier. Paste that connection string into the "Connection string" box, and Azure Storage Explorer will prepopulate the "Display name" box with your Blob Storage account name. If you wish to change the display name, you have the option to do so. Then click the "Next" button again, confirm that your details are correct, and complete the wizard. Figure 2-5 shows the end result of this: a storage account connected via key rather than Azure account.

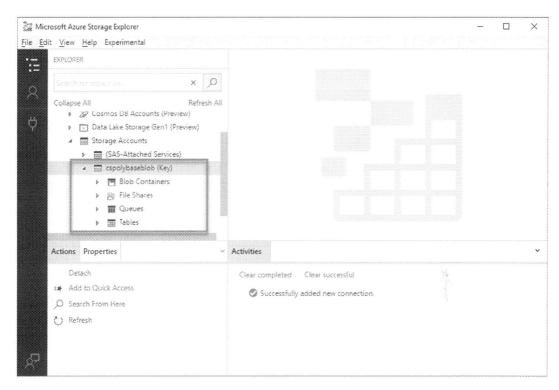

Figure 2-5. *Here we see the newly added account, cspolybaseblob*

Upload Data

In order to access Azure Blob Storage data with PolyBase, we will need to create at least one Blob Container. To do this, right-click the "Blob Containers" node and select "Create Blob Container." You will then be able to fill in the name of the Blob Container you would like to create. Figure 2-6 shows the two Blob Containers we will work with, ncpop and visits.

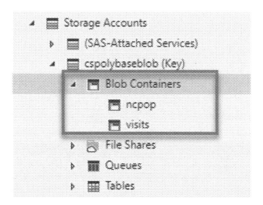

Figure 2-6. *Create two Blob Containers named ncpop and visits, respectively*

Inside the ncpop Blob Container, we will upload a file with the population for each city and county in North Carolina. You can obtain a copy of this file from the book's code repository; it is in the Data folder and named NorthCarolinaPopulation.csv. Back in Azure Storage Explorer, click the "Upload" button and upload the NorthCarolinaPopulation.csv file, making sure to select the blob type of Block Blob and uploading to a folder named Census. The end result should look something like Figure 2-7.

Caution   Azure Blob Storage folder and file names are case sensitive. There is a community norm to keep all names lowercased, so if my capitalization causes you unease, make everything lowercase, but remember to keep it lowercased when we get to the point of integrating with SQL Server via PolyBase.

After you upload this file, go to the visits Blob Container and upload the file named Visits.txt into a folder named Visits. This file contains a small, made-up data set which we will use later in the chapter.

Now that we have our sample data in place, it is time to move back to SQL Server and begin our task of integration.

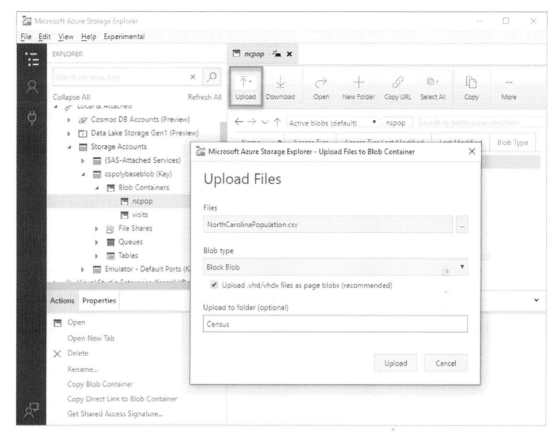

Figure 2-7. *Uploading a file to Azure Blob Storage*

Building a Link

The first thing I want to do in SQL Server is ensure that I know which database I wish to use when connecting to the outside world. Unlike linked servers, PolyBase objects are database specific. This may seem a bit weird at first if you are used to linked servers—which connect to a remote **server**, after all—but there are benefits to this. For example, suppose you have totally separate databases, perhaps one per customer, each of which connects to some independent, customer-specific resource on a remote server. With the linked server model, every database on the server will use the same linked server. With PolyBase, your remote objects live in the database, so database users can access their remote resources but will not be able to peek at remote resources.

Of course, this is not the only security pattern available. If you happen to have a large number of databases which need to talk to the same outside resource, you might prefer to create a single database which reaches out to that external resource and perform cross-database queries from your application. In the simplest scenario, you have a single database which needs to connect to an external resource, which we will demonstrate in this section.

To that end, our first goal is to build a database. Listing 2-1 has us create a new database called PolyBaseRevealed. At first, this will be an empty database, but throughout the book, we will fill it with normal tables as well as external tables.

Listing 2-1. Create a PolyBaseRevealed database

```
CREATE DATABASE PolyBaseRevealed
GO
```

Now that we have a database, we can connect to Azure Blob Storage. To do so, we will need four things: credentials, an external data source, an external file format, and an external table. Let's take a look at each in turn.

Credentials

SQL Server uses Database Scoped Credentials to authenticate with resources outside of SQL Server. These credentials do not tie to any particular login, user, or other database resources. In addition to PolyBase, you might use Database Scoped Credentials when working with cross-database querying in Azure SQL Database or using BULK INSERT or OPENROWSET operations to access data in Azure Blob Storage, or even with StretchDB. In order to create a Database Scoped Credential, you must have the CONTROL permission on the current database.

There are two steps required to create a Database Scoped Credential. The first step is to create a database master key. Listing 2-2 shows the syntax for this.

Listing 2-2. Create a database master key

```
USE PolyBaseRevealed
GO
CREATE MASTER KEY ENCRYPTION BY PASSWORD = '<Some PWD>';
GO
```

Naturally, you will want to use a strong password when creating your database master key, as this key protects all other private keys and certificates created on this database, including the Database Scoped Credential that we will create in Listing 2-3.

Caution   Be sure to back up your database master key with the BACKUP MASTER KEY command and store that backed-up key in a secure location. If you lose the database master key, you will lose access to your private keys and certificates created off of this database master key.

Listing 2-3. Create a Database Scoped Credential

```
CREATE DATABASE SCOPED CREDENTIAL AzureStorageCredential
WITH IDENTITY = '<Your Azure blob name>',
SECRET = '<Your Azure Secret>';
GO
```

Your Azure blob name will be the name of the storage account—in my case, that was *cspolybaseblob*. Your Azure secret will be the "Key" field on the *Access keys* page for your Azure storage account, an example of which you can see in Figure 2-3.

Once you have created your Database Scoped Credential, you are ready to create the next major item: an external data source.

External Data Sources

The purpose of an external data source is to define the thing to which SQL Server will connect. This could be an Azure storage blob, a Hadoop cluster, an Oracle or Teradata database, or even another SQL Server instance. Like with credentials, you will need the CONTROL permission to create an external data source.

Listing 2-4 creates a new Azure Blob Storage data source called *AzureNCPopBlob*, which connects to the *ncpop* blob on the *cspolybaseblob* Azure storage account using the *AzureStorageCredential* Database Scoped Credential created earlier.

Listing 2-4. Create an external data source

```
IF NOT EXISTS
(
    SELECT 1
    FROM sys.external_data_sources e
    WHERE
        e.name = N'AzureNCPopBlob'
)
BEGIN
    CREATE EXTERNAL DATA SOURCE AzureNCPopBlob WITH
    (
        TYPE = HADOOP,
        LOCATION = 'wasbs://ncpop@cspolybaseblob.blob.core.windows.net',
        CREDENTIAL = AzureStorageCredential
    );
END
GO
```

Note   There is an external data store type named BLOB_STORAGE, but this external data source only connects to Azure Blob Storage as part of bulk insert operations. To query data in Azure Blob Storage, as we will do here, the type must be HADOOP. The reason for this is that Azure Blob Storage's Windows Azure Storage Blob (WASB) protocol extends the Hadoop Distributed File System (HDFS), allowing PolyBase to treat blobs as though they were files in Hadoop.

As long as you have created the Database Scoped Credential, you should be able to create this external data source. As a quick note, creating the data source does not validate anything, meaning that you might receive an error further down the line when trying to query an external table due to a typo in the external data source location. Another thing worth noting is that credentials are technically optional—if you are connecting to a blob which allows anonymous public access, you do not need to pass a credential along. In most cases, however, the credential will be necessary.

With an external data source in place, we should look at the third piece of the puzzle: an external file format.

External File Formats

An external file format is simply the type of file that you expect to retrieve from your external data source. One example of an external file format is a delimited file, such as a comma-separated values file. PolyBase supports four external file formats. Three of the four types are Hadoop centric, so we will defer discussion of those until Chapter 3. In this chapter, we will focus on delimited files.

Delimited Files

Delimited files are the most common file type when working outside of Hadoop. The comma-separated values (CSV) file is ubiquitous in public data sets, followed by tab-separated, semicolon-separated, and more exotic field terminators such as the pipe (|) and tilde (~). PolyBase will also support multicharacter delimiters.

In addition to the field terminator, PolyBase supports string delimiters, which allow you to include a field terminator within a string. By default, PolyBase does not use a string delimiter, but you will often see the quotation mark (") in the wild.

Caution   There is no way to escape a string delimiter in PolyBase at this time. For example, if you use the quotation mark as a string delimiter, PolyBase will successfully parse `"Some Value"` by removing the quotation marks. It will, however, fail to parse `"Some " Value"` as you might expect. When working with delimited files, you commonly see people double up on the string delimiter to indicate to the parser that this is a normal character rather than a control character, but `"Some "" Value"` will also fail, as will `"Some \" Value."` Be sure to pick a string delimiter which does not show up in your data set.

Another format option which you can choose is the encoding. PolyBase supports two encodings: UTF-8 (the default) and UTF-16. If you are dealing with ASCII formatted files, you can safely stick with the default of UTF-8.

The final format option of interest for PolyBase on SQL Server is the date format, which defines how the dates in your flat file should look. This date format parameter is the source of a number of flat file import problems with PolyBase because PolyBase only supports a limited set of date and time formats and the parser is unforgiving when it comes to dates, rejecting values which you might otherwise expect to be acceptable.

Given these date-related pain points, if you do not need to filter on date values, it could be better to import the fields as strings rather than DATE, DATETIME2, or other date or time data types and then perform conversions as needed within SQL Server.

Flat File Compression

PolyBase supports a few compression algorithms for flat files. The primary compression algorithm—and the one which you will find on Microsoft Docs—is gzip compression. This venerable compression algorithm works well for text files but comes at a cost: decompressing and reading data in gzip is single threaded, meaning that only one reader will be able to work with a single gzipped file. You can get around this limitation by compressing your data into a larger number of gzipped files, where the number is at least the number of readers. This means that if you have a six-node Scale-Out Group, you would want at least six gzipped files.

Instead of using gzip, you can use the bzip2 format. This format provides superior compression compared to gzip and is splittable, meaning you can have multiple readers work off of parts of the file. The downside to the bzip2 format is that it is much more CPU intensive than gzip, and the time you save in reduced network bandwidth might end up being less than the time you spend waiting for files to decompress.

There are several compression formats which PolyBase does not support for delimited files, including zip (the most common compression format on Windows), 7z, Snappy, and LZ4. Hadoop supports the latter two compression formats, and certain external file formats can support Snappy, but not delimited files. PolyBase also does not handle tar files perfectly—it removes the first row from the file but does read all remaining rows.

Define an External File Format

Listing 2-5 provides an example of an external file format. In this case, we will create a file format for reading CSVs with quotation marks around strings.

Listing 2-5. Creating an external file format

```
IF NOT EXISTS
(
    SELECT 1
    FROM sys.external_file_formats e
```

```
    WHERE
        e.name = N'CsvFileFormat'
)
BEGIN
    CREATE EXTERNAL FILE FORMAT CsvFileFormat WITH
    (
        FORMAT_TYPE = DELIMITEDTEXT,
        FORMAT_OPTIONS
        (
            FIELD_TERMINATOR = N',',
            USE_TYPE_DEFAULT = TRUE,
            STRING_DELIMITER = '"',
            ENCODING = 'UTF8'
        )
    );
END
GO
```

The USE_TYPE_DEFAULT parameter defines whether we want the PolyBase engine to insert default values for data types if those fields are missing. For numeric values, the default is 0. For strings, the engine emits an empty string. And for dates, we would get 1900-01-01 back. If you set USE_TYPE_DEFAULT to False, then the PolyBase engine will return NULL wherever it finds a value is missing.

Now that we have an external data source and an external file format, we can move to the final step: creating an external table.

External Tables

An external table behaves to the end user like a regular table, but has one key difference: the data is stored somewhere other than SQL Server. Otherwise, the behavior as part of a SELECT statement is the same, even down to using two-part naming for tables (i.e., dbo.MyTable) vs. the four-part naming that you would use for a linked server (like MyServer.MyExternalDatabase.dbo.MyTable).

The syntax for creating an external table is fairly simple, as Listing 2-6 shows. The first half of the table creation statement is just like creating any other table save for the EXTERNAL keyword. But once we get past the column definition section, things start to change.

Listing 2-6. Creating an external table

```
IF (OBJECT_ID(N'dbo.NorthCarolinaPopulation') IS NULL)
BEGIN
    CREATE EXTERNAL TABLE dbo.NorthCarolinaPopulation
    (
        SumLev INT NOT NULL,
        County INT NOT NULL,
        Place INT NOT NULL,
        IsPrimaryGeography BIT NOT NULL,
        [Name] VARCHAR(120) NOT NULL,
        PopulationType VARCHAR(20) NOT NULL,
        Year INT NOT NULL,
        Population INT NOT NULL
    )
    WITH
    (
        LOCATION = N'Census/NorthCarolinaPopulation.csv',
        DATA_SOURCE = AzureNCPopBlob,
        FILE_FORMAT = CsvFileFormat,
        REJECT_TYPE = VALUE,
        REJECT_VALUE = 5
    );
END
GO
```

Inside the WITH block, we define five parameters. The first parameter is our file location, and this can represent either an individual file or an entire folder. In the preceding external table, we are going to read from a single file, NorthCarolinaPopulation.csv. If we had Census data for a number of states, we could simply reference the Census/ folder, and the PolyBase engine is smart enough to retrieve all files underneath that folder.

After the LOCATION parameter, we have the two external references that we just defined: DATA_SOURCE and FILE_FORMAT. These tell the PolyBase engine where the data lives and in what format it exists, respectively.

The final two parameters explain how we want to handle row rejection. When working with Big Data systems, invalid data is a way of life. The reason for this is that Big Data systems tend to store data in a semistructured format. This means that we do not define a data structure when writing the data; instead, we define it when reading the data, otherwise known as "schema on read." By contrast, relational databases are examples of structured data sets (or "schema on write"), where we predefine the number of columns, data types, nullability, primary and unique key constraints, foreign key constraints, check constraints, and triggers to guarantee the structure of our data. This guarantee comes at a performance cost, however: it takes time and CPU cycles to check all of these things upfront, so we defer the checks in Big Data systems until later to allow our writers to push data as quickly as possible.

If those checks fail when querying an external table—that is, if the format of the data differs from our definition—PolyBase rejects the row, and it does not appear in our final result set. In the preceding case, if the engine rejects more than five rows, then the entire query fails and we get an error like the one in Figure 2-8. In this case, to force an error, I changed the value of REJECT_VALUE from 5 to 1 by dropping and re-creating the external table with the new rejection value setting.

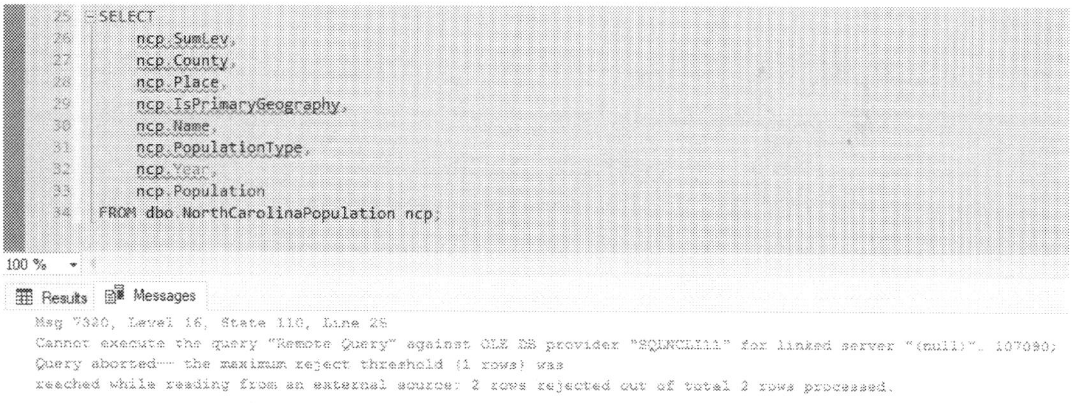

Figure 2-8. *If we have more rows fail than the REJECT_VALUE setting allows, the database engine returns an error with message number 7320*

There are two possible values for REJECT_TYPE: VALUE and PERCENTAGE. The VALUE setting is straightforward: if, during processing, the PolyBase engine encounters more than that number of rows with errors, it will end query processing and return an error with message number 7320. Because the engine throws an error, the SQL client—whether

SQL Server Management Studio, Azure Data Studio, or something else—will clear out the result set, meaning that if processing is 99% of the way through and errors out at the very end, you get none of the data back. For long-running queries, this can be a frustrating outcome.

The alternative is to use the PERCENTAGE rejection type. If you decide to set REJECT_TYPE = PERCENTAGE, then REJECT_VALUE becomes the percent of records which must fail before the PolyBase engine returns an error. If you do use this type, you must also set a parameter REJECT_SAMPLE_VALUE, an integer value which determines how many rows to pull in before recalculating the rejection percentage. For example, suppose you set the value of REJECT_SAMPLE_VALUE to 5000 and REJECT_VALUE to 20. The PolyBase engine will retrieve the first 5000 rows, determine how many of those rows fail to fit our external table structure, and determine if that failure percentage is above 20%. If the first batch has 750 failures out of 5000, our failure percentage is 15%. Because this is below 20%, the engine will pull the next 5000 rows. Suppose that there are 1100 failures in this second batch. The PolyBase engine will then calculate the **total** failure rate, meaning (750 + 1100) / (5000 + 5000), or 18.5%. Because this is still below 20%, we retrieve the next 5000 rows. If that batch has 1500 errors, our new failure rate is 22.3% (3350 / 15,000), and so processing stops.

Tip   I recommend setting rejection value counts rather than percentages as long as the number of rows does not fluctuate wildly over time. When first creating an external table, I like to set the rejection threshold extremely high—I want to pull in all of the data and see how many records I get back. If there is a large discrepancy between my expected row counts and actual row counts, I can investigate the matter, fix my input data (or my external table definition), and try again until I have a reasonable number of rows. Once I have that in place, I drop and re-create the external table definition with a much more restrictive rejected row count. This gives me a warning if the incoming data structure has changed in a way which violates my external table design.

Now that we have created all of the necessary components for Azure Blob Storage integration, we can begin writing T-SQL queries against the data.

Querying External Data

One of the best features about PolyBase is that it takes the same T-SQL syntax for querying internal (as opposed to external), relational SQL Server tables and extends that functionality to external data sources without consideration for where that data really lives. For example, in Listing 2-7, we can see that selecting all columns and rows from the external table is the same as selecting from a regular table in the PolyBaseRevealed database—in fact, if we had not spent much of this chapter setting everything up, you might not have known this was an external table at all!

Listing 2-7. Querying data from an external table

```
SELECT
    ncp.SumLev AS SummaryLevel,
    ncp.County,
    ncp.Place,
    ncp.IsPrimaryGeography,
    ncp.name,
    ncp.PopulationType,
    ncp.year,
    ncp.Population
FROM dbo.NorthCarolinaPopulation ncp;
GO
```

Something interesting if you run this query is that it returns back 13,607 rows, but if you open the original CSV file in Excel, you will notice that there are 13,611 rows including the header. The header accounts for one of these four rows, but as for the remainder of the rows, PolyBase tells us little. We will see in Chapter 9 some special functionality in Azure Synapse Analytics which makes this discovery process easier, and Chapter 5 will show a technique for discovering errors when creating external tables against the on-premises product. In this chapter, we will investigate the data ourselves without any help from the PolyBase services. In Figure 2-9, I have narrowed down the search to find the three offending rows: records with a character "A" instead of a valid integer for that area's population. Because the Population attribute has a data type of integer, and because there is no valid conversion from "A" to an integer, the row fails its data quality check, and PolyBase silently ignores the row while incrementing an internal rejected row counter.

SUMLEV	COUNTY	PLACE	PRIMGEO_FLAG	NAME	POPTYPE	YEAR	POPULATION
162	0	23980	0 Fontana Dam town		CENSUSPOP	2010	A
157	75	23980	1 Fontana Dam town		CENSUSPOP	2010	A
157	125	10120	1 Candor town (pt.)		CENSUSPOP	2010	A

Figure 2-9. *One header row and three invalid population values fail data quality checks*

Narrowing down our external table is also easy because the WHERE clause works exactly the same way as with regular tables. Listing 2-8 shows us that we can filter data in external tables with no special effort.

Listing 2-8. The WHERE clause works the same as with standard tables in SQL Server

```
SELECT
    ncp.name,
    ncp.Population
FROM dbo.NorthCarolinaPopulation ncp
WHERE
    ncp.year = 2017
    AND ncp.PopulationType = 'POPESTIMATE'
    AND ncp.County = 0
    AND ncp.SumLev = 162
ORDER BY
    Population DESC,
    name ASC;
GO
```

We can even join external tables to regular SQL Server tables. In Listing 2-9, we have two tables in the PolyBaseRevealed database, one called dbo.PopulationCenter and the other named dbo.CityPopulationCenter, which tables you can create from the book's source code repository. The population center table has two rows representing a pair of regions in North Carolina: the Triangle area, which includes cities like Raleigh, Durham, and Chapel Hill; and the Triad area, which includes cities like Greensboro, High Point, and Winston-Salem. The specific cities which make up each region show up in the city to population center junction table.

Note   For those aggrieved parties who will insist that I have sullied their honor by not including their towns of residence in this table, I included only the largest cities and towns in each population center, selecting as a cutoff those cities and towns with approximately 50,000 or more residents. If your town is not in this list, you have my word that I fully agree that you are a resident of the Triad or Triangle and a fantastic person to boot.

Listing 2-9. Retrieving data by region in North Carolina. Towns and cities outside of our two population centers will appear but display NULL instead of a population center name

```
SELECT
    ncp.name,
    cpc.PopulationCenterName,
    ncp.Population
FROM dbo.NorthCarolinaPopulation ncp
    LEFT OUTER JOIN dbo.CityPopulationCenter cpc
        ON ncp.name = cpc.CityName
WHERE
    ncp.year = 2017
    AND ncp.PopulationType = 'POPESTIMATE'
    AND ncp.County = 0
    AND ncp.SumLev = 162
ORDER BY
    Population DESC,
    name ASC;
GO
```

Figure 2-10 shows the first few results of this query. We can see that some of the largest cities in the state make up these two population centers, but the largest city in the state—Charlotte—is in neither center.

▲ RESULTS	Name	PopulationCent...	Population
1	Charlotte city	*NULL*	859035
2	Raleigh city	Triangle	464758
3	Greensboro city	Triad	290222
4	Durham city	Triangle	267743
5	Winston-Sale...	Triad	244605
6	Fayetteville city	*NULL*	209889
7	Cary town	Triangle	165904
8	Wilmington city	*NULL*	119045
9	High Point city	Triad	111513
10	Greenville city	*NULL*	92156

Figure 2-10. *The largest cities in North Carolina based on population estimates from 2017*

Once we have this data available to us in SQL Server, we can use the full range of T-SQL syntax and, at least as far as functionality goes, ignore the actual location of this data. Listing 2-10 aggregates city populations by population center, leaving out cities like Charlotte which do not belong in either center.

Listing 2-10. We can aggregate external table data with regular tables exactly the same way that we would aggregate two regular tables

```
SELECT
    cpc.PopulationCenterName,
    SUM(ncp.Population) AS TotalPopulation
FROM dbo.NorthCarolinaPopulation ncp
    INNER JOIN dbo.CityPopulationCenter cpc
        ON ncp.name = cpc.CityName
WHERE
    ncp.year = 2017
    AND ncp.PopulationType = 'POPESTIMATE'
    AND ncp.County = 0
```

```
    AND ncp.SumLev = 162
GROUP BY
    cpc.PopulationCenterName;
GO
```

Figure 2-11 gives us the results, showing that the Triangle area is the larger of the two population centers.

⊿ RESULTS		
	PopulationCent...	TotalPopulation
1	Triad	699417
2	Triangle	1008718

Figure 2-11. *Population estimates for the Triangle and Triad population centers for the year 2017. This might help you win a bar bet someday*

In addition to retrieving data from external tables, PolyBase also gives us the ability to insert data into external tables.

Inserting into External Tables

In order to insert data into Azure Blob Storage via PolyBase, we need to set one configuration option first. Listing 2-11 shows us how to enable PolyBase data export.

Listing 2-11. Enable PolyBase data export functionality

```
EXEC sp_configure
    @configname = 'allow polybase export',
    @configvalue = 1;
GO
RECONFIGURE
GO
```

Once we enable this setting, we can now insert data. To motivate this example, I will create two tables in SQL Server which contain information on people and locations. Listing 2-12 builds out these two tables in the PolyBaseRevealed database.

Listing 2-12. Create two SQL Server–based tables with sample data

```sql
USE [PolyBaseRevealed]
GO
CREATE TABLE dbo.Person
(
    PersonID INT NOT NULL,
    FirstName NVARCHAR(75) NOT NULL,
    LastName NVARCHAR(75) NOT NULL
);

INSERT INTO dbo.Person
(
    PersonID,
    FirstName,
    LastName
)
VALUES
(1, N'Test', N'User'),
(2, N'Second', N'User'),
(3, N'Another', N'Person');

CREATE TABLE dbo.Location
(
    LocationID INT PRIMARY KEY NOT NULL,
    LocationName NVARCHAR(75) NOT NULL
);

INSERT INTO dbo.[Location]
(
    LocationID,
    LocationName
)
VALUES
(1, N'Sheboygan'),
(2, N'Walla Walla'),
(3, N'Okeechobee');
```

We also have data showing when the people in our data set visited these various locations, which you can find in the Visits.txt file in the provided code repository's Data folder. Move this Visits.txt file up to a new Blob Container on your Azure storage account called visits and then run the code in Listing 2-13 to create a new external data source and external table, replacing cspolybaseblob with the name of your storage account.

Listing 2-13. Create a new external data source for the new Blob Container and an external table which uses it

```
CREATE EXTERNAL DATA SOURCE AzureVisitsBlob WITH
(
    TYPE = HADOOP,
    LOCATION = 'wasbs://visits@cspolybaseblob.blob.core.windows.net',
    CREDENTIAL = AzureStorageCredential
);
GO
CREATE EXTERNAL TABLE dbo.Visits
(
    PersonID INT NOT NULL,
    LocationID INT NOT NULL,
    VisitDate DATE NOT NULL
)
WITH
(
    LOCATION = N'Visits/',
    DATA_SOURCE = AzureVisitsBlob,
    FILE_FORMAT = CsvFileFormat,
    REJECT_TYPE = VALUE,
    REJECT_VALUE = 1
);
GO
```

To ensure that you have loaded the data properly, run Listing 2-14, which joins the data in SQL Server with the Visits external table. You should get five rows back.

Listing 2-14. Query the Visits external table and enrich its results with data from SQL Server

```
SELECT
    v.PersonID,
    p.FirstName,
    p.LastName,
    v.LocationID,
    l.LocationName,
    v.VisitDate
FROM dbo.Visits v
    INNER JOIN dbo.Person p
        ON v.PersonID = p.PersonID
    CROSS APPLY
    (
        SELECT TOP(1)
            l.LocationName
        FROM dbo.Location l
        WHERE
            l.LocationID = v.LocationID
    ) l;
GO
```

Note   The reason this query contains a CROSS APPLY rather than another INNER JOIN is to show that the PolyBase engine covers parts of T-SQL which are outside the ANSI SQL standard.

Figure 2-12 shows the results of this query.

	PersonID	FirstName	LastName	LocationID	LocationName	VisitDate
1	1	Test	User	1	Sheboygan	2019-03-07
2	1	Test	User	2	Walla Walla	2019-03-08
3	2	Second	User	1	Sheboygan	2019-02-06
4	2	Second	User	3	Okeechobee	2019-03-04
5	3	Another	Person	3	Okeechobee	2019-03-01

Figure 2-12. Five rows in the Visits table

We can now insert rows into this external table like we would any other table.
Listing 2-15 shows an example of inserting a new row.

Listing 2-15. Insert a new row into the Visits table

```
--Insert a new visitation
INSERT INTO dbo.Visits
(
          PersonID,
          LocationID,
          VisitDate
)
VALUES
    (1,1,'1900-01-01');
GO
```

Running the query from Listing 2-14 again, we get six results this time, as Figure 2-13 shows.

	PersonID	FirstName	LastName	LocationID	LocationName	VisitDate
1	1	Test	User	1	Sheboygan	1900-01-01
2	2	Second	User	1	Sheboygan	2019-02-06
3	3	Another	Person	3	Okeechobee	2019-03-01
4	2	Second	User	3	Okeechobee	2019-03-04
5	1	Test	User	1	Sheboygan	2019-03-07
6	1	Test	User	2	Walla Walla	2019-03-08

Figure 2-13. *A new row appears in our Visits external table*

Over in Azure, we can see in Figure 2-14 that inserting a single record resulted in the creation of four new files, three of which are empty.

Name	Access Tier	Access Tier Last Modified	Last Modified	Blob Type	Content Type	Size	Status
QID513_20190114_133126_0.txt	Hot (inferred)		1/14/2019, 1:31:36 PM	Block Blob	application/octet-stream	15 B	Active
QID513_20190114_133126_1.txt	Hot (inferred)		1/14/2019, 1:31:36 PM	Block Blob	application/octet-stream	0 B	Active
QID513_20190114_133126_2.txt	Hot (inferred)		1/14/2019, 1:31:35 PM	Block Blob	application/octet-stream	0 B	Active
QID513_20190114_133126_3.txt	Hot (inferred)		1/14/2019, 1:31:36 PM	Block Blob	application/octet-stream	0 B	Active
Visits.txt	Hot (inferred)		12/29/2018, 4:06:32 PM	Block Blob	text/plain	109 B	Active

Figure 2-14. *Inserting a row resulted in the creation of four files*

The PolyBase engine will create at least four files when inserting to Azure Blob Storage regardless of the number of records you insert. The format of the resulting set of file names is the execution ID (such as QID513), followed by the date and time of insertion, followed by a unique number for each thread or process working on exporting this data. Depending upon the number of rows of data to insert and how PolyBase internally distributes the data to different threads and machines, each of these files may have a different number of rows. As data sizes grow larger, the files will remain similar in size but are never guaranteed to be exactly the same number of rows or the same data size.

Now that we have looked at the basics of inserting data, we will now cover a few gotchas around data insertion.

PolyBase Data Insertion Considerations

You may run into a few issues when trying to insert data into PolyBase. The purpose of this section is to cover some of the most common issues.

PolyBase Is Insert-Only

PolyBase only allows you to insert data into an external table; it does not allow for updating, deleting, or merging data. If you attempt to run an UPDATE, DELETE, or MERGE statement, you will receive an error message 46519 like in Figure 2-15.

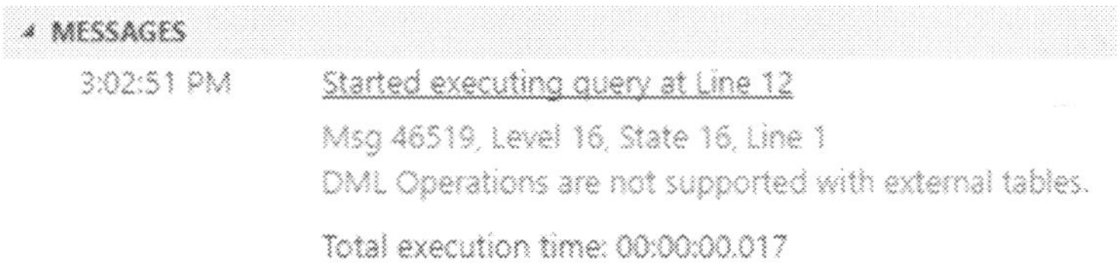

Figure 2-15. *PolyBase does not support Data Manipulation Language (DML) operations aside from data insertion*

The reason for this is that the Hadoop Distributed File System (HDFS) is append-only, meaning that you can add to files but cannot update existing rows or delete rows in individual files. This is fairly normal for data analytic engines, which—in contrast to OLTP systems—are typically Write-Once Read-Many (WORM) by design. PolyBase uses WASB, an extension of HDFS, to write data to Azure Blob Storage. Therefore, the same rules apply here as with a proper Hadoop cluster.

Insert Only into Folders

PolyBase will only allow you to insert into an Azure Blob Storage folder. If you define your external table location as an existing file and attempt to insert into the external table, you will receive the error message shown in Figure 2-16. If you try to beat the system and create an external table with a location like Visits/MyVisits.txt, PolyBase will create a new folder called MyVisits.txt underneath the Visits folder and will write multiple files.

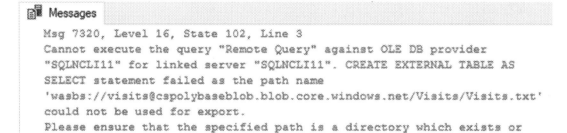

Figure 2-16. *PolyBase only supports inserting into directories*

Conclusion

In this chapter, we looked at how PolyBase integrates with Azure Blob Storage. We started by creating an Azure storage account and uploading data to it. After that, we walked through the critical mechanisms behind PolyBase: the external data source, external file format, and external table. We saw that querying an external table is just as easy as querying a regular table using T-SQL, and we can use proprietary T-SQL constructs like CROSS APPLY with our external table calls. Finally, we covered inserting into external tables, including coverage of some of the most common insertion errors.

Our work in this chapter will set us up well for Chapter 3, where we will take a look at the original use case for PolyBase: integration with Hadoop.

CHAPTER 3

Connecting to Hadoop

Chapter 2 showed us how to use PolyBase to integrate SQL Server with Azure Blob Storage. In this chapter, we will integrate to the original external data source: Hadoop. In the first part of this chapter, we will take a peek at an already-built Hadoop cluster. Then, we will configure PolyBase to work with the two key variants of Hadoop (pending the release of an on-premises version of Cloudera Data Platform). Next, we will review what changes in terms of PolyBase functionality between Azure Blob Storage and Hadoop. After this review, we will create the infrastructure needed to query a Hadoop external data source. Finally, we will query this external data source and confirm that data retrieval and data insertion both work as they do in Azure Blob Storage.

Caution   If you skipped over Chapter 2 because you have no plans to use Azure Blob Storage, you might miss out on important PolyBase concepts. Start with the section entitled "Building a Link" for material which applies not only to Azure Blob Storage but to many other external data sources as well.

Hadoop Prerequisites

In this chapter, I will assume that you already have a Hadoop cluster in place. Supported cluster configurations include the Hortonworks Data Platform (HDP) and Cloudera Distribution of Hadoop (CDH). PolyBase does not officially support clusters built off of the MapR Converged Data Platform, the Amazon Hadoop distribution, or a custom-built Hadoop cluster, although I have seen successful cases of custom-built Hadoop clusters working. Importantly, PolyBase does not support Azure's HDInsight, Amazon's Elastic MapReduce, or the Cloudera Data Platform cloud, all of which are prebuilt, scalable

© Kevin Feasel 2020
K. Feasel, *PolyBase Revealed*, https://doi.org/10.1007/978-1-4842-5461-5_3

cloud-based Hadoop clusters. The PolyBase engine requires access to certain ports which are locked down on managed Hadoop cluster platforms, so if you have spun up a cluster in preparation for this chapter, save yourself the money and get rid of it.

In order to follow along, the easiest approach is to build out your own cluster using Ambari for HDP or deploying CDH through the Cloudera Manager. Hortonworks and Cloudera both provide great instructions for installing Hadoop from scratch, so if you want a weekend project which inevitably drags out for a month as you try to fix a seemingly never-ending series of weird issues, look at the installation guide for either of those.

Another alternative is to use a sandbox: a single-node Hadoop cluster with everything preinstalled and configured. Cloudera provides sandbox virtual machines for Hortonworks Data Platform and the Cloudera Distribution of Hadoop on their web site. Using a sandbox can be easier, but if you decide to download the Hortonworks Data Platform sandbox for any version from HDP 2.5 on, be forewarned that you will experience issues because the sandboxed data nodes are actually Docker containers. Chapter 5 includes a detailed discussion on how to configure such a system. By contrast, the CDH QuickStart VM does not use Docker to separate its data node from the name node, and so the PolyBase engine and data movement service are capable of connecting without issue. If you would like to try out a Hadoop cluster and have no experience building one, the CDH QuickStart is probably the better option (and I say that as a long-time fan of the Hortonworks Data Platform distribution of Hadoop).

Assuming you have a Hadoop cluster already in place, we will now review the necessary components for PolyBase, including the Hadoop Distributed File System (HDFS), YARN, and MapReduce.

Preparing Files in HDFS

Before we begin configuring PolyBase on the SQL Server side, we will need to prepare our Hadoop cluster. In this section, I will use for my Hadoop cluster a Hortonworks Data Platform 3.0 installation. If you have a Cloudera Distribution of Hadoop installation, the screenshots will differ a little from what your distribution has to offer, but in this section, the work will fundamentally be the same.

The first thing we need to do is upload the data sets we would like to use into HDFS. For this chapter, we will use three data sets, two of which are in the Data folder of the accompanying code repository. Our first data set comes from the city of Raleigh,

North Carolina's Open Data initiative and includes 232,127 police incidents from the year 2014 into the beginning of January 2019. If you would like to obtain a more recent version of this file, the Open Data Raleigh web site hosts this police incident data at `http://data-ral.opendata.arcgis.com/datasets/raleigh-police-incidents-nibrs`.

The second accompanying data set contains 177,738 reports of incidents from the various fire departments of Raleigh, North Carolina. Open Data Raleigh hosts this data set as well, and you can obtain a recent version at `https://data-ral.opendata.arcgis.com/datasets/fire-incidents`.

Note   The Raleigh fire incidents data set is a particularly difficult one for PolyBase to parse. The version in the book's accompanying code repository includes several changes to reduce the number of errors, including removing newlines from address line 2, changing the formatting to tab-separated values, and converting dates to a format PolyBase can read. I also modified the Raleigh police incidents data set to change dates to a PolyBase-supported format.

The third data set we will use in this chapter is a much larger data set: parking violations in New York City for fiscal years 2015 through 2017. This adds up to approximately 6.5 GB of data in uncompressed text files and compresses down to just under 1 GB when using the 7z compression format. You can also grab a copy of the original data set from the New York City Open Data initiative web site at `https://data.cityofnewyork.us/browse?q=parking+violations`. This link will include the Parking Violations Issued data sets for several fiscal years, as well as a few other data sets which are unnecessary for this chapter.

Once you have your data sets ready and unzipped, you will want to create a directory in HDFS called PolyBaseData. To do this, you will need to open a terminal session to your cluster and run the commands in Listing 3-1.

Listing 3-1. Commands to create a new directory called PolyBaseData in HDFS and grant full access to everybody. In a production environment, you might want to limit access to this folder to certain users or groups

```
sudo -u hdfs hadoop fs -mkdir /PolyBaseData
sudo -u hdfs hadoop fs -chmod 777 /PolyBaseData
```

The first command runs the mkdir command against the Hadoop Distributed File System as the hdfs user, which is the default name for this user in HDP. We create the new directory and then run chmod to grant all users read, write, and execute permissions to this folder. That way, our lesser-privileged user accounts can upload and read data without permission issues.

On the topic of user accounts, we will need to decide whether to use the default pdw_user account for PolyBase or use a separate account. If you decide to use the default account, create a new user on your name node and a user directory in HDFS like in Listing 3-2.

Note   Separate accounts only come into play if you have configured your Hadoop cluster to work with Kerberos. If you do not have Kerberos enabled on your Hadoop cluster, then the PolyBase engine will only use the pdw_user account.

Listing 3-2. Create a new pdw_user account

```
sudo useradd pdw_user
sudo passwd pdw_user
sudo -u hdfs hadoop fs -mkdir /user/pdw_user
sudo -u hdfs hadoop fs -chown pdw_user /user/pdw_user
```

If you are following along, your terminal will look something like Figure 3-1 after you have created the pdw_user account.

```
 kevin@clusterino: /
kevin@clusterino:/$ sudo useradd pdw_user
[sudo] password for kevin:
kevin@clusterino:/$ sudo passwd pdw_user
Enter new UNIX password:
Retype new UNIX password:
passwd: password updated successfully
kevin@clusterino:/$ sudo -u hdfs hadoop fs -mkdir /user/pdw_user
kevin@clusterino:/$ sudo -u hdfs hadoop fs -chown pdw_user /user/pdw_user
kevin@clusterino:/$ █
```

Figure 3-1. *Creating a pdw_user account for PolyBase to use as its default account*

If you would instead like to use an existing user account, you will need to create the appropriate credential later when building your external data source in SQL Server.

Now that we have our HDFS directory and user accounts prepared, we can begin to push files into HDFS. There are several techniques to do this, but the easiest one when working with HDP is to upload using the Files View in Ambari. Figure 3-2 shows where you can find the Files View in the Views menu located in the top-right corner of the Ambari user interface.

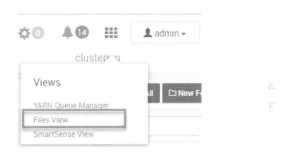

Figure 3-2. *The Files View comes with Ambari and works for all supported versions of HDP*

The Files View shows an Explorer-style listing of files in HDFS. You can navigate down by clicking one of the folder links, such as the PolyBaseData link. You can navigate back up the tree using the breadcrumbs in the status bar near the top of the page. Once you have navigated into the PolyBaseData folder, Figure 3-3 shows the button you can use to upload a file.

Name >	Size >	Last Modified >	Owner >	Group >	Permission	Erasure Coding	Encrypted
Fire_Incidents.csv	64.5 MB	2019-01-06 11:56	admin	ndfs	-rw-r--r--		No

Figure 3-3. *Uploading files is as easy as pressing a button*

Clicking this button will pop up a modal dialog which asks you to upload a single file at a time. You can click the box in the middle of the screen to select a file, or drag a file from Windows Explorer onto the file box. Whichever method you choose, you will see something like Figure 3-4, a dialog with a progress bar showing you how far along you are in loading this data. Depending upon the file size and your network connection, this might take some time, so be patient.

Figure 3-4. *Uploading a file. This dialog can sit at 100% for a few seconds as processing finalizes*

Upload the Raleigh fire incident and police incident data sets into the main PolyBaseData directory. If you decide to use the New York City parking incident data sets, I recommend creating two additional folders: NYCParkingTickets and NYCParkingTicketsORC. We will use the ORC folder later, but for now, upload the uncompressed CSV files into NYCParkingTickets.

Now that we have data, we can obtain important configuration details that we will need to bring back to SQL Server.

Gather Configuration Settings

In order to connect to Hadoop, we are going to need a few pieces of information. If you are using the Hortonworks Data Platform, we first will need to know the version of HDP installed. To get this information, navigate to /usr/hdp/ and look for a directory name. In my case, it is 3.0.1.0-187 but your version will likely differ.

The next thing we need to know, regardless of the distribution, is the address and port for HDFS. In Ambari, go to the HDFS service and then click the "Configs" button. Navigate to the Advanced configurations section, expand the Advanced core-site section, and copy the value for `fs.defaultFS`. Figure 3-5 shows this process in Ambari.

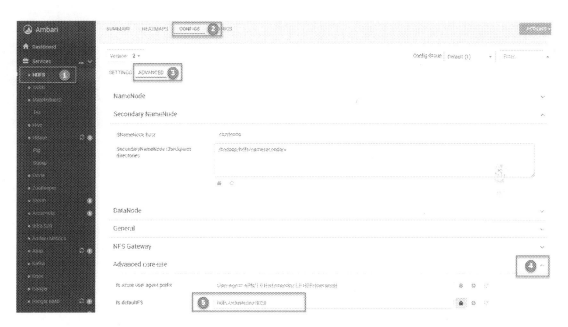

Figure 3-5. *Obtain the location where HDFS is listening from Ambari*

Alternatively, on a terminal, you can navigate to `/etc/hadoop/conf` and run `grep -n1 fs.defaultFS core-site.xml`, and this will show the address as well.

After obtaining the address and port for HDFS access, we will need the location and port for YARN, Hadoop's resource manager. In the same terminal window as earlier, type `grep -n1 yarn.resourcemanager.address yarn-site.xml`, and you will see the appropriate server name and port. By default, this will be your name node on port 8050, but you will want to make sure of this.

If you prefer to use Ambari to find this information, navigate to the YARN service, and in the advanced configuration settings, expand the Advanced yarn-site section and look for the appropriate key. Figure 3-6 shows the end result of this search.

yarn.nodemanager.vmem-check-enabled	false			
yarn.nodemanager.webapp.cross-origin.enabled	true			
yarn.resourcemanager.address	clusterino:8050			
yarn.resourcemanager.admin.address	clusterino:8141			
yarn.resourcemanager.am.max-attempts	2			
yarn.resourcemanager.bind-host	0.0.0.0			
yarn.resourcemanager.display.per-user-apps				

Figure 3-6. *The YARN resource manager address will be important for running jobs in Hadoop*

This resource manager address is technically not necessary for integrating with Hadoop, but it does enable something which can be quite valuable: predicate pushdown. Predicate pushdown is the topic for Chapter 4, so we will defer discussion of the topic until then.

Now that we have the key pieces of information for connecting to Hadoop, let's return to our SQL Server instances for further configuration.

Configuring SQL Server

In Chapter 2, we saw that we needed to create four things in order for SQL Server to interact with Azure Blob Storage via PolyBase: a credential, an external data source, an external file format, and an external table. We will still need to create three of these four, but we will need to do some additional work beforehand.

The first thing to do is ensure that your Hadoop connectivity setting is correct. If you are using a recent version of the Cloudera Distribution of Hadoop, you should use a value of 6. Alternatively, if you are using the Hortonworks Data Platform distribution, use a value of 7. Listing 3-3 shows us how to configure the Hadoop connectivity option in SQL Server.

Listing 3-3. Set the Hadoop connectivity setting to a value of 6 if you are connecting to a CDH cluster or 7 if you are connecting to an HDP cluster

```
EXEC sp_configure
    @configname = 'hadoop connectivity',
    @configvalue = 7;
GO
RECONFIGURE
GO
```

After that, we need to ensure that we can communicate with our Hadoop services through their hostnames, not just IP addresses. For example, my Hadoop cluster is named clusterino, so any SQL Server instances which should be able to communicate with my Hadoop cluster must know how to reach clusterino on the network. In a corporate environment, this would likely include appropriate DNS aliases; for a home lab, you can also modify values in the Windows hosts file, which is located at `%WINDIR%\system32\drivers\etc\hosts`. You will need to open this file with administrative privileges if you wish to save changes. Figure 3-7 shows sample entries from a host file, including two valid host lines and one commented out.

```
# localhost name resolution is handled within DNS itself.
#        127.0.0.1          localhost
#        ::1                localhost
192.168.100.116            clusterino
#192.168.100.104           sandbox-hdp.hortonworks.com
192.168.100.104            quickstart.cloudera
```

Figure 3-7. *Clusterino and the Cloudera QuickStart VM have entries in this hosts file*

If you can ping your Hadoop cluster from the server hosting SQL Server and get a response back, then this is set up correctly, and you can move to the next step in Hadoop configuration for PolyBase.

Update PolyBase Configuration Files

The next step when configuring PolyBase to connect to a Hadoop cluster is to set your yarn-site.xml and mapred-site.xml files. Assuming that you installed SQL Server to the default location and have installed SQL Server 2019, you will find the configuration files in `%PROGRAMFILES%\Microsoft SQL Server\MSSQL15.MSSQLSERVER\ MSSQL\Binn\Polybase\ Hadoop\conf`. For versions prior to SQL Server 2019, the directory will be `MSSQL14` (for SQL Server 2017) or `MSSQL13` (for SQL Server 2016), and if you have a named instance installed but no default, you will need to replace `MSSQLSERVER` with the name of your instance.

Inside this directory, there are two files of interest to us: mapred-site.xml and yarn-site.xml. The mapred-site.xml configuration file handles configuration settings for MapReduce jobs and will be necessary for predicate pushdown in Chapter 4. Replace your mapred-site.xml in SQL Server's configuration folder with the contents of the *Sample mapred-site.xml* file in the accompanying code repository. You can find *Sample mapred-site.xml* in the accompanying code repository by navigating to the Chapter 03 folder and then the conf folder underneath that.

Inside that conf folder, we have two sample yarn-site.xml files, one for CDH and the other for HDP. If you are using CDH, copy the contents of *Sample yarn-site_CDH.xml* into your PolyBase yarn-site.xml configuration file. If you are using HDP, first open the *Sample yarn-site_HDP.xml* file and ensure that all references in `yarn.application.classpath` point to the version of the Hortonworks Data Platform that you have installed. This is the directory you made note of earlier in this chapter and will look something like `/usr/hdp/3.0.1.0-187/`. Find and replace the version in the config file with your version, and then you can copy the contents of this file into your PolyBase yarn-site.xml configuration file.

Caution   Some of the documentation you will find online will have you use `/usr/ hdp/current` as the starting directory for your classpath references. This may not work as expected because the PolyBase engine assumes the location of certain libraries and Java binaries, and the symbolic links in `/usr/hdp/current` differ from what we need. The safer route is to reference a specific version of the Hortonworks Data Platform. If you wish to upgrade HDP without needing to change PolyBase configuration files, you can also create a symbolic link to your HDP version in `/usr/hdp` and reference that folder in the configuration file. That way, when you upgrade HDP, you need only switch the symbolic link's pointer to allow PolyBase to use the new version.

Now that we have everything configured, we can begin to create external objects in SQL Server.

External PolyBase Objects for Hadoop

In Chapter 2, we looked at the core of external PolyBase objects: credentials, external data sources, external file formats, and external table. In this section, we will briefly cover the overlap between Azure Blob Storage and Hadoop objects, but our focus will be on what PolyBase brings to the table specifically for Hadoop.

Credentials

Credentials are only needed if you have Kerberos enabled on your Hadoop cluster and wish to link an external data source to a specific user account rather than the default pdw_user account. Listing 3-4 shows how you can create a Database Scoped Credential based off of some user account.

Listing 3-4. Create a new Database Scoped Credential if you are using Kerberos on your Hadoop cluster

```
CREATE DATABASE SCOPED CREDENTIAL HadoopSomeUserAccount
WITH IDENTITY='<SomeUserAccount>',
SECRET='<SomePassword>';
```

If you wish to use the default user account, you do not need to create a credential.

External Data Sources

External data sources for Hadoop look similar to those for Azure Blob Storage, except that we have one new parameter: the resource manager location. This is the server and port on which YARN is listening and will be critical for running MapReduce jobs against the cluster. If you do not have YARN installed or enabled on your Hadoop cluster, the PolyBase data movement service will still be able to pull data from your Hadoop cluster like it would Azure Blob Storage. What you lose, however, is the ability to offload some of the work onto your Hadoop cluster and away from expensive SQL Server instances.

Listing 3-5 gives an example of an external data source connecting to a Hadoop cluster named clusterino. Clusterino is running Hortonworks Data Platform 3.0, and the name node handles both HDFS and YARN.

Note   If you have a Cloudera Distribution of Hadoop cluster running, your resource manager port might be 8032 instead of the 8050 listed in the following. Be sure to review the configuration section earlier in this chapter if you do not know the port number for YARN.

Listing 3-5. Create a new external data source for Hadoop

```
IF (DB_ID('PolyBaseRevealed') IS NULL)
BEGIN
    CREATE DATABASE PolyBaseRevealed;
END
GO
USE [PolyBaseRevealed]
GO
IF NOT EXISTS
(
    SELECT 1
    FROM sys.external_data_sources s
    WHERE
        s.name = N'Clusterino'
)
BEGIN
    CREATE EXTERNAL DATA SOURCE Clusterino WITH
    (
        TYPE = HADOOP,
        LOCATION = 'hdfs://clusterino:8020',
        RESOURCE_MANAGER_LOCATION = N'clusterino:8050'
    );
END
GO
```

In this case, I will not connect to Hadoop via Kerberos, so I do not need to specify a credential. If you do not have Kerberos configured and still specify a credential, PolyBase queries will work, but they will run as pdw_user instead of your credential.

External File Formats

The biggest difference between Azure Blob Storage and Hadoop concerns file formats. Azure Blob Storage can technically support the same set of file formats as Hadoop, but we typically see delimited files dominate in Azure Blob Storage. In Hadoop, however, the popularity of SQL interfaces like Hive and Impala have driven developers to come up with file formats more suitable for data storage and retrieval than delimited files. PolyBase supports three of these file formats: RCFile, ORC, and Parquet. Table 3-1 shows all four formats and provides a quick summary for each.

Table 3-1. *A comparative listing of valid PolyBase external file formats*

File Format	Benefits	Drawbacks	Best Uses
Delimited file	Easy to use	Less efficient Slower performance	Getting started Reading row-major data
RCFile	Columnar	Two strictly superior options exist	Don't use this unless you have legacy data
ORC	Great aggregate performance	Columnar not always a good fit Slower to write than Parquet	Non-nested files you aggregate frequently
Parquet	Great aggregate performance	Columnar not always a good fit Often larger than ORC	Aggregating nested data

Now we will look at each file format, starting with delimited files.

Delimited Files

Public data sets typically come as delimited files, often in comma-separated values (CSV) format but sometimes using delimiters like the tab, semicolon, pipe (|), or tilde (~). For more details on delimited files, review the section entitled "Delimited Files" in Chapter 2.

In the following examples, we will use two file formats, one which reads comma-separated files and one which reads tab-separated files. Listing 3-6 includes the code to create both of these format file specifications.

Listing 3-6. Create external file formats for two delimited file types

```
IF NOT EXISTS
(
    SELECT 1
    FROM sys.external_file_formats e
    WHERE
        e.name = N'CsvFileFormat'
)
BEGIN
    CREATE EXTERNAL FILE FORMAT CsvFileFormat WITH
    (
        FORMAT_TYPE = DELIMITEDTEXT,
        FORMAT_OPTIONS
        (
            FIELD_TERMINATOR = N',',
            USE_TYPE_DEFAULT = True,
            STRING_DELIMITER = '"',
            ENCODING = 'UTF8'
        )
    );
END
GO
IF NOT EXISTS
(
    SELECT 1
    FROM sys.external_file_formats e
    WHERE
        e.name = N'TsvFileFormat'
)
BEGIN
    CREATE EXTERNAL FILE FORMAT TsvFileFormat WITH
```

```
    (
        FORMAT_TYPE = DELIMITEDTEXT,
        FORMAT_OPTIONS
        (
            FIELD_TERMINATOR = N'\t',
            USE_TYPE_DEFAULT = True,
            STRING_DELIMITER = '"',
            ENCODING = 'UTF8'
        )
    );
END
GO
```

RCFile

Record Columnar File, also known as RCFile, dates from early versions of Apache Hive. It was the first columnar format supported in the Hadoop ecosystem, and at the time it was an innovative solution, guaranteeing that row details would remain on the same Hadoop node while performing efficient aggregations.

If you have existing data in RCFile format, PolyBase can support it; if you do not already have existing data in RCFile format, use the ORC or Parquet formats instead. Both of these newer formats are more efficient, both in terms of data size and retrieval speed. Aside from legacy support, there is little reason to use RCFile today.

ORC

Optimized Row Columnar (ORC) format is an efficient columnar file format. You are most likely to see this format in Apache Hive warehouses, particularly when working with the Hortonworks Data Platform. ORC is similar to SQL Server columnstore indexes in that both store data in a modified column-major order, both offer nice levels of compression, and both work best at performing aggregations against a few columns rather than querying dozens or hundreds of columns efficiently. To give a quick idea of how well ORC compresses, the three years of New York City parking violations data we will analyze in this chapter are 2.6, 1.9, and 1.9 gigabytes, respectively. In ORC format using the default options, these same files are 419, 258, and 405 MB in size, respectively. In 7z format—an excellent format for compressing text and a great point of comparison—the files are 387, 274, and 359 MB in size. Unlike 7z format, however, Hadoop can process ORC files and can do so quickly.

When creating an ORC external file format in PolyBase, we have fewer parameters available to us than with comma-separated values. The only optional setting is DATA_COMPRESSION, which can use Google's Snappy compression format or the default zlib format. In general, the default zlib format tends to compress better than Snappy, and performance is similar with Snappy being faster in some cases and zlib in others. Our file format in this chapter will use the default zlib codec. Listing 3-7 shows how to create an external file format for ORC.

Listing 3-7. Create an external file format to access ORC files

```
IF NOT EXISTS
(
    SELECT 1
    FROM sys.external_file_formats e
    WHERE
        e.name = N'OrcFileFormat'
)
BEGIN
    CREATE EXTERNAL FILE FORMAT OrcFileFormat WITH
    (
        FORMAT_TYPE = ORC,
        DATA_COMPRESSION = 'org.apache.hadoop.io.compress.DefaultCodec'
    );
END
GO
```

Parquet

Parquet is, like ORC, an efficient columnar file format. You are more likely to see this format when working with Impala warehouses and the Cloudera Distribution of Hadoop. Parquet tends to be better than ORC when working with nested data and worse when working with flat data like our examples in this chapter. Because we will not show any nested data in this chapter, we will skip showing examples of this file format.

If you do have Parquet files, PolyBase supports two compression codecs: Snappy and gzip. If you build Parquet files from Apache Impala, the default compression format is Snappy, but you have the choice between gzip, bzip2, LZO, Snappy, and Deflate formats. Files compressed with the Snappy codec tend to be a bit larger than their gzip equivalents but also tend to be faster, leaving Snappy as a good default choice.

Listing 3-8 gives an example of creating an external file format using Parquet and Snappy compression. Even if you do not currently use the Parquet file format, you can still safely create this external file format. Like ORC, there is only one parameter to set when creating a Parquet external file format: the compression codec.

Listing 3-8. Create an external file format to access Parquet files

```
IF NOT EXISTS
(
    SELECT 1
    FROM sys.external_file_formats e
    WHERE
        e.name = N'ParquetFileFormat'
)
BEGIN
    CREATE EXTERNAL FILE FORMAT ParquetFileFormat WITH
    (
        FORMAT_TYPE = PARQUET,
        DATA_COMPRESSION = 'org.apache.hadoop.io.compress.SnappyCodec'
    );
END
GO
```

Now that we have our file formats configured, we can create external tables and start querying our data.

External Tables

Creating external tables is the same for Hadoop as it is for Azure Blob Storage: we define columns and data types like normal tables and then include a WITH clause which references the relevant external data source and external file format, as well as rejection type and number or percent of rows before the PolyBase engine rejects a query. For a refresher on how external tables work, review the section entitled "External Tables" in Chapter 2.

The accompanying code project includes scripts for four external tables: Raleigh police incidents, Raleigh fire incidents, FY 2016 New York City parking violations, and FY 2015–2017 New York City parking violations. Listing 3-9 includes a sample from Raleigh police incidents.

Listing 3-9. Create an external table to reference Raleigh police incident data

```
IF (OBJECT_ID('dbo.RaleighPoliceIncidents') IS NULL)
BEGIN
    CREATE EXTERNAL TABLE dbo.RaleighPoliceIncidents
    (
        ObjectID INT NOT NULL,
        GlobalID VARCHAR(36) NULL,
        CaseNumber VARCHAR(100) NULL,
        CrimeCategory VARCHAR(130) NULL,
        CrimeCode VARCHAR(10) NULL,
        CrimeDescription VARCHAR(250) NULL,
        CrimeType VARCHAR(100) NULL,
        ReportedBlockAddress VARCHAR(150) NULL,
        CityOfIncident VARCHAR(100) NULL,
        City VARCHAR(100) NULL,
        District VARCHAR(50) NULL,
        ReportedDate DATETIME2(3) NULL,
        ReportedYear INT NULL,
        ReportedMonth TINYINT NULL,
        ReportedDay TINYINT NULL,
        ReportedHour TINYINT NULL,
        ReportedDayOfWeek VARCHAR(15) NULL,
        Latitude VARCHAR(30) NULL,
        Longitude VARCHAR(30) NULL,
        Agency VARCHAR(50) NULL,
        UpdatedDate DATETIME2(3) NULL
    )
```

```
    WITH
    (
        LOCATION = N'/PolyBaseData/Raleigh_Police_Incidents_NIBRS.csv',
        DATA_SOURCE = Clusterino,
        FILE_FORMAT = CsvFileFormat,
        REJECT_TYPE = VALUE,
        REJECT_VALUE = 5000
    );
END
GO
```

The GlobalID column in the table is actually a uniqueidentifier data type, but PolyBase does not support this data type, so we have to bring it in as VARCHAR(36) instead. In addition, it is important to note that PolyBase has a stringent definition of what is valid as a date and time. Many flat files store date and time in the ISO 8601 format yyyy-MM-ddTHH:mm:ssZ, where T is a separator between date and time, and Z defines that the time stored is actually in UTC rather than a local time zone. An example of a date and time in this format is 2019-04-16T08:36:49Z, which represents April 16, 2019, at 8:36 and 49 seconds AM in UTC time. PolyBase, however, does not support dates in this format, but it will accept dates in the format yyyy-MM-dd HH:mm:ss, so we can convert our dates into this format. Microsoft includes the rather limited list of supported date and time formats on Microsoft Docs (https://docs.microsoft.com/en-us/sql/t-sql/statements/create-external-file-format-transact-sql).

If your source data stores dates and times in an unsupported format and you cannot alter the source data to use one of the supported date and time formats, you still have two options available. The first option is to convert the input file to ORC or Parquet format. ORC and Parquet readers tend to be much more flexible about handling date and time types than PolyBase, so formats like the one earlier are no problem. From there, you can query the data using an external file format of ORC or Parquet rather than the delimited source file.

Alternatively, if you would prefer to keep the file as a delimited file and do not need to use date-based filters when querying the data, you can define the date columns as VARCHAR rather than date or time types. This is more useful in cases where the dates are metadata which you might include in a result set but would not directly query, such as added or modified times for records. If you do need to filter these dates, however, you will want to modify the source file upstream or convert the file to ORC or Parquet format.

Note   There are several techniques you can use for modifying dates in existing files. If you have relatively small files, you can open them up in a tool like Notepad++ and build a regular expression to replace values. I have a blog post on the topic at `https://CSmore.info/on/dateregex`. You can run larger files through a stream editor like sed or process them with a tool such as SQL Server Integration Services as well. If you have control over the extraction routine, it would be easiest just to modify it to write out dates in a format acceptable to PolyBase.

At this point, we have a series of external tables we can use to discover PolyBase functionality when working with Hadoop. In the next section, we will write queries to retrieve data from these files, learning about a few of PolyBase's rougher edges along the way.

Querying Data in Hadoop

In this section, we will query data from different Hadoop data sources. First, we will look at Raleigh police incident data. Then, we will look at a file which is trickier for the PolyBase engine to handle: Raleigh fire incident data. After that, we will review parking violations in New York City and compare performance between flat files and ORC files. Finally, we will write data from SQL Server into Hadoop using PolyBase.

Row Counts with Police Incident Data

The first file we will look at is a set of police incident data. There are in total 232,128 rows in the data set including the header. Running a count operation, as in Listing 3-10, shows that PolyBase returns a simple line count without performing validation. Figure 3-8 shows the result.

Listing 3-10. A simple count operation returns the total number of rows

```
SELECT COUNT(1) AS NumberOfIncidents
FROM dbo.RaleighPoliceIncidents;
```

	NumberOfIncidents
1	232128

Figure 3-8. *There are 232,128 rows in the file, but this includes the header row*

Looking at a breakdown by year, however, we get back a sum of 232,127, which is the actual number of data rows. Listing 3-11 shows the data and Figure 3-9 the result.

Listing 3-11. A count by year filters out the header row

```
SELECT
    rpi.ReportedYear,
    COUNT(1) AS NumberOfIncidents
FROM dbo.RaleighPoliceIncidents rpi
GROUP BY
    rpi.ReportedYear
ORDER BY
    rpi.ReportedYear;
```

	ReportedYear	NumberOfIncid...
1	2014	30306
2	2015	51978
3	2016	49415
4	2017	50142
5	2018	49736
6	2019	550

Figure 3-9. *There are 232,127 incidents in the data set, though you might want to check my math*

This leads to an important lesson: counts of rows in PolyBase may not be the same as results when querying data. In this case, we streamed all of the data over from HDFS into SQL Server but did not apply any transformation rules when getting the total number of rows. The `sys.dm_exec_distributed_requests` and `sys.dm_exec_distributed_request_steps` Dynamic Management Views (DMVs), two of the DMVs available for troubleshooting PolyBase queries, will let us see what really happened during this query.

Note   We will cover PolyBase DMVs in depth in Chapter 10.

The distributed requests DMV provides us execution information for queries against external data sources or against some of the PolyBase DMVs. Figure 3-10 shows a sample output, where execution ID QID747 is the aggregation query we ran against HDFS and other execution IDs with handles like QID750 and QID753 are cases where I queried DMVs to collect screenshots.

	sql_handle	execution_id	status	error_id	start_time	end_time	total_elapsed_time
3	NULL	QID754	Completed	NULL	2019-01-22 17:31:07.053	2019-01-22 17:31:07.053	0
4	0x020000002...	QID753	Completed	NULL	2019-01-22 17:22:56.397	2019-01-22 17:22:56.447	50
5	NULL	QID752	Completed	NULL	2019-01-22 17:22:56.390	2019-01-22 17:22:56.390	0
6	NULL	QID751	Completed	NULL	2019-01-22 17:22:56.383	2019-01-22 17:22:56.383	0
7	0x02000000C...	QID750	Completed	NULL	2019-01-22 17:22:51.643	2019-01-22 17:22:51.687	43
8	NULL	QID749	Completed	NULL	2019-01-22 17:22:51.640	2019-01-22 17:22:51.640	0
9	NULL	QID748	Completed	NULL	2019-01-22 17:22:51.630	2019-01-22 17:22:51.630	0
10	0x020000004...	QID747	Completed	NULL	2019-01-22 17:22:37.947	2019-01-22 17:22:43.097	5151

Figure 3-10. *Finding the correct execution ID for our aggregation query*

Once we have the ID, the `sys.dm_exec_distributed_request_steps` DMV will tell us what happened during processing for this operation. There were 12 total operations, which we will cover in more detail in Chapter 10. The short version of this is that the PolyBase data movement service streamed data from HDFS into our SQL Server instance, wrote placeholder values to a temporary table, and then counted the number of placeholder rows. We can see the most important commands in Listing 3-12.

Listing 3-12. Operations the PolyBase engine performs to get a count of the number of rows in an external table. Note that these commands are one part of the whole PolyBase execution operation

```
CREATE TABLE [tempdb].[dbo].[TEMP_ID_89] ([col] TINYINT ) WITH(DATA_
COMPRESSION=PAGE);
CREATE TABLE [tempdb].[dbo].[TEMP_ID_90] ([col] BIGINT ) WITH(DATA_
COMPRESSION=PAGE);
SELECT
    CONVERT (TINYINT, 0, 0) AS [col]
FROM    [PolyBaseRevealed].[dbo].[RaleighPoliceIncidents] AS T1_1
SELECT [T1_1].[col] AS [col]
FROM (
    SELECT
        COUNT_BIG(CAST ((1) AS INT)) AS [col]
    FROM (
        SELECT 0 AS [col]
        FROM [tempdb].[dbo].[TEMP_ID_89] AS T3_1
    ) AS T2_1
    GROUP BY [T2_1].[col]
) AS T1_1
```

In these commands, we can see that the temporary tables PolyBase uses for this query simply contain a single numeric value to represent a row, and so rows which do not fit the external table schema will still count. By contrast, the query which returns columns from the police incident data file rejects one row due to data type mismatch, leading to the expected 232,127 results.

If you decide to query a specific column, you might see different numbers. Listing 3-13 shows two queries, one getting the count of districts and the other getting the count of updated dates. District has a type of VARCHAR(50), whereas updated date has a type of DATETIME2(3), meaning that the header row will work just fine for district but will fail to convert to the required data type for updated date. These two queries end up having a different number of rows returned, which is similar to what happens when you get the count of rows based off of a column containing NULLs.

Listing 3-13. Querying individual columns returns the number of non-NULL rows for that column

```
--232,128 rows returned.
SELECT COUNT(District) AS NumberOfIncidents
FROM dbo.RaleighPoliceIncidents;
--232,127 rows returned.
SELECT COUNT(UpdatedDate) AS NumberOfIncidents
FROM dbo.RaleighPoliceIncidents;
```

The moral of this story is that you cannot always trust simple counts to return exactly the same number of rows as operations which require operating on the data. The results are technically accurate, but if you have auditing code expecting the numbers to tie, the results could be surprising.

Newlines and Quotes with Fire Incident Data

The next data set to investigate is a collection of Raleigh Fire Department incidents. You can find two files in `Fire_Incidents.zip`, one CSV file and one TSV file. The CSV file is the original format for this data, and the TSV file is after postprocessing.

Comparing line counts between the two files, the TSV contains 177,738 data rows and 1 header row. By contrast, the CSV has 180,219 rows in total. Figure 3-11 shows the reason for this discrepancy: newlines in the file.

	X	Y	OBJECTID	incident_number	address2
49093	-78.5746	35.84251	521856	07-0016459	NEW HOPE BAPTIST CHURCH
49094	-78.6057	35.89949	521857	09-0008063	STONEGATE GROUP HOME
49095	-78.6947	35.78922	521858	14-0023416	NCSU GREENHOUSE 3
49096	-78.619	35.86094	521859	07-0033293	ST RAPHAEL (46.433476346000475, -64.01539991399966)
49097	-78.6359	35.78108	521860	08-0012760	EDENTON ST METHODIST
49098	-78.5869	35.78138	521861	08-0009378	WAKE COUNTY GOVERNMENT

Figure 3-11. *Some of the rows in this data set have newlines*

In the original CSV, there is a break between "ST RAPHAEL" and the coordinates, as you can see in Figure 3-12.

```
491..  -78.69474244,35.78922451,521858,14-0023416,745,A1    :00.000Z,0,C,8,"3131 LIGON ST R
4916.  -78.61902068,35.86094111,521859,07-0033293,,NULL,.   NC 27601","ST RAPHAEL
49169  (46.433476346000475, -64.01539991399966)",,b90ea2.   justin.greco@raleighnc.gov_ral
```

Figure 3-12. *Address line 2 spills over to the next line*

In fairness to the people maintaining this data set, this file is still a valid CSV because it uses a string delimiter of quotation marks to indicate what is within a string. These delimiters are supposed to allow any character, including newlines and field terminators, to appear without confusing a CSV parser. PolyBase, however, cannot handle newlines within fields and will try to consider this as two separate rows, rejecting both because neither row fits the data structure on its own.

Another problem that PolyBase has is that it cannot handle string delimiters within a string delimiter. In other words, if you use the quotation mark as your string delimiter, quotation marks cannot appear within the string itself. The standard for handling delimited files is that if you use a string delimiter, doubling up that delimiter acts to inform the parser that this is just a regular quotation mark rather than a string delimiter character. For example, one of the rows in this data set has an address line 2 value of ** IN FRONT OF ""PANDORA"". A CSV parser should interpret this and set the value of address line 2 to ** IN FRONT OF "PANDORA" but PolyBase is unable to parse the line and fails the row automatically, meaning it will not even show up when selecting COUNT(1) from the table. Figure 3-13 shows the six records with extra quotation marks.

	incident_number	address2
1	13-0014743	SCANA "CAYCE TOC"
2	10-0004579	SCANA "CAYCE TOC"
3	11-0036949	** IN FRONT OF "PANDORA"
4	10-0016102	SCANA "CAYCE TOC"
5	15-9008425	Actual Street name is "Wakebrook"
6	09-0019563	SCANA "CAYCE TOC"

Figure 3-13. *There are six rows with quotation marks in the text itself. The PolyBase engine cannot parse these six rows and will ignore them even when counting the number of rows*

To get around these limitations in the engine, I created a version of the fire incident data set without newlines or quotation marks and saved the file as a tab-separated values (TSV) file instead of comma-separated values. Doing this gets us to the 177,738 rows plus a header that we expect, and running a SELECT * statement shows all of the rows.

Troubleshooting these types of issues, as well as data length and data type issues, can be difficult with the SQL Server edition of PolyBase. The reason for this difficulty is that this version of PolyBase does not return any row information for rejected records. By contrast, if you are using Azure Synapse Analytics, you can output rejected rows into a folder and review the results later. Chapter 9 shows how we can use this to find data irregularities in Azure Synapse Analytics. Chapter 5 includes a way of finding these irregularities on-premises as error messages.

Going Faster with Parking Violations Data

Our last data set is New York City parking violations data for fiscal years 2015 through 2017. In total, this is 33,239,162 rows—including 3 header rows—spread out over three files. Listing 3-14 shows how we can specify a folder and query against all of the files in that folder.

Listing 3-14. Creating an external table which reads against an entire folder instead of a single file

```
CREATE EXTERNAL TABLE ParkingViolations
(
    SummonsNumber VARCHAR(50),
    ...
)
WITH
(
    LOCATION = N'/PolyBaseData/NYCParkingTickets/',
    DATA_SOURCE = Clusterino,
    FILE_FORMAT = CsvFileFormat,
    REJECT_TYPE = VALUE,
    REJECT_VALUE = 5000
);
```

In my test environment, running a simple SELECT COUNT(1) from the parking violations external table shows that there are 33,239,162 rows in the external table, but it takes 8 minutes and 18 seconds to retrieve this result when pulling from a Hadoop cluster with a single data node to a SQL Server instance with a standalone PolyBase installation. In addition to the simple count, Listing 3-15 shows a query which returns the count of results by the violator's registration state. This is a fairly straightforward query which takes 8 minutes and 32 seconds to run with that same setup.

Listing 3-15. A query which breaks out parking violations by registration state. This serves as a simple but realistic query we might run for reporting or data analysis

```
SELECT
    RegistrationState,
    COUNT(*) AS NumberOfViolations
FROM dbo.ParkingViolations2016
GROUP BY
    RegistrationState
ORDER BY
    RegistrationState;
```

We have a few ways that we can speed these types of queries up, including some combination of

- Improving hardware, especially available network bandwidth.

- Using predicate pushdown to run MapReduce jobs against Hadoop. This will be the topic of Chapter 4.

- Increasing the number of Hadoop data nodes.

- Increasing the number of PolyBase compute nodes.

- Using a column-based file format such as ORC or Parquet.

In this section, we will focus on the last two options. The first of these two is to increase the number of PolyBase compute nodes, which you can only do if you have a PolyBase Scale-Out Group. If you have already installed PolyBase standalone or if your machines are not on an Active Directory domain, you will not be able to scale out PolyBase nodes. Supposing you do have a Scale-Out Group set up, we can see the benefit that brings in this particular scenario.

When running the same queries against a three-node Scale-Out Group, getting a count of rows took 8 minutes and 30 seconds, and querying by state took 8 minutes and 29 seconds. This is approximately the same amount of time as a standalone PolyBase installation took. One reason we did not see any performance improvement is that, under the covers, PolyBase is streaming all of this data from Hadoop to SQL Server instances. When streaming data, the PolyBase data movement service connects directly to Hadoop data nodes, as we will prove in Chapter 4. With fewer Hadoop data nodes than PolyBase Scale-Out Group compute nodes, the Hadoop data node needs to satisfy all Scale-Out Group compute nodes directly, limiting our ability to take advantage of this direct connection. In addition, there is a limit to how fast we can move data across a network, and if you saturate the network shifting data from HDFS into SQL Server, adding more compute will not improve the situation. This turns out to be the more important reason, as we will see.

Another option we have, outside of adding additional servers or network capacity, is to use a columnar file format like ORC or Parquet. In this case, I will convert these files to ORC format, build a new external table off of the ORC files, and test performance once more. The easiest way to convert files from a delimited format into ORC is through Apache Hive, a warehousing technology in the Hadoop ecosystem. Hive implements its own flavor of SQL called Hive Query Language (HiveQL), but it is close enough to ANSI SQL that familiarity with one translates to the other. In the accompanying code repository, there is a HiveQL script called `Chapter 03\hive\Convert CSV to ORC.sql`. This script contains the code needed to create two Hive external tables and pipe data from CSV format into ORC files. Listing 3-16 shows a summarized version of this script.

Listing 3-16. Convert a set of CSV files into ORC format using Apache Hive, **not** PolyBase

```
CREATE EXTERNAL TABLE IF NOT EXISTS ParkingViolations
(
    SummonsNumber STRING,
    ...
)
ROW FORMAT DELIMITED
FIELDS TERMINATED BY ','
STORED AS TEXTFILE
location '/PolyBaseData/NYCParkingTickets/'
```

```
tblproperties ("skip.header.line.count"="1");

CREATE EXTERNAL TABLE IF NOT EXISTS ParkingViolationsORC
(
    SummonsNumber STRING,
    ...
)
ROW FORMAT DELIMITED
FIELDS TERMINATED BY ','
STORED AS ORC
location '/PolyBaseData/NYCParkingTicketsORC/';

INSERT INTO ParkingViolationsORC
SELECT * FROM ParkingViolations;
```

This may take a while depending upon how many data nodes you have and how powerful your machines are. Figure 3-14 shows the new file sizes, where we drop from approximately 6.4GB of data to just over 1GB of data, a nice compression ratio.

Name >	Size >		Name >	Size >
⤶			⤶	
Parking_Violations_Issued_-_Fiscal_Ye...	2.6 GB		000000_0	419.0 MB
Parking_Violations_Issued_-_Fiscal_Ye...	1.9 GB		000001_0	406.5 MB
Parking_Violations_Issued_-_Fiscal_Ye...	1.9 GB		000002_0	257.7 MB

Figure 3-14. *Converting CSVs to ORC gave us a compression ratio of better than 6 to 1*

Because the ORC file format is fundamentally different from delimited files, we need to make sure that we have created the appropriate external file format. Review Listing 3-7 for an example of this format. When working with data in ORC format with a standalone PolyBase installation, our count of rows takes a mere 10 seconds, and our aggregation by state completes in 26 seconds. When running against a Scale-Out Group with three nodes, the count of rows takes 8 seconds, and aggregation by state takes just 12 seconds. In this case, where we spend relatively less time shuffling data and relatively more time performing CPU-intensive aggregation work, we can see the value of the Scale-Out Group in sharing that computational load and reducing the overall time required to complete this query.

Finally, as a way of comparison, the aggregation by state query takes 12–13 seconds when running natively in Hive against a single data node, which is a great result for PolyBase: in this scenario, it achieved processing time parity with native tools despite needing to exfiltrate data from HDFS over the network, something Hive did not need to do. These results depend, of course, on a number of factors, and PolyBase queries will not always be as fast as native queries, but it does show that the best-case scenario of "as fast as native queries" is possible.

Now that we have looked at retrieving data from Hadoop, we will finish the chapter by looking at inserting data into Hadoop.

Inserting Data into Hadoop

Inserting data into Hadoop involves the same process as inserting data into Azure Blob Storage. If you have not already configured SQL Server to allow PolyBase to export data, run the commands in Listing 3-17. If you do not do this before attempting to insert data into an external table, you will receive an error message.

Listing 3-17. Enable PolyBase data export functionality

```
EXEC sp_configure
    @configname = 'allow polybase export',
    @configvalue = 1;
GO
RECONFIGURE
GO
```

Once you have enabled PolyBase export, you can insert into external tables whose LOCATION is a folder. Like with Azure Blob Storage, PolyBase only allows INSERT operations. If you attempt to run an UPDATE, DELETE, or MERGE operation to modify data in an external table, you will receive error message 46519 like in Figure 3-15. Note that a MERGE operation will still fail even if it simply tries to insert data and performs no update or delete operations.

```
◢ MESSAGES
    3:02:51 PM        Started executing query at Line 12
                      Msg 46519, Level 16, State 16, Line 1
                      DML Operations are not supported with external tables.

                      Total execution time: 00:00:00.017
```

Figure 3-15. *Only insert operations are allowed with external tables*

For more information on how to insert into PolyBase and limitations around insertion, review the section entitled "Inserting into External Tables" in Chapter 2. Because Azure Blob Storage uses the same HDFS-based API, functionality works the same between these two products.

Conclusion

In this chapter, we learned how to integrate SQL Server with Hadoop. We walked through configuration options unique to Hadoop, including the resource manager location on external data sources. We also reviewed three columnar file formats which are popular in the Hadoop ecosystem: RCFile, ORC, and Parquet. We learned when to use ORC and Parquet and to ignore RCFile for new development. We also learned about some of the tricky bits when working with PolyBase, including issues with date formatting, when counts might be off from expectations, and some options for making PolyBase queries faster (although we will cover more in Chapters 4 and 11). We wrapped up this chapter with brief coverage of inserting into external tables.

In the next chapter, we will look at a key feature of PolyBase: the ability to perform predicate pushdown against Hadoop. We will see how the PolyBase engine builds a MapReduce job and is able to offload compute onto a Hadoop cluster.

CHAPTER 4

Using Predicate Pushdown to Enhance Query Performance

In Chapters 2 and 3, we looked at using PolyBase to retrieve data from Azure Blob Storage and Hadoop, respectively. In both of those cases, we allowed the PolyBase data movement service to pull all of the data from our external data source and then applied filters and performed aggregations within SQL Server. This is our only option for Azure Blob Storage, but when working with Hadoop, there is another technique: predicate pushdown. This chapter will dive into the concept of predicate pushdown and look at the mechanisms available in PolyBase to offload compute requirements onto Hadoop. We will first cover what predicate pushdown means and why it is important. Next, we will use a packet capture tool to understand exactly what is happening on the network during queries against external tables, both with and without predicate pushdown. This will help us gain an understanding of what PolyBase predicate pushdown has to offer as well as its limitations. Finally, we will look at situations when predicate pushdown makes sense to use.

The Importance of Predicate Pushdown

To understand why predicate pushdown is so important, let's begin with a quick story about relational databases. Relational databases are made up of relations, aka. tables. Suppose we have two tables, Person and Company. We would like to build a set of people who work at a specific company. One way that we can do this is to perform a Cartesian join of Person and Company: one row for each combination of Person and

© Kevin Feasel 2020
K. Feasel, *PolyBase Revealed*, https://doi.org/10.1007/978-1-4842-5461-5_4

Company. After we create this cross product of all combinations of person and company, we can then filter where the person's employer is the company name, which leaves us one row per person at a company. From there, we can apply another filter, where the company is the firm we care about. This leaves us with our final result: only people who work at the specific company in our query.

This is an elegant conceptual solution to the problem, but would be a terrible way to query data because you would need to retrieve all of the Person and Company records before filtering down. Suppose we had a database with every resident in the New York City metropolitan area—all 20 million or so—and every business establishment in the United States—approximately 6 million—according to the United States Census Bureau.[1] We want to find out how many New Yorkers work at a corner grocery store in Harlem. To do this using the technique outlined earlier, we would need to read 20 million Person records from disk, followed by 6 million Company records. We need to store this data in memory and use CPU cycles to winnow down to the five or six employees we care about. This is a tremendous waste of resources and would not allow us to scale beyond small data sets.

Predicate pushdown is one of the key tools we have to scale out because it lets us ignore some of the unnecessary data. In the preceding scenario, instead of pulling in all 6 million businesses, we can **push down** the predicate and operate on it earlier. If we lay out the data the right way—which we typically implement as indexes—we can pull back just the record for our corner grocery store of interest. From there, if the Person data has an appropriate index on the company identifier, we can filter on that predicate without needing to scan through 20 million rows. This is one of the core performance tuning techniques data professionals internalize: filter out as much of the data you can as soon as possible. Doing so reduces hardware requirements and generally allows you to run more queries in less time.

When it comes to accessing data across different data platform technologies, we still have a concept of predicate pushdown, but it does change slightly when dealing with PolyBase.

---

[1]The Census Bureau's Statistics of US Businesses data is available at www.census.gov/data/tables/2016/econ/susb/2016-susb-annual.html

Predicate Pushdown in PolyBase

To understand predicate pushdown in PolyBase (or, frankly, any data platform technology of serious scale, like Amazon Redshift, Databricks Unified Analytics Platform, Apache Hive, as well as SQL Server linked server queries), suppose we go through the same corner grocery store example, but this time, our Company relation is an external table stored in Hadoop, and our Person relation is a normal table in SQL Server. If we want to perform the same filtered query as before, PolyBase gives us two options. The first option is to stream the Company data from Hadoop into a temporary table in SQL Server and then join that temporary table to our Person table, filtering on the relevant company once that data is in a temporary table. In effect, this is similar to the first preceding example: we need to retrieve all of the data from Company, but in addition to the disk, memory, and CPU costs, we have additional network costs: the time and bandwidth it takes to move Company data from HDFS into SQL Server. This is still reasonably efficient when dealing with smaller data sets of hundreds of thousands or maybe even millions of rows, but really falls apart when you look at an external table with billions of rows. Figure 4-1 gives us an example of this streaming model.

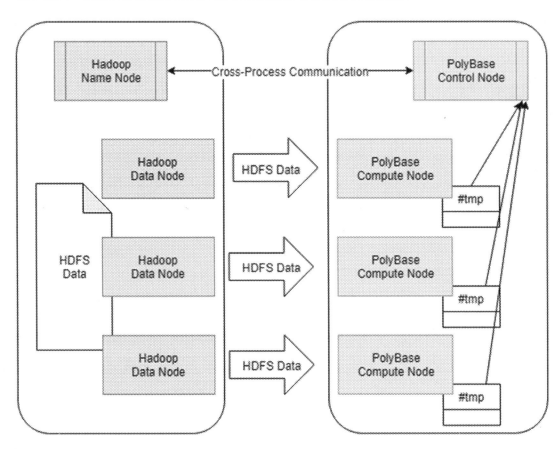

Figure 4-1. *With the streaming model, we pull all six million Company rows from files in HDFS and push it into temporary tables in compute nodes, where we apply filters and return the one company to the control node for final processing*

By contrast, we can also use PolyBase's breed of predicate pushdown. Instead of pulling back all of the data and loading it into a temporary table, we have the ability to make our Hadoop cluster do the work of filtering and then send the filtered result back to SQL Server. In doing this, we have two potential benefits. First, on-premises SQL Server tends to be a more expensive product than an on-premises Hadoop cluster on a per-core basis due to licensing costs. If you can offload compute from your relatively more expensive SQL Server instances onto relatively less expensive Hadoop data nodes, that can reduce IT costs over time. Second, external data sources have their own tools to filter data efficiently. For example, when running MapReduce jobs, having a filter operation in a Map job step will allow the data nodes to scan through file blocks and write fewer rows out. Filtering data stored in an external source is often more efficient than spending the network and hardware costs of pulling that data into SQL Server for filtering even in the event that SQL Server is much more efficient at doing this task. Figure 4-2 shows an architectural-level example of predicate pushdown in action.

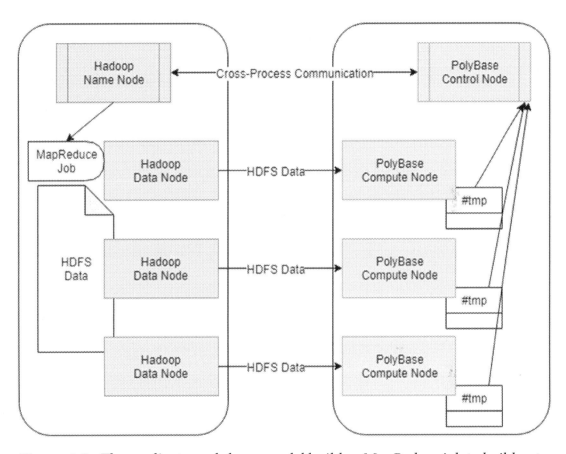

Figure 4-2. *The predicate pushdown model builds a MapReduce job to build out only the one Company row we need and send that row over to PolyBase compute nodes. This reduces the amount of data sent over the network and reduces the risk of one of the Compute Node SQL Server instances from running out of disk space when reading giant files*

Predicate pushdown can also work on the Reduce side of MapReduce jobs: we can aggregate data in Hadoop and send those aggregated results back. Our Hadoop cluster, which may have compute power available, might be able to aggregate data faster than a single SQL Server instance. Even if it cannot, the idea of opportunity cost comes into play: the amount of compute we spend sending data from Hadoop and aggregating in SQL Server is compute resources that we cannot use to satisfy other users' queries. Offloading some of the burden can help balance out resource requirements across a broad array of systems and user personas.

Note   For additional information on the theory behind PolyBase, I recommend a pair of papers from Microsoft's Gray Systems Lab, entitled Split Query Processing in Polybase and Indexing HDFS Data in PDW: Splitting the data from the index, both available at the Gray Systems Lab web site at `http://gsl.azurewebsites. net/Projects/Polybase.aspx`. These papers came out in 2013 and 2014, respectively, and cover the version of PolyBase in SQL Server Analytics Platform System (APS), so some of the behavior the authors describe will differ from the PolyBase in SQL Server or Azure Synapse Analytics. In particular, the concepts behind the second paper—on splitting indexes from data—are not available outside of APS. Instead, we will see in Chapter 11 that we have the ability to generate statistics, but all external data remains external.

With this academic understanding of the two processing modes available to us, we can learn more about the practical implementation with the use of an execution plan, a pair of Dynamic Management Views, and the packet capture tool Wireshark.

Diving into Predicate Pushdown

Before we execute a query with predicate pushdown, we need to ensure that we have Wireshark installed on a machine running SQL Server. Wireshark is a popular packet capture tool, meaning it allows us to observe network traffic between systems. We will use it in this chapter to trace what is happening when we write a T-SQL query which uses predicate pushdown. You can obtain a copy of Wireshark, licensed under GNU's General Public License version 2, from `www.wireshark.org`.

Caution   If you install Wireshark on a corporate machine, be sure that you have approval from your security and executive teams. I know of one former colleague who was fired for installing Wireshark without permission on a desktop machine at an insurance company. There is nothing innately evil about Wireshark, and it is a go-to tool for diagnosing network problems, but be safe nonetheless. This might be a place where you just want to read along and see or try out at home.

In order to see the differences between a query with predicate pushdown and without, we will execute the same query against the same instance using the Raleigh police incident data set from Chapter 3, differing only in whether we enable pushdown.

Packet Capture Without Predicate Pushdown

Listing 4-1 shows the query we will run without predicate pushdown.

Listing 4-1. Group the number of Raleigh police incidents by year using the direct access technique

```
SELECT
    rpi.ReportedYear,
    COUNT(1) AS NumberOfIncidents
FROM dbo.RaleighPoliceIncidents rpi
GROUP BY
    rpi.ReportedYear
ORDER BY
    rpi.ReportedYear;
```

With Wireshark open and running against our network interface, we can see the interactions between our SQL Server instance (IP address 172.17.146.51) and the Hadoop cluster (IP address 192.168.100.116). Figure 4-3 shows the beginning of this process, which spanned approximately 14.1 seconds from start to finish.

Note   All of the times and ports in this section come from me running the query against machines on my network. If you attempt to replicate these results, your numbers may differ from mine. In particular, execution times will depend upon compute power and network bandwidth, and the number of packets per operation will depend on factors such as packet size and your networking infrastructure. These numbers are intended to be indicative rather than conclusive.

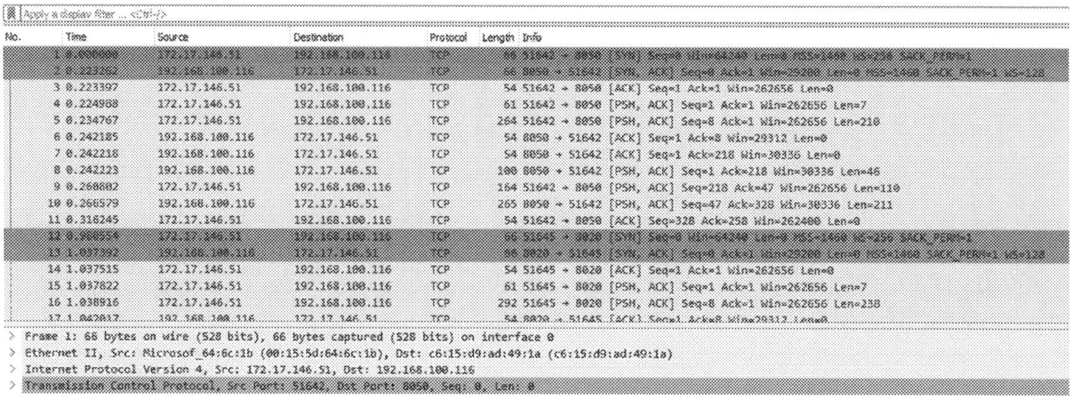

Figure 4-3. *A packet capture containing interactions between SQL Server and Hadoop to solve a PolyBase query*

In the Info field, we see the source and destination ports for each individual TCP stream. For example, the first packet comes from SQL Server on port 51642—PolyBase tends to use ports above 50000 for its ephemeral activities—and connects to port 8050 on the Hadoop name node. Port 8050 is the default port for YARN on Hortonworks Data Platform. We can right-click a packet and navigate to Follow ➤ TCP Stream as in Figure 4-4.

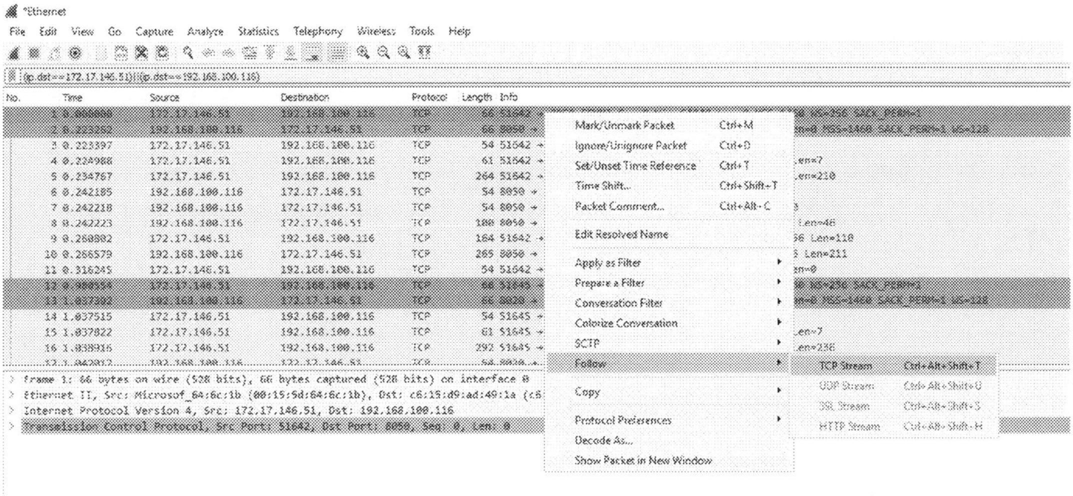

Figure 4-4. *Follow the TCP streams to understand how everything fits together*

This first stream connects to YARN and calls a function called getClusterNodes, which returns the names of available nodes. This response takes approximately a quarter of a second and leads into the second stream. In this second stream, Figure 4-5 shows that SQL Server connects from port 51645 to the name node's HDFS port (8020) and requests basic information on the file Raleigh Police Incidents NIBRS.csv to ensure that the file exists and that the pdw_user account has sufficient permissions to access this file.

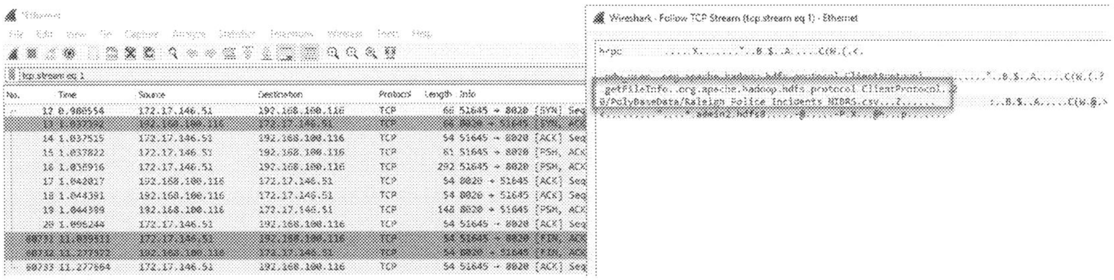

Figure 4-5. *The PolyBase engine requests file information as the first step in data retrieval*

After this, the third stream comes from SQL Server on port 51712 and once again makes a request of the name node's HDFS port, but this time asking for block locations for where on data nodes our requested file lives. Figure 4-6 shows this in action.

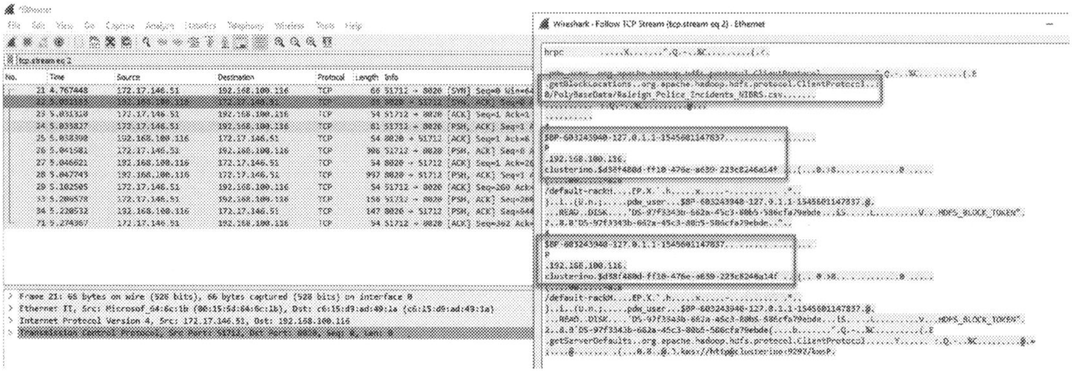

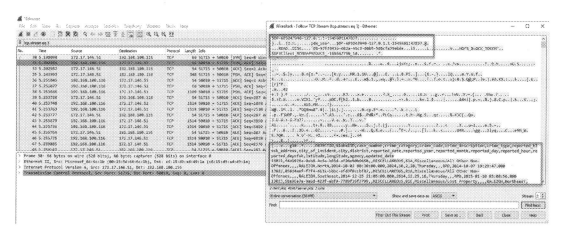

Figure 4-6. *The PolyBase engine then asks for data node addresses*

Once the PolyBase engine has information on where the data lives, it makes a non-MapReduce call to HDFS on the data node data transfer port (50010) and requests all of the data back. In this case, it takes 40,417 server packets and approximately 5 seconds to stream this data across the network over to SQL Server. Figure 4-7 shows this TCP stream.

Figure 4-7. *The PolyBase data movement service requests the entire police incident file*

SQL Server then loads this data into a temporary table and runs our initial T-SQL query, returning a grouped result set by year. If we want to run this as a MapReduce job, the underlying process is quite different.

Packet Capture with Predicate Pushdown

Our query to retrieve incident counts by year will be the same as in the prior example save for a single query hint: the FORCE EXTERNALPUSHDOWN hint. When we use this query hint against a Hadoop external data source, the PolyBase engine will generate a MapReduce job regardless of whether any internal signals indicate that streaming the data into SQL Server would be quicker. Listing 4-2 shows this new query.

Caution   I consider the term "query hints" in SQL Server as a misnomer. These are, in fact, query commands. The downside to writing a query hint/command is that the database engine will do what you tell it to do, even if what you tell it to do is a bad idea or physically impossible. In this case, if you do not have a resource manager location configured on your external data source, using the FORCE EXTERNALPUSHDOWN hint will result in outright query failure rather than falling back to a no-pushdown query. Query hints are useful in certain scenarios—such as this one—but use them with appropriate caution.

Listing 4-2. Use a query hint to force PolyBase to generate a MapReduce job

```
SELECT
    rpi.ReportedYear,
    COUNT(1) AS NumberOfIncidents
FROM dbo.RaleighPoliceIncidents rpi
GROUP BY
    rpi.ReportedYear
ORDER BY
    rpi.ReportedYear
OPTION(FORCE EXTERNALPUSHDOWN);
```

In this case, the operation took approximately 21 seconds from start to finish with much more activity. Stream 0 begins similar to the no-pushdown scenario but is considerably more sophisticated, including two separate sets of requests. The first set of requests asks for file information on the Raleigh police incident data set from the name node via port 8020, but at approximately 4 seconds in, this stream asks for data on a folder in /user/pdw_user/.staging/. Figure 4-8 shows this behavior.

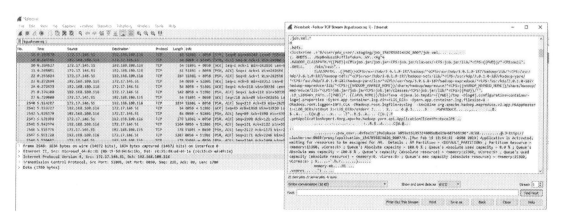

Figure 4-8. *The file info stream now contains two separate operations*

Stream 1 is quite different from its no-pushdown counterpart, as this stream is responsible for building a new YARN task. Figure 4-9 shows a segment of this, where PolyBase builds an XML file elaborating on the job contents and receives back confirmation that the application is ready for work. Similar to stream 0, stream 1 has a multisecond gap, starting nearly at the same time as stream 0 but taking a five-second hiatus until it can submit this job request.

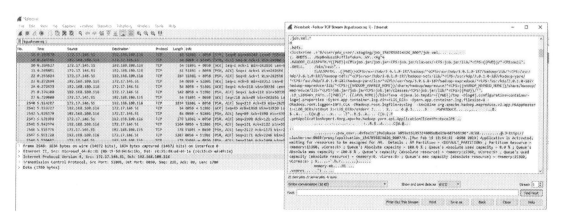

Figure 4-9. *The job creation stream is relatively short but critical*

As streams 0 and 1 reach the hiatus between actions, stream 2 comes into play. This stream contains Microsoft's JAR file and weighs in at 27 MB of data. It takes approximately 2.5 seconds for this stream to complete pushing the file to WebHDFS. In Figure 4-10, we can see the beginnings of this file and references to various Microsoft Java classes in the com.microsoft.polybase namespace.

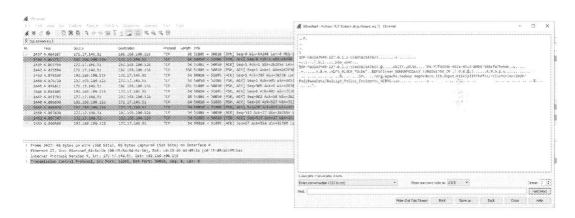

Figure 4-10. *The vast majority of packets in this data stream come from stream 2, which transfers Microsoft's JAR file over to the Hadoop cluster*

After a hefty stream 2, streams 3 and 4 are rather light in comparison. Their purpose is to specify the source location for our MapReduce job via WebHDFS. Figure 4-11 reveals this detail for stream 3.

Figure 4-11. *Stream 3 begins after stream 2 ends but before stream 1 can create a YARN job*

Stream 5 runs right before the YARN job begins and transmits a configuration XML file. Of interest to us is the InputFormatBaseColumnSchemas property, which includes an encoded XML representation for each of the columns we defined in the external table. Figure 4-12 shows this part of stream 5.

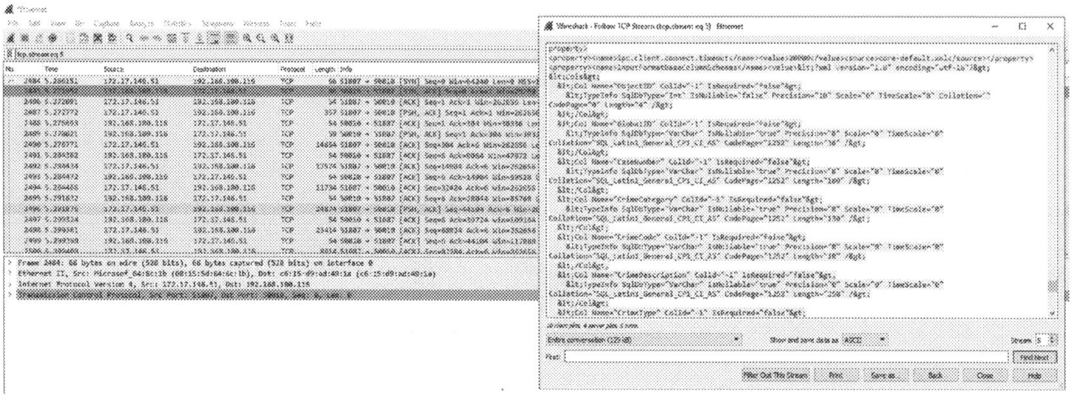

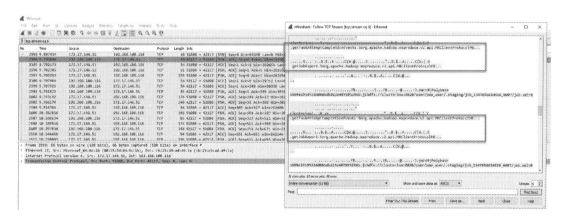

Figure 4-12. *Stream 5 transmits expected schema information as well as other YARN configuration details*

Once the YARN job has begun, stream 6 communicates with the name node on a new port, 42117. Here, the PolyBase engine repeatedly calls two functions named `getTaskAttemptCompletionEvents` and `getJobReport`, as we can see in Figure 4-13. Once those function calls return a completed status, this stream pulls counters and job details back. All in all, this takes approximately seven seconds to run.

Figure 4-13. *Stream 6 serves as a status check stream, waiting until the MapReduce job has completed and retrieving basic job statistics at the end*

After the YARN job completes, stream 7 queries the name node via HDFS port 8020 and lists files in the job's Output directory. Of particular notice are the files in PPAX format. PPAX is a proprietary format which PolyBase uses to migrate MapReduce results back into SQL Server. Figure 4-14 shows this file listing. From there, stream 8 queries for block locations for any PPAX files. Because we have already seen this type of stream before, I did not include a separate image.

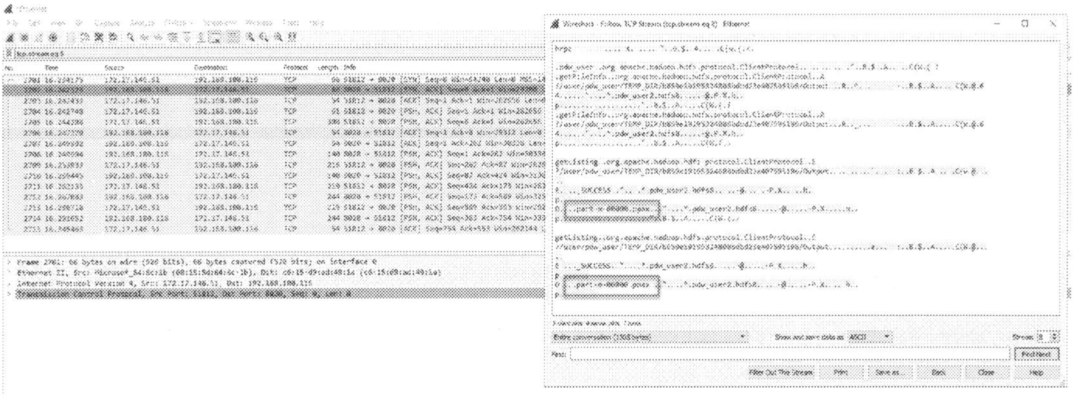

Figure 4-14. *Our MapReduce payload at last: we have the PPAX files in sight*

Finally, in stream 10, we retrieve the results of these PPAX files. Because the files are in a non-ASCII format, we cannot see their outputs directly, but we know that the final payload will be small because we get back six rows of two numeric values, as we see in Figure 4-15.

	ReportedYear	NumberOfIncid...
1	2014	30306
2	2015	51978
3	2016	49415
4	2017	50142
5	2018	49736
6	2019	550

Figure 4-15. *Instead of sending over all of the data, the MapReduce result is a trivial six rows of two integers*

Now that we have a more detailed understanding of the mechanisms behind predicate pushdown, we can take a look at several queries of varying complexity to determine when and where predicate pushdown makes sense.

When Predicate Pushdown Makes Sense

Predicate pushdown does not make sense in all circumstances. In this section, we will look at several queries of differing levels of complexity and try to build principles around when pushdown can make sense.

Small Data: Raleigh Police Incidents

The Raleigh police incident data set from Chapter 3 contains 232,127 data rows and 1 header row and weighs in at approximately 55.6MB in size. We already saw in Listings 4-1 and 4-2 that it took longer to run a MapReduce job returning six rows than streaming the data and aggregating in SQL Server.

Similarly, we can try a different query which is slightly more complex than our first example. Listing 4-3 shows the version without predicate pushdown. The version with predicate pushdown is Listing 4-3 with OPTION(FORCE EXTERNALPUSHDOWN) appended before the semi-colon.

Listing 4-3. A query with multiple levels of filtering and a complex predicate

```
SELECT
    rpi.City,
    rpi.District,
    COUNT(1) AS NumberOfIncidents
FROM dbo.RaleighPoliceIncidents rpi
WHERE
    rpi.ReportedYear = 2017
    AND
    (
        rpi.ReportedHour BETWEEN 21 AND 23
        OR rpi.ReportedHour BETWEEN 0 AND 5
    )
GROUP BY
```

```
    rpi.City,
    rpi.District
HAVING
    COUNT(1) > 10
ORDER BY
    NumberOfIncidents DESC;
```

Running this query three separate times, it took approximately 5.6 seconds per execution. As a MapReduce job, it took 14 seconds against a single-node cluster. Other queries have similar behavior, including a simple SELECT * which takes approximately 8.5 seconds to stream and 26 seconds as a MapReduce job.

What the small data example tells us is that we need to be able to absorb the upfront costs of pushing Microsoft's JAR file over (2–2.5 seconds on my machines over my network), starting up a YARN job (roughly 6 seconds), and executing the MapReduce code (variable, depending upon the nature of the query and filters). With small files, it is unlikely that we ever meet that minimum cost criterion; let's instead move on to a bigger data set and see how things change.

Bigger Data: New York City Parking Violations

The New York City parking ticket data set is considerably larger, with 6.5GB of formatted text covering 33,239,159 data rows and 3 header rows. With this much larger data set, we will begin to see the value that predicate pushdown via MapReduce can bring us.

Listing 4-4 shows us a fairly constrained query, where we include only vehicles with Ohio tags with model years ranging from 2005 through 2010.

Listing 4-4. Including a narrow filter which we expect to return very few rows

```
SELECT
    ViolationPrecinct,
    COUNT(*) AS NumberOfViolations
FROM dbo.ParkingViolations pv
WHERE
    pv.RegistrationState = 'OH'
    AND pv.VehicleYear IN ('2005', '2006', '2007', '2008', '2009', '2010')
```

```
GROUP BY
    ViolationPrecinct
ORDER BY
    NumberOfViolations DESC;
```

This query returns 70 distinct precincts, with 2482 violations in precinct 0, 21 in precinct 44, 17 in precinct 75, and no other precinct with more than 13 violations. Running this as a simple streaming query without predicate pushdown, it takes 8 minutes and 38 seconds to complete. When forcing PolyBase to run this query as a MapReduce job, it takes 2 minutes and 14 seconds. Now we're starting to see a difference!

As we move to larger and larger data sets, the upfront costs for processing that we saw in the smaller data set end up smaller than the cost of moving the entire data set across the network from HDFS into temp tables in SQL Server. But there's one nasty trick: we never really pushed down the predicate.

Limitations in Pushdown-Eligible Predicates

Figure 4-16 shows the MapReduce job outputs in PPAX format. Weighing in at approximately 200MB, we can already see that our WHERE clause does not make it all the way down to Hadoop, considering that we are expecting 70 rows of two integers back.

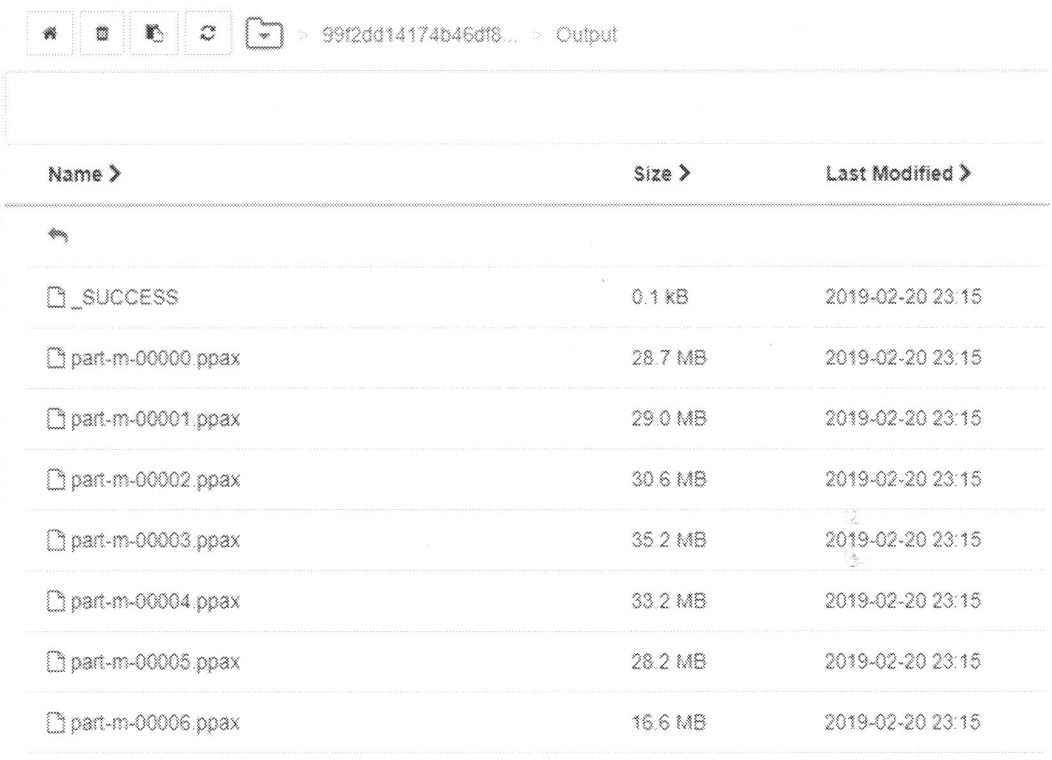

Name >	Size >	Last Modified >
↰		
▯ _SUCCESS	0.1 kB	2019-02-20 23:15
▯ part-m-00000.ppax	28.7 MB	2019-02-20 23:15
▯ part-m-00001.ppax	29.0 MB	2019-02-20 23:15
▯ part-m-00002.ppax	30.6 MB	2019-02-20 23:15
▯ part-m-00003.ppax	35.2 MB	2019-02-20 23:15
▯ part-m-00004.ppax	33.2 MB	2019-02-20 23:15
▯ part-m-00005.ppax	28.2 MB	2019-02-20 23:15
▯ part-m-00006.ppax	16.6 MB	2019-02-20 23:15

Figure 4-16. *These six output files show that our MapReduce job returned far more than 70 records*

For further corroboration, we can use the code in Listing 4-5 to see how many rows each step in the PolyBase query handled. This gives us a result that we can see in Figure 4-17.

Listing 4-5. Find the number of rows for each step in the PolyBase external query. Note that execution ID QID1549 is a particular execution ID. If you run this yourself, you can find the appropriate execution ID from the sys.dm_exec_distributed_requests DMV

```
SELECT
    execution_id,
    step_index,
    total_elapsed_time,
    row_count,
```

```
    command
FROM sys.dm_exec_distributed_request_steps
WHERE
    execution_id = 'QID1549';
```

	execution_id	step_index	total_elapsed_ti...	row_count	command
1	QID1549	0	0	-1	TEMP_ID_33
2	QID1549	1	54471	-1	*NULL*
3	QID1549	2	0	-1	TEMP_ID_34
4	QID1549	3	46	-1	CREATE TABLE [tempdb].[dbo].[TEMP_ID_34] ([Regi...
5	QID1549	4	15	-1	EXEC [tempdb].[sys].[sp_addextendedproperty] @n...
6	QID1549	5	15	-1	UPDATE STATISTICS [tempdb].[dbo].[TEMP_ID_34] ...
7	QID1549	6	0	-1	TEMP_ID_35
8	QID1549	7	15	-1	CREATE TABLE [tempdb].[dbo].[TEMP_ID_35] ([Viol...
9	QID1549	8	82953	-1	*NULL*
10	QID1549	9	82953	33239162	HDFS import - External RoundRobin
11	QID1549	10	82797	212	SELECT [T1_1].[ViolationPrecinct] AS [ViolationPreci...

Figure 4-17. *Our MapReduce operation returned 33,239,162 rows to SQL Server, meaning every row in all of the files*

With this proof in hand, it is worth looking at Microsoft's documentation on predicate pushdown, which you can find at `https://docs.microsoft.com/en-us/sql/relational-databases/polybase/polybase-pushdown-computation`. Specifically, in the section entitled "Pushdown for basic expressions and operators," it lays out what is eligible for pushdown. Included in this list is the set of equality and inequality operators but only for numeric, date, and time data types. Because our query filters are all against VARCHAR columns, none of the predicates are eligible for pushdown according to this documentation. If our vehicle year column were an integer rather than a string, we might see predicate pushdown eliminate rows and send SQL Server fewer records for secondary processing.

In order to test this conjecture, we will need a new table. Included in the code section for this chapter is an external table called dbo.ParkingViolationsNum, which is exactly the same as dbo.ParkingViolations except that its VehicleYear attribute is an INT data type instead of VARCHAR. Listing 4-6 is the new query against this table.

Listing 4-6. This new query now has part of its WHERE clause eligible for predicate pushdown

```
SELECT
    ViolationPrecinct,
    COUNT(*) AS NumberOfViolations
FROM dbo.ParkingViolationsNum pv
WHERE
    pv.RegistrationState = 'OH'
    AND pv.VehicleYear >= 2005 AND pv.VehicleYear <= 2010
GROUP BY
    ViolationPrecinct
ORDER BY
    NumberOfViolations DESC
OPTION(FORCE EXTERNALPUSHDOWN);
```

The filter on vehicles registered in the state of Ohio is still not eligible for pushdown, but at least we limit our results to vehicles with model years ranging from 2005 through 2010. This leads to a much nicer looking Figure 4-18, where instead of 200 MB of data, we process just over 26 MB of data to send back to SQL Server.

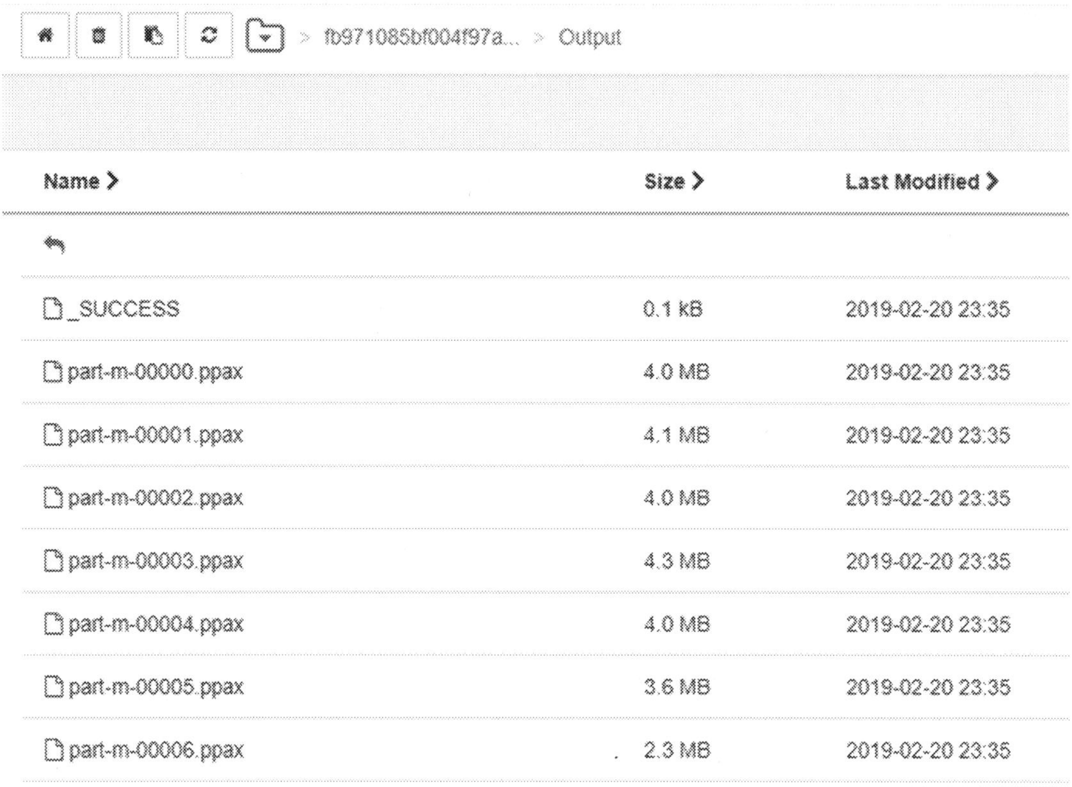

Figure 4-18. *Our MapReduce job definitely filtered out rows this time around*

Furthermore, Figure 4-19 confirms that SQL Server imported less than a quarter of the total number of rows thanks to this filter.

	execution_id	step_index	total_elapsed_ti...	row_count	command
1	QID1567	0	0	-1	TEMP_ID_39
2	QID1567	1	38415	-1	*NULL*
3	QID1567	2	0	-1	TEMP_ID_40
4	QID1567	3	15	-1	CREATE TABLE...
5	QID1567	4	31	-1	EXEC [tempd...
6	QID1567	5	15	-1	UPDATE STATI...
7	QID1567	6	0	-1	TEMP_ID_41
8	QID1567	7	15	-1	CREATE TABLE...
9	QID1567	8	12698	-1	*NULL*
10	QID1567	9	12698	7794895	HDFS import ...
11	QID1567	10	12541	222	SELECT [T1_1]...

Figure 4-19.   Instead of importing 33 million rows, we retrieve 7.8 million

Given this limitation in what kinds of filters can enable predicate pushdown, we will want to structure external tables to have as many numeric values as possible. We do run a higher risk of rejection with non-string fields because of data not fitting the data type, so if data is coming from a nonrelational system or from flat files, we might want to perform cleanup before trying to bring it into SQL Server as a PolyBase external table.

This is not the only limitation with predicate pushdown. In addition, there are limitations around query complexity.

Limitations on Pushdown with Complex Filters

Suppose we have some of our data in SQL Server and some of our data in external tables. We have already seen in Chapter 2 that PolyBase allows us to join data from different sources together seamlessly. We can also, in some circumstances, perform predicate pushdown with joined data. Listing 4-7 creates a temporary table named #Season which lists what season it is in Raleigh for a particular month. We will then join that data to the Raleigh police incident external table and pull back results for the summers of 2015 and 2016.

Listing 4-7. Create a temporary table with seasonal data and join to police incidents with a filter

```
CREATE TABLE #Season
(
    Month INT,
    Season VARCHAR(20)
);
INSERT INTO #Season
(
    Month,
    Season
)
VALUES
    (1, 'Winter'), (2, 'Winter'), (3, 'Spring'),
    (4, 'Spring'), (5, 'Spring'), (6, 'Summer'),
    (7, 'Summer'), (8, 'Summer'), (9, 'Summer'),
    (10, 'Fall'), (11, 'Fall'), (12, 'Winter');

SELECT
    rpi.ReportedYear,
    rpi.ReportedMonth,
    s.Season,
    COUNT(1) AS NumberOfIncidents
FROM dbo.RaleighPoliceIncidents rpi
    INNER JOIN #Season s
        ON rpi.ReportedMonth = s.Month
WHERE
    rpi.ReportedYear IN (2015, 2016)
    AND rpi.ReportedMonth IN (6, 7, 8, 9)
GROUP BY
    rpi.ReportedYear,
    rpi.ReportedMonth,
    s.Season
```

```
ORDER BY
    rpi.ReportedYear,
    rpi.ReportedMonth
OPTION(FORCE EXTERNALPUSHDOWN);
```

Running this query returns 101,393 records from Hadoop, as we can see in Figure 4-20. We get back 34,455 rows, which is exactly the number of incidents in our result set.

	execution_id	step_index	total_elapsed_ti...	row_count	command
1	QID1597	0	0	~1	TEMP_ID_52
2	QID1597	1	12327	~1	NULL
3	QID1597	2	0	~1	TEMP_ID_53
4	QID1597	3	31	~1	CREATE TABLE...
5	QID1597	4	15	~1	EXEC [tempd...
6	QID1597	5	0	~1	UPDATE STATI...
7	QID1597	6	608	~1	NULL
8	QID1597	7	575	34455	HDFS import ...
9	QID1597	8	343	34455	SELECT [T1_1]...
10	QID1597	9	0	~1	DROP TABLE [...

Figure 4-20. *Predicate pushdown succeeded, returning only the rows needed for processing*

I might not want to hard-code the summer months, however, especially if I have data for Raleigh and Sydney, Australia, where the summer months have no overlap. Instead, I might write something like Listing 4-8, which takes the existing temp table and filters on season. Conceptually, I'd like the SQL Server Database Engine to work with the PolyBase service to determine that s.Season = 'Summer' is equivalent to rpi.ReportedMonth IN (6, 7, 8, 9) and ensure that we can continue benefiting from predicate pushdown.

Listing 4-8. A more logical filter for developers might end up causing performance problems

```
SELECT
    rpi.ReportedYear,
    rpi.ReportedMonth,
    s.Season,
    COUNT(1) AS NumberOfIncidents
FROM dbo.RaleighPoliceIncidents rpi
    INNER JOIN #Season s
        ON rpi.ReportedMonth = s.Month
WHERE
    rpi.ReportedYear IN (2015, 2016)
    AND s.Season = 'Summer'
GROUP BY
    rpi.ReportedYear,
    rpi.ReportedMonth,
    s.Season
ORDER BY
    rpi.ReportedYear,
    rpi.ReportedMonth
OPTION(FORCE EXTERNALPUSHDOWN);
```

The reality is not as pleasant. Figure 4-21 shows that we get from Hadoop 101,393 rows, which is the total number of police incidents for the years 2015 and 2016 combined. The PolyBase engine did successfully push down the predicate for reported year, but it did not make the time-saving translation.

	execution_id	step_index	total_elapsed_ti...	row_count	command
◢ RESULTS					
1	QID1606	0	0	-1	TEMP_ID_56
2	QID1606	1	12789	-1	*NULL*
3	QID1606	2	0	-1	TEMP_ID_57
4	QID1606	3	125	-1	CREATE TABLE...
5	QID1606	4	171	-1	EXEC [tempd...
6	QID1606	5	15	-1	UPDATE STATI...
7	QID1606	6	390	-1	*NULL*
8	QID1606	7	327	101393	HDFS import ...
9	QID1606	8	233	101393	SELECT [T1_1]...
10	QID1606	9	31	-1	DROP TABLE [...

Figure 4-21. *An equivalent but easier-to-maintain filter results in significantly more rows moving from Hadoop to SQL Server. On a large data set, this could mean a major performance hit*

Based on this limitation, the best advice is to keep filters simple, even if it means writing code which is less robust. For another example of complex filters causing us to migrate additional rows from HDFS, review Listing 4-9.

Listing 4-9. The CASE statement in the WHERE clause prevents predicate pushdown

```
SELECT
    rpi.ReportedYear,
    rpi.ReportedMonth,
    s.Season,
    COUNT(1) AS NumberOfIncidents
FROM dbo.RaleighPoliceIncidents rpi
    INNER JOIN #Season s
        ON rpi.ReportedMonth = s.Month
WHERE
    rpi.ReportedMonth =
```

```
            CASE
                WHEN rpi.ReportedYear = 2015 THEN 2
                WHEN rpi.ReportedYear = 2016 THEN 4
                ELSE NULL
            END
GROUP BY
    rpi.ReportedYear,
    rpi.ReportedMonth,
    s.Season
ORDER BY
    rpi.ReportedYear,
    rpi.ReportedMonth
OPTION(FORCE EXTERNALPUSHDOWN);
```

In this case, running the query forces us to retrieve all 232,127 rows from HDFS before winnowing them down to 7938 in SQL Server. Figure 4-22 shows us the gory details.

	execution_id	step_index	total_elapsed_ti...	row_count	command
1	QID1615	0	0	-1	TEMP_ID_60
2	QID1615	1	12519	-1	NULL
3	QID1615	2	0	-1	TEMP_ID_61
4	QID1615	3	20	-1	CREATE TABLE...
5	QID1615	4	15	-1	EXEC [tempd...
6	QID1615	5	0	-1	UPDATE STATI...
7	QID1615	6	444	-1	NULL
8	QID1615	7	443	232127	HDFS import ...
9	QID1615	8	350	7938	SELECT [T1_1]...
10	QID1615	9	7	-1	DROP TABLE [...

▲ RESULTS

Figure 4-22. *A complex filter leads to a full HDFS file scan and a wasted MapReduce job*

In this case, we can rewrite the query into something like Listing 4-10. This gives us exactly the same results but is easier on our SQL Server instance.

Listing 4-10. An equivalent query to Listing 4-9, except this time the PolyBase service is able to push down our predicate

```
SELECT
    rpi.ReportedYear,
    rpi.ReportedMonth,
    s.Season,
    COUNT(1) AS NumberOfIncidents
FROM dbo.RaleighPoliceIncidents rpi
    INNER JOIN #Season s
        ON rpi.ReportedMonth = s.Month
WHERE
    (rpi.ReportedYear = 2015 AND rpi.ReportedMonth = 2)
    OR (rpi.ReportedYear = 2016 AND rpi.ReportedMonth = 4)
GROUP BY
    rpi.ReportedYear,
    rpi.ReportedMonth,
    s.Season
ORDER BY
    rpi.ReportedYear,
    rpi.ReportedMonth
OPTION(FORCE EXTERNALPUSHDOWN);
```

Reviewing this query's request steps in Figure 4-23, we can see that our MapReduce job performed the filter, returning only the rows necessary for processing.

Note   The PolyBase service is capable of performing predicate pushdown if we use s.Month = 2 instead of rpi.ReportedMonth = 2. In this case, because both columns are part of a join together, the optimizer can translate one into the other. In general, however, it is best to make it as easy as possible for the database engine and PolyBase service by specifying external table columns in the WHERE clause, as this translation may not necessarily happen on more complex queries.

---

	execution_id	step_index	total_elapsed_ti...	row_count	command
1	QID1624	0	0	-1	TEMP_ID_64
2	QID1624	1	13380	-1	NULL
3	QID1624	2	0	-1	TEMP_ID_65
4	QID1624	3	46	-1	CREATE TABLE...
5	QID1624	4	15	-1	EXEC [tempd...
6	QID1624	5	0	-1	UPDATE STATI...
7	QID1624	6	218	-1	NULL
8	QID1624	7	203	7938	HDFS import ...
9	QID1624	8	109	7938	SELECT [T1_1]...
10	QID1624	9	0	-1	DROP TABLE [...

Figure 4-23. *The query in Listing 4-10 returns exactly the right number of rows, speeding up data importation and processing in SQL Server compared to Figure 4-22*

With these lessons in mind, we can summarize the lessons learned.

MapReduce and Pushdown in Summary

When working with external tables in Hadoop, keep the following points in mind:

- There is a ramp-up time for any MapReduce job. For smaller data sets, it is likely faster simply to pull all of the data from HDFS without running a job. The exact amount of time will depend on your network speed and Hadoop cluster size (and utilization), but if it takes less than 20 seconds to retrieve data, a MapReduce job likely will not finish much faster.

- Try to use as many numeric, date, and time data types in your WHERE clause as possible. PolyBase predicate pushdown only works with these data types.

- Keep your filters simple whenever possible. The optimizer is not always smart enough to transform your query into one which supports predicate pushdown even if such a transformation is possible.

- Filter as much as possible against external tables rather than SQL Server–based tables. Filters against normal tables apply only after data arrives from HDFS.

Conclusion

In this chapter, we took a detailed look at how PolyBase implements predicate pushdown. We looked at TCP streams using Wireshark to gain an understanding of the differences between the two possible techniques for moving data from a Hadoop cluster into SQL Server: streaming all of the data from HDFS vs. executing a MapReduce job to build PPAX files containing the data we need. We investigated the requirements for predicate pushdown, noting in particular that string columns are ineligible for pushdown and that the optimizer will not always perform predicate pushdown if a filter is sufficiently complicated. We wrapped up this chapter with a quick list of guidelines for writing optimal queries involving Hadoop-based external tables.

In Chapter 5, we will wrap up our detailed investigation of PolyBase V1 by covering common integration errors between SQL Server and Hadoop or Azure Blob Storage. From there, starting with Chapter 6, we will look at the new PolyBase functionality as of SQL Server 2019.

CHAPTER 5

Common Hadoop and Blob Storage Integration Errors

Over the past few chapters, we have learned how to integrate SQL Server with both Azure Blob Storage and Hadoop and learned about the concept of predicate pushdown with Hadoop clusters. In this chapter, we will wrap up our analysis of PolyBase V1 by diving into troubleshooting techniques and solving common issues.

PolyBase is a technology which connects together complicated technologies, so it should not be surprising that complications can arise. When complications do come up, knowing where to look is critical, so we will first focus on where to find the most helpful logs in SQL Server and Hadoop. From there, we will look at general configuration issues. After that, we will cover working with Docker, particularly with the Hortonworks Data Platform sandbox. After that, we will cover one of the most common classes of problems with PolyBase: data issues. Then, we will look at predicate pushdown failure modes. Finally, we will touch on common issues with Scale-Out Groups.

Note This chapter in particular assumes that you have some experience working with SQL Server, but limited experience with Hadoop or Kerberos. Many PolyBase errors come from some combination of incorrect PolyBase, Hadoop, and Kerberos settings, and this chapter will not teach you how to become a Hadoop administrator or a Kerberos wizard. Instead, the purpose of this chapter is to help you troubleshoot some of the more common issues and provide you with the techniques needed to take an issue to your Hadoop or Kerberos administrator with a reasonable expectation that the issue does not lie in misconfiguration on the SQL Server side.

© Kevin Feasel 2020
K. Feasel, *PolyBase Revealed*, https://doi.org/10.1007/978-1-4842-5461-5_5

Finding the Real Logger

One of the toughest issues when troubleshooting problems in PolyBase is that the immediate error is rarely helpful. SQL Server exposes many of the issues like in Figure 5-1: a Msg 7320 error which reads `Cannot execute the query "Remote Query" against OLE DB provider "SQLNCLI11" for linked server "(null)"`.

Started executing query at Line 1

Msg 7320, Level 16, State 110, Line 1

Cannot execute the query "Remote Query" against OLE DB provider "SQLNCLI11" for linked server "(null)".

Total execution time: 00:00:26.379

Figure 5-1. *PolyBase often surfaces this generic error instead of explaining the real problem*

We will not get very far with just this information; we need real details. Fortunately, we can get these real details from various logs. One of the first places to look is the PolyBase logs.

PolyBase Log Files

There are seven log files the PolyBase Engine and Data Movement services use. The default location for these logs is `%PROGRAMFILES%\Microsoft SQL Server\MSSQL[##].MSSQLSERVER\MSSQL\Log\Polybase`, where `[##]` is the two-digit number representing your SQL Server version and `MSSQLSERVER` is your instance name. Figure 5-2 shows an example of these seven log files on my machine named `SQLWIN10`.

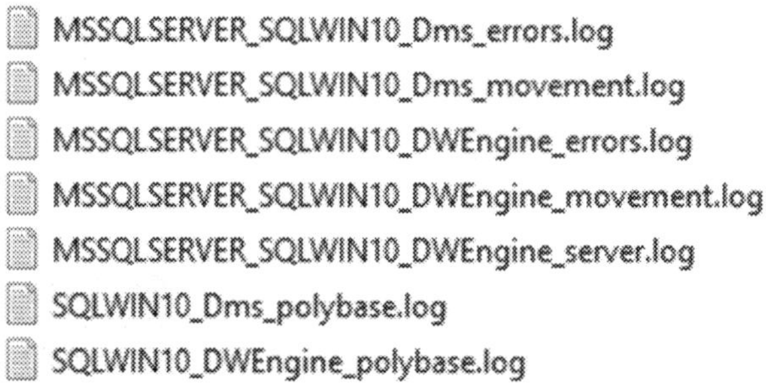

MSSQLSERVER_SQLWIN10_Dms_errors.log
MSSQLSERVER_SQLWIN10_Dms_movement.log
MSSQLSERVER_SQLWIN10_DWEngine_errors.log
MSSQLSERVER_SQLWIN10_DWEngine_movement.log
MSSQLSERVER_SQLWIN10_DWEngine_server.log
SQLWIN10_Dms_polybase.log
SQLWIN10_DWEngine_polybase.log

Figure 5-2. *PolyBase stores useful data in seven log files*

Let's take each one of these in turn and understand what information the file provides and when that information is most useful.

DMS Errors

The DMS error log gives stack traces when an exception occurs in the data movement service. One of the more common errors you might find when reading through this log is `System.Data.SqlClient.SqlException: Operation cancelled by user`. This exception occurs when a user or application stops a query, such as when a user hits the "Stop" button in Azure Data Studio. You can safely ignore this error.

This particular log file tends to give you a high-level view of when errors occur but little information on the root cause or even the specific error. One of the more common errors I tend to see in this log is `Internal Query Processor Error: The query processor encountered an unexpected error during the processing of a remote query phase`. This phrase will not help me diagnose the problem, but this log file does tend to include information like the query ID and plan ID, which I can use to figure out which queries are failing.

DMS Movement

The data movement service writes a good amount of information to the DMS Movement log and includes detailed information on what data moves over from Azure Blob Storage or Hadoop to SQL Server. This includes the SQL queries the PolyBase data movement service generates, configuration settings such as the number of readers the DMS will use to migrate data, and detailed operation at each step. Combined with the DMS error log, we can start to piece together our errors.

DWEngine Errors

Like the DMS error log, the DWEngine error log gives a higher-level overview of when errors occur, as well as stack traces. This file can help you pinpoint when an error occurs. The errors in this file tend to be a bit more descriptive than the ones in the DMS error log. For example, we can find errors relating to the maximum reject threshold in this file: `Query aborted-- the maximum reject threshold (1 rows) was reached while reading from an external source: 2 rows rejected out of total 2 rows processed`.

DWEngine Movement

This log provides us with more detail on queries and errors which the DWEngine error log captures. In some cases, this file has enough information to drive to the root cause. In Figure 5-3, we see an example of a clear error message where I defined a column in an ORC file as a string data type but am trying to use an integer data type to access it via PolyBase.

```
3/5/2019 9:57:42 PM [Thread:5656] [CommandWorker:ErrorEvent] (Error, High): TRACE FROM DMS:
Microsoft.SqlServer.DataWarehouse.Common.ErrorHandling.MppSqlException: HdfsBridge::recordReaderFillBuffer - Unexpected
error encountered filling record reader buffer: HadoopUnexpectedException: class com.microsoft.pp.converter.RawCharArray
cannot be cast to INT ---> Microsoft.SqlServer.DataWarehouse.Hadoop.HadoopBridge.JavaBridgeAccessException: Java exception
raised on call to HdfsBridge_RecordReaderFillBuffer. Java exception message:
HdfsBridge::recordReaderFillBuffer - Unexpected error encountered filling record reader buffer: HadoopUnexpectedException:
class com.microsoft.pp.converter.RawCharArray cannot be cast to INT
```

Figure 5-3. *An invalid conversion attempt fails, and we have enough information to track it down*

I can combine this error with my knowledge of the query to trace down exactly which table this is and fix the external table definition.

DWEngine Server

The DWEngine Server log contains a few pieces of useful information. One of the most useful is that it contains the create statements for external data sources, file formats, and tables. We can use this log to determine what our external resources looked like at the time of exception, just in case somebody changed one of them during troubleshooting.

This log also contains information on failed external table access attempts. If you have firewall or connection problems, this should be your first log to review. Figure 5-4 shows an example of a common HDFS bridge error whose root cause is insufficient permissions granted to the PolyBase `pdw_user` account.

```
1/6/2019 12:28:27 PM [Thread:7908] [EngineInstrumentation:EngineExecuteQueryErrorEvent] (Error, High):
Microsoft.SqlServer.DataWarehouse.Common.ErrorHandling.MppSqlException: EXTERNAL TABLE access failed due to internal error:
'Error occurred while accessing HDFS: Java exception raised on call to HdfsBridge_IsDirExist. Java exception message:
HdfsBridge::isDirExist - Unexpected error encountered checking whether directoy exists or not: ConnectException: Connection
refused: no further information' ---->
Microsoft.SqlServer.DataWarehouse.DataMovement.Common.ExternalAccess.HdfsAccessException: Error occurred while accessing
HDFS: Java exception raised on call to HdfsBridge_IsDirExist. Java exception message:
```

Figure 5-4. *This error message, typo included, can help us troubleshoot directory and permissions errors*

DMS PolyBase

The DMS PolyBase log shows us something extremely important: any data translation failure. Figure 5-5 gives us three examples of data translation errors, including column conversion errors, data length errors, and string delimiter errors. We can also find cases where values are NULL, but the external table requires a non-nullable field, invalid date conversion attempts, and more.

```
[2019-01-23 20:28:50,375] [WARN ] [Thread-265] [com.microsoft.pp.converter.ToPaxBlockConverter] Column ordinal: 1,
Expected data type: FLOAT(53), Offending value: X  [Column Conversion Error] Error: Error converting date type VARCHAR to
FLOAT.
[2019-01-23 20:30:31,200] [WARN ] [Thread-271] [com.microsoft.pp.converter.ToPaxBlockConverter] Column ordinal: 15,
Expected data type: VARCHAR(30) collate SQL_Latin1_General_CP1_CI_AS, Offending value:  THOMAS DR DDS
[Column Conversion Error], Error: String or binary data would be truncated
[2019-01-23 20:30:46,830] [WARN ] [Thread-274] [com.microsoft.pp.converter.ToPaxBlockConverter] Column ordinal: 15,
Expected data type: VARCHAR(30) collate SQL_Latin1_General_CP1_CI_AS, Offending value:  THOMAS DR DDS
[Column Conversion Error], Error: String or binary data would be truncated.
[2019-01-23 22:20:27,335] [WARN ] [Thread-371] [com.microsoft.pp.converter.ToPaxBlockConverter] Column ordinal: 39,
Expected data type: VARCHAR(30) collate SQL_Latin1_General_CP1_CI_AS, Offending value: "01 nppes_provider_street1""
[Tokenization failed], Error: Could not find a delimiter after string delimiter.
```

Figure 5-5. *Three sample data errors show the importance of the DMS PolyBase log file*

This information can greatly reduce the amount of effort needed to fix data issues in a relatively low-use environment like a test server. On a busy system, the sheer size of the data file will likely make detailed analysis prohibitively expensive.

DWEngine PolyBase

This file is much less interesting than most of the other logs. In my work, I have not seen it stretch to more than a few lines, and the most interesting thing in this log is the location of new Hadoop clusters as you create external data sources.

Hadoop Log Files

In this section, we will look at some of the important resource locations to review when diagnosing issues between SQL Server and Hadoop. These logs can provide additional critical information needed to solve a problem with the help of a good Hadoop administrator. In each example, we will cover where you can find these resources on the Hortonworks Data Platform distribution of Hadoop; if you are using the Cloudera Distribution of Hadoop, the exact ports may differ. For each service, we will use a Hadoop cluster whose name node is called clusterino and all relevant servers run on it.

Job Tracker

You can find the Job Tracker UI at `http://clusterino:8088/cluster`. This service shows the status of all MapReduce jobs on the server, making it an important resource for issues around predicate pushdown. Figure 5-6 shows an example of the Job Tracker UI, which shows job users, application types (you will see MAPREDUCE or TEZ as options here, but PolyBase only supports MapReduce operations), and status.

Figure 5-6. *The Job Tracker UI is critical for diagnosing MapReduce issues*

Clicking an application ID takes you to a job status page, which then lets you see the logs for each application attempt. Those logs include prelaunch, launch, and runtime logs, including whatever the MapReduce job wrote to the output (as syslog) or to the standard error (stderr) output.

YARN Resource Manager

YARN has its own resource manager UI in HDP 3.0, which you can find at `http://clusterino:8088/ui2/`. Selecting the Applications link will show you the various MapReduce and Tez jobs including their progress and status. Figure 5-7 shows you a sample list.

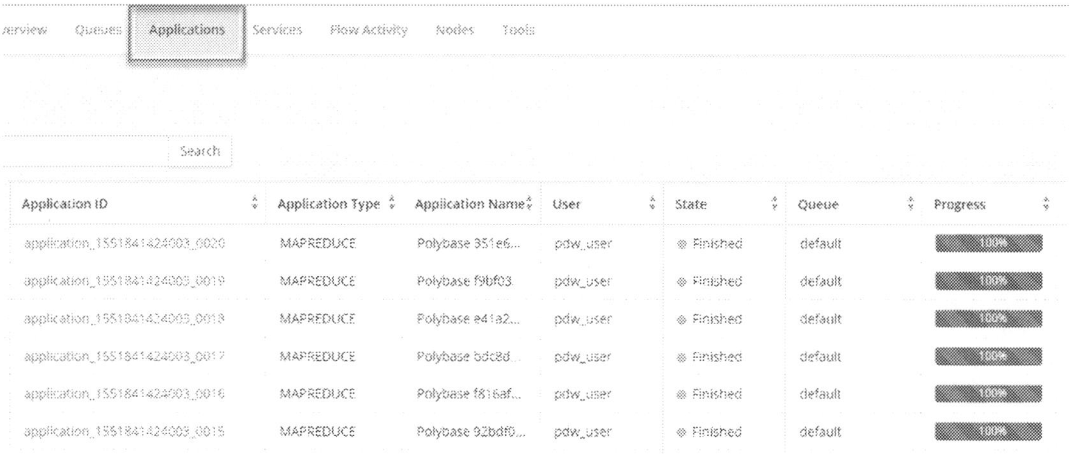

Application ID	Application Type	Application Name	User	State	Queue	Progress
application_1551841424003_0020	MAPREDUCE	Polybase 351e6...	pdw_user	Finished	default	100%
application_1551841424003_0019	MAPREDUCE	Polybase f9bf03...	pdw_user	Finished	default	100%
application_1551841424003_0018	MAPREDUCE	Polybase e41a2...	pdw_user	Finished	default	100%
application_1551841424003_0017	MAPREDUCE	Polybase bdc8d...	pdw_user	Finished	default	100%
application_1551841424003_0016	MAPREDUCE	Polybase f816af...	pdw_user	Finished	default	100%
application_1551841424003_0015	MAPREDUCE	Polybase 92bdf0...	pdw_user	Finished	default	100%

Figure 5-7. *The YARN resource manager log shows the status of various MapReduce and Tez jobs, including PolyBase jobs with predicate pushdown*

Clicking one of these application links brings you to a page where you can look up information on resource utilization for active jobs, diagnostics, and logs for jobs in progress as well as completed jobs. Figure 5-8 shows an example log entry for a completed PolyBase job using MapReduce.

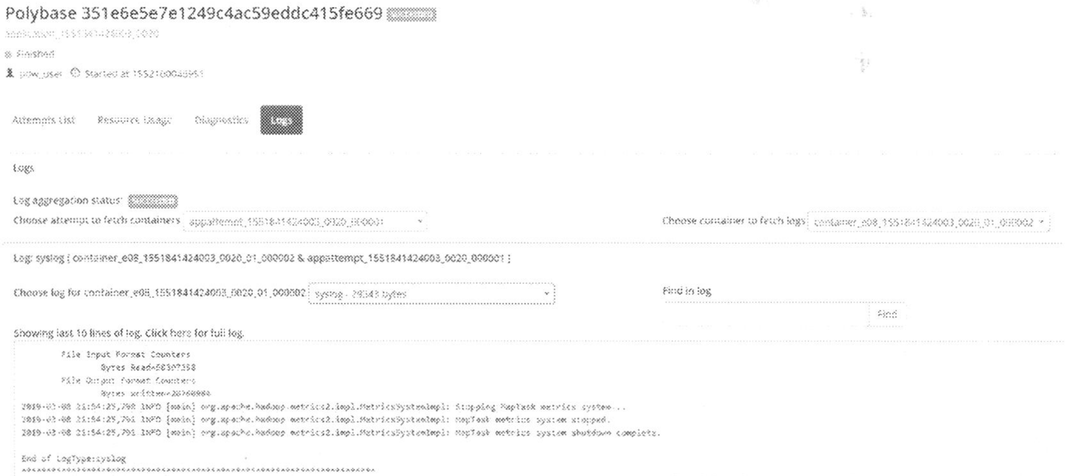

Figure 5-8. *This UI provides a nicer interface than the Job Tracker UI*

The YARN resource manager UI is functionally similar to the Job Tracker UI, but it provides a fresher experience. I have found the YARN resource manager UI better for watching jobs in progress, but the older Job Tracker UI tends to be better for finding an error, as it combines together the logs from various YARN containers which perform Map and Reduce actions, whereas the new UI splits each of these out via a drop-down list, requiring more clicks to analyze the entire log.

JobHistory UI

The JobHistory UI runs on `http://clusterino:19888` and shows log data from MapReduce jobs. Figure 5-9 gives us an idea of how the JobHistory interface looks.

Retired Jobs

Show 20 ▾ entries

Submit Time ⬍	Start Time ⬍	Finish Time ⬍	Job ID ⬍	Name ⬍	User ⬍	Queue ⬍	State ⬍	Maps Total ⬍
2019.03.08 21:54:08 EST	2019.03.08 21:54:13 EST	2019.03.08 21:54:25 EST	job_1551841424003_0020	Polybase 351e6e5e7e1249c4ac59eddc415fe669	pdw_user	default	SUCCEEDED	1
2019.03.08 21:38:49 EST	2019.03.08 21:38:53 EST	2019.03.08 21:39:00 EST	job_1551841424003_0019	Polybase f9bf0307efd04876b9a3f36060fda9e9	pdw_user	default	KILLED	0
2019.03.08 21:37:43 EST	2019.03.08 21:37:47 EST	2019.03.08 21:37:54 EST	job_1551841424003_0018	Polybase e41a20b6c2844367b6154cf3fd98500c	pdw_user	default	KILLED	0
2019.03.08 18:49:58 EST	2019.03.08 18:50:03 EST	2019.03.08 18:50:54 EST	job_1551841424003_0017	Polybase bdc8d4473e7c490db1f3bc4c68c4a7ba	pdw_user	default	SUCCEEDED	3
2019.03.08 18:42:02 EST	2019.03.08 18:42:07 EST	2019.03.08 18:42:58 EST	job_1551841424003_0016	Polybase f816afb52ca341aaa898f0621d347cfc	pdw_user	default	SUCCEEDED	3
2019.03.08 18:39:34 EST	2019.03.08 18:39:38 EST	2019.03.08 18:41:42 EST	job_1551841424003_0015	Polybase 92bdf00171e1481b89f05b1e6cec46aa	pdw_user	default	KILLED	0
2019.03.07 23:10:04 EST	2019.03.07 23:10:08 EST	2019.03.07 23:10:25 EST	job_1551841424003_0013	Polybase be0471d0df51413abab4b4cf2ea62a54	pdw_user	default	FAILED	0

Figure 5-9. *The JobHistory UI gives us information on MapReduce jobs, including failures*

Clicking a job link takes us to a log page similar to the Job Tracker UI. From here, we can see specific details on what happened during an operation and why a job might have failed.

Some of the errors that SQL Server returns will include a link to the JobHistory UI if the error occurred during a MapReduce job.

NameNode Logs

If you have a basic configuration issue with Hadoop, you might learn more information in the NameNode logs, located at `http://clusterino:50070/logs`. This includes messages from your name node, from data nodes, and from HDFS audits. These logs can be useful if you are unable even to stream data from HDFS into SQL Server.

Log Files

Any investigation of Hadoop logs would be remiss without a mention of /var/log, which hosts log files for many of the key Hadoop services. Two log locations of note are the Hive logs and the Ranger logs.

You can find Hive logs at /var/log/hive. Hive is a product which provides warehousing in Hadoop and offers users access through a SQL dialect called Hive Query Language (HiveQL). PolyBase V1 makes very little direct use of Hive—for example, you cannot use PolyBase in Hadoop mode to connect directly to a Hive table. Instead, you must connect via HDFS to the files which make up your Hive table. Still, you might run into an issue with PolyBase around—see the "Predicate Pushdown Failure" section for one such example.

Another set of logs which might be helpful are Ranger logs, which you can obtain at /var/log/ranger. Ranger is the key data security tool in the Hadoop ecosystem and manages Kerberos authentication. If you believe you might have Kerberos-related issues, the Ranger logs are often a good place to look.

Configuration Issues

The most common issues around PolyBase tend to be configuration issues. In this section, we will look at several errors related to service configuration. This section should serve as a checklist: when troubleshooting PolyBase problems, ensure that these settings are right before diving down the rabbit hole.

SQL Server Configuration

This first set of configuration steps all relate to ensuring that SQL Server has everything set up appropriately. First, if this is a standalone instance or the head node of a scale-out cluster, ensure that the PolyBase Data Movement Service and PolyBase Engine service are both running, like in Figure 5-10.

SQL Server (MSSQLSERVER)	Provides sto...	Running	Automatic	NT Service\MSSQLSERVER
SQL Server Agent (MSSQLSERVER)	Executes jo...		Manual	NT Service\SQLSERVERAGENT
SQL Server Browser	Provides SQ...		Disabled	Local Service
SQL Server CEIP service (MSSQLSERVER)	CEIP service...	Running	Automatic	NT Service\SQLTELEMETRY
SQL Server PolyBase Data Movement (MSSQLSERVER)	Manages co...	Running	Automatic	CSMore\PolyBaseService
SQL Server PolyBase Engine (MSSQLSERVER)	Creates, co...	Running	Automatic	CSMore\PolyBaseService

Figure 5-10. *Ensure that the PolyBase services are running*

If these services are stopped, attempting to query external tables can result in the error message in Figure 5-11.

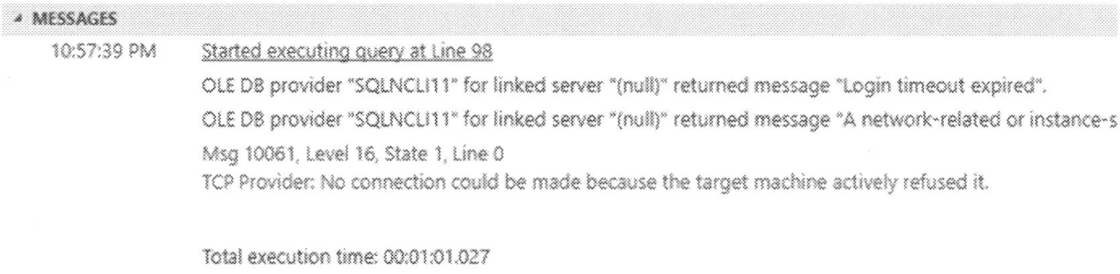

Figure 5-11. *Msg 10061, TCP provider: No connection could be made because the target machine actively refused it*

If you see this message, try starting the PolyBase services. You may also need to restart the SQL Server service if you just enabled PolyBase and have not restarted the SQL Server service yet. If you are running SQL Server Developer Edition, you will also need to enable TCP/IP as a valid protocol in the SQL Server Configuration Manager's protocols for your instance. This is enabled by default in Standard and Enterprise Editions, but you might also want to confirm that an overzealous administrator did not disable the ability to use TCP/IP to connect to SQL Server.

In addition to ensuring that the services are started, ensure that your Hadoop connectivity configuration settings are correct and they reference the correct data source. Reference Chapter 1 for more details on initial configuration and Chapters 2 and 3 for Azure Blob Storage and Hadoop configuration, respectively.

Check External Resources

The next thing to look at is your external resources—that is, your external data source, file format, and table definitions. Any typos or mistakes in these external resources could result in an unintuitive error message, so take care and review these resources.

For external data sources, ensure that if you are connecting to Azure Blob Storage or to Hadoop with Kerberos running, you have a Database Scoped Credential with your identity and secret. SQL Server will accept anything here and does not attempt to validate what you enter, so you will not see an error until you try to query the external table. On the Azure Blob Storage side, ensure that your WASBS link is correct and the credentials you use have at least read access. On the Hadoop side, ensure that your location is the name node and fill out the resource manager location if you wish to use predicate pushdown. You can find more on Hadoop configuration in Chapter 3.

For external file formats, ensure that you have the correct field terminator and string delimiter. If your files are pipe delimited, having a comma-delimited file format will not work. This advice might sound obvious, but neither Hadoop nor Azure Blob Storage performs any kind of validation checking on files, so if one of a thousand files sneaks into a folder and has the wrong field terminator, your job might fail.

For external tables, ensure that your source files are using the file format you chose and that they are available to the PolyBase user. If you have Kerberos enabled, this will be the Database Scoped Credential for the account you configure; otherwise, this will be a Hadoop user called `pdw_user` which will need read and possibly write access to folders. In addition to these basic checks, you should also spot check the files to ensure that they have the right number of columns and data types you expect.

Check SQL Server Configuration Files

After reviewing external resources, you might next check your configuration files in `%PROGRAMFILES%\Microsoft SQL Server\MSSQL[##].MSSQLSERVER\MSSQL \Binn\ Polybase\Hadoop\conf`, where [##] is the two-digit number representing your SQL Server version and MSSQLSERVER is your instance name. The two most important files here are `mapred-site.xml` and `yarn-site.xml`. You might need to configure other files in this directory depending upon your Hadoop configuration. For tips on how to configure these files, review Chapter 3.

Note   In some cases, you might need to modify one of these files outside of what Chapter 3 recommends. For example, you might need to change the Java VM default size in `mapred-site.xml` if you frequently encounter Java heap space errors. Work with your Hadoop administrator to determine what the correct value should be based on the `mapred-site.xml` on your Hadoop cluster. If you are your Hadoop administrator, work with yourself on it.

Hadoop-Side Configuration

The next set of configuration errors are Hadoop-side configuration errors. Here, we will look at four of the most common configuration issues.

Invalid User Permissions or Missing Account

By default, Hadoop does not have a user named `pdw_user`, but this is the account PolyBase uses when Kerberos is turned off. If you have not created this user on your Hadoop cluster and provided it read access to the files or folders you wish to use as the source for external tables, you will get an error like in Figure 5-12.

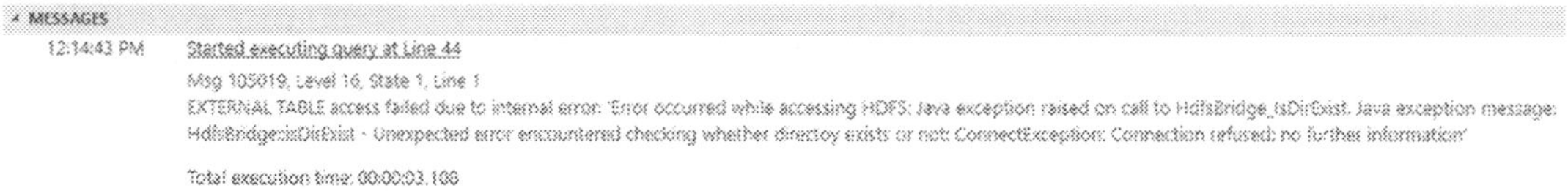

Figure 5-12. Msg 105019, Java exception message: HdfsBridge::isDirExist – Unexpected error encountered checking whether directoy exists or not

In the case of Figure 5-12, that error can occur when the folder does not exist, but if you can independently confirm that the directory exists in HDFS, the `pdw_user` account likely does not have permission to access it.

Could Not Obtain Block

The next error I run into frequently includes text like: `Could not obtain block: BP-333635372-127.0.0.1-1508779710286:blk_1073744640_3824`. This error message indicates that the PolyBase service was not able to read a particular block of data from a data node. The PolyBase compute nodes communicate directly with data nodes in Hadoop, which can speed up data transfer drastically with a scale-out cluster but requires that PolyBase compute nodes be able to reach those data nodes. In this case, the data node has an IP address of 127.0.0.1, which is an unroutable IP address.

There are two potential solutions to this problem. The first solution is to add the configuration setting in Listing 5-1 to your SQL Server's `hdfs-site.xml` file.

Listing 5-1. Use hostnames for data nodes instead of IP addresses

```
<property>
  <name>dfs.client.use.datanode.hostname</name>
  <value>true</value>
</property>
```

Alternatively, you can fix your data node references to use routable IP addresses.

Host File Pointing to 127.0.0.1

The third issue you might run into is most common on sandboxes like the Hortonworks Data Platform sandbox or the Cloudera Distribution of Hadoop sandbox. In these cases, the host `quickstart.cloudera` or `sandbox-hdp.hortonworks.com` points to 127.0.0.1 or 127.0.1.1. This causes Hadoop services to route locally instead of going through a routable IP address, which can also lead to the issue in Figure 5-12. If you run into this, change your `/etc/hosts` file to point your externally accessible IP address out as your hostname. For example, if your routable IP address is 192.168.100.104, make that the IP address for `sandbox-hdp.hortonworks.com` or `quickstart.cloudera`.

Kerberos Should Be On or Off, Not Both

Kerberos configuration is complicated enough that it is beyond the scope of this book. For this section, it is enough to mention that there are several files you need to modify to enable Kerberos support with PolyBase. Modifying some of the files while leaving others untouched will result in errors.

PolyBase and Dockerized Data Nodes

As of Hortonworks Data Platform 2.5, the HDP sandbox now uses Docker containers to host the name node and data node services. PolyBase needs to be able to communicate directly with data nodes, so there is some process involved with configuring the HDP sandbox (or any other containerized solution) to work with PolyBase. In this section, I will cover getting the Hortonworks Data Platform 3.0 sandbox running. The specific instructions will differ slightly for versions of HDP prior to 2.6.5, but the general concepts are the same.

In order for this to work, we will need to make a configuration change on the SQL Server side and several changes on the Hadoop side. First, on the SQL Server side, open up the hdfs-site.xml configuration file in `%PROGRAMFILES%\Microsoft SQL Server\ MSSQL[##].MSSQLSERVER\MSSQL \Binn\Polybase\Hadoop\conf`, where `[##]` is the two-digit number representing your SQL Server version and `MSSQLSERVER` is your instance name. Inside this file, add the property in Listing 5-2.

Listing 5-2. A new property for `hdfs-site.xml` on the SQL Server side

```
<property>
  <name>dfs.client.use.datanode.hostname</name>
  <value>true</value>
</property>
```

This forces PolyBase to use hostnames rather than IP addresses when addressing data nodes. We can do this because `/etc/hosts` on the HDP sandbox has a route from the defined hostname to the IP address on its Docker subnet.

After we make this change, there are several changes we will need to perform on the Hadoop side. To make these changes, ssh into your Hadoop cluster's name node; for the HDP 3.0 sandbox, the username is `root` and the password `hadoop`. Listing 5-3 walks us through the first couple of steps.

Listing 5-3. The first steps needed to open necessary ports for PolyBase on the HDP 3.0 sandbox

```
cd /sandbox/deploy-scripts/
cp /sandbox-flavor .
vi assets/generate-proxy-deploy-script.sh
```

Once you have opened the deploy script, scroll down to the bottom of the `tcpPortsHDP` list and add entries for ports 8050, 50010, and 10020. Save the file and then run the scripts in Listing 5-4 to build a new proxy file and put it into place.

Listing 5-4. Generate a new proxy deploy script and copy it to the right location

```
./generate-proxy-deploy-script.sh
cd /sandbox
mv proxy/proxy-deploy.sh proxy/proxy-deploy.sh.old
cp deploy-scripts/sandbox/proxy/proxy-deploy.sh proxy/
```

At this point, you should be able to run `./sandbox-stop.sh` to stop the sandbox. After this script finishes, run `docker ps` to make sure that all of the images are gone, running `docker kill` commands if there are any still running. See Figure 5-13 as an example of running `docker kill`.

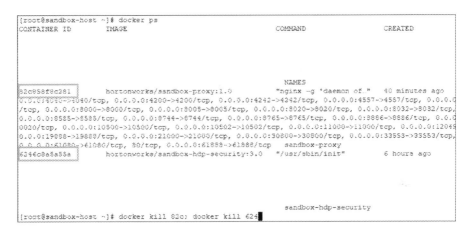

Figure 5-13. *Find running Docker images and kill them*

Now that all of the images are gone, run the command `./proxy/proxy-deploy.sh` to build a new image with our expanded port range in mind. Run docker ps again and check the output of the port forwarding list to ensure that you see entries for our new ports, like `0.0.0.0:50010->50010/tcp`. If you see that, shut down the sandbox and restart Linux. Once your sandbox reboots, you should be able to connect to Ambari and configure this server like a regular Hortonworks Data Platform cluster.

Data Issues

Data issues comprise the next major class of problems. Azure Blob Storage and Hadoop are semistructured systems, meaning that readers imbue the data with a sense of structure rather than writers. By contrast, SQL Server is a structured system, meaning that writers cannot insert invalid data—data which fails column type, length, nullability, or key constraints. Because SQL Server is a much tougher grader than Hadoop or Azure Blob Storage, we frequently see errors trying to read data. In this section, I will classify several of the major issues and describe what you can do to fix them.

Structural Mismatch

The first common data problem is structural mismatch—that is, when you define your external table one way but the data does not comport to that structure. For example, you might define an external table as having eight columns, but the underlying data set has seven or nine columns. In that case, the PolyBase engine will reject rows because they do not fit the expected structure.

Caution   In production Hadoop systems, developers are liable to change the structure of files and leave old files as is. For example, a report with eight columns might suddenly populate with nine columns on a certain date. The PolyBase engine cannot support multiple data structures for the same external table and will reject at least one of the two structures. This might cause a previously working external table query suddenly and unexpectedly to fail.

Aside from column totals, there are several other mismatch problems which can cause queries to fail. For example, text files might have different schemas or delimiters: one type might be comma-delimited and another pipe-delimited. Some text files might use the quotation mark as a string delimiter, and others might use brackets or tildes. Any lack of consistency will cause the PolyBase engine to fail processing. If you do run into this scenario, an easy solution would be to create several external tables—one for each distinct file structure—and use a view to combine them together as one logical unit.

Unsupported Characters or Formats

PolyBase supports only a limited number of date formats. The safest route is to limit your text file dates to use supported formats. You can find these on Microsoft Docs (`https://docs.microsoft.com/en-us/sql/t-sql/statements/create-external-file-format-transact-sql`).

PolyBase also struggles with newlines in text fields, so strip those out before trying to load data. Even within a quoted delimiter, newlines will cause the PolyBase engine to think it is starting a new record.

PolyBase Data Limitations

PolyBase also has limits to what data it can support. From Microsoft Docs (`https://docs.microsoft.com/en-us/sql/relational-databases/polybase/polybase-versioned-feature-summary`), we can see that the maximum row size cannot exceed 32KB for SQL Server or 1MB for Azure Synapse Analytics. In addition, if you save your data in ORC format, you might receive Java out-of-memory exceptions due to data size. For text-heavy files, it might be best to keep them as delimited files rather than ORC files.

Curate Your Data

One way to fix structural mismatches, unsupported characters, and data limitations is to curate the data going to SQL Server. Instead of trying to process raw text files in a Hadoop directory, transform and clean the data in these files so it fits a common structure. Hadoop developers have more flexible tools for working with semistructured data, so take advantage of these tools and use SQL Server for processed data.

If you know you can trust your data writers to follow a given convention, this is not necessary, but in most practical applications, adding this cleansing layer in Hadoop helps a lot, particularly because of PolyBase's limitations in exposing invalid data for users to correct.

This point about knowledge leads to a broader conclusion: know your data. PolyBase is not a good technology for arbitrary data discovery because it requires known, structured data sets like a relational database would have. The better you know your data processes, data distributions, and areas where oddities can crop up, the less frustrating the process will be. Like any data project, most of your effort will go into cleaning the data.

Predicate Pushdown Failure

The next common class of errors relates to predicate pushdown to Hadoop. We can see an example of the first error in this class in Figure 5-14.

```
Msg 7320, Level 16, State 110, Line 84
Cannot execute the query "Remote Query" against OLE DB provider "SQLNCLI11" for linked server "(null)".
Query processor could not produce a query plan because of the hints defined in this query.
Resubmit the query without specifying any hints.
```

Figure 5-14. *Without a resource manager, you get this generic-looking error message when you attempt to force predicate pushdown on an external table*

If you receive this error almost instantly after trying to execute a query with the `OPTION(FORCE EXTERNALPUSHDOWN)` hint, check the definition of your external data source, specifically its resource manager location. Ensure that the port number is correct, as this will differ between Hortonworks and Cloudera distributions and could even differ between the sandbox and standalone installations. Most likely, your external data source does not have a resource manager location, and PolyBase needs that to configure and execute MapReduce jobs.

The most common symptom of a predicate pushdown issue other than a missing resource manager location is an error like the one in Figure 5-15. This error contains a tracking URL, which is a giveaway that the PolyBase engine did communicate with the Hadoop cluster's resource manager, YARN.

```
Msg 7320, Level 16, State 110, Line 3
Cannot execute the query "Remote Query" against OLE DB provider "SQLNCLI11" for linked server "(null)". Hadoop Job Execution failed.
Tracking URL is http://clusterino:8088/proxy/application_1651841424003_0013/
Messages from failed tasks:

Task ID: task_1651841424003_0013_m_000000, Message = Error converting data type VARCHAR to INT.
```

Figure 5-15. *A failure trying to execute a MapReduce job*

In this case, the issue is that in an ORC file, a particular column is of type string, but PolyBase is attempting to force the MapReduce job to convert implicitly that string value to an integer. This implicit conversion attempt causes the MapReduce job to throw an exception which comes back to SQL Server in the preceding guise.

In the event that you do not know why SQL Server received the error it did, click the link it provides to go to Hadoop's JobHistory UI server for your specific job. In Figure 5-16, we see a sample error. I have highlighted the most important part of the error message: `Could not find or load main class org.apache.hadoop.mapreduce.v2.app.MRAppMaster`.

This particular error is telling you that the MapReduce job that the PolyBase engine created cannot find necessary Java classes, including the MapReduce application master class. This class is fundamental for execution of MapReduce jobs, and the error is indicative of a setup problem, as every Hadoop distribution will have this class.

If you get this error, there are four likely solutions. The first is to ensure that your mapred-site.xml on the machine hosting SQL Server has a property called mapreduce. app-submission.cross-platform with a value of true. If you are missing this property, add it; otherwise, PolyBase cannot execute MapReduce jobs.

If your mapred-site.xml is correct, next check the SQL Server side's yarn-site.xml file. Ensure that you have the right yarn.application.classpath and that it is pointing to the right folders. For a refresher on this, review the section in Chapter 3 entitled "Update PolyBase Configuration Files" for more information on what this classpath variable should look like.

```
Diagnostics:   Application application_1550698566423_0001 failed 2 times due to AM Container for appattempt_1550(
               Failing this attempt.Diagnostics: [2019-02-20 16:37:05.287]Exception from container-launch.
               Container id: container_e05_1550698566423_0001_02_000001
               Exit code: 1
               [2019-02-20 16:37:05.290]Container exited with a non-zero exit code 1. Error file: prelaunch.err.
               Last 4096 bytes of prelaunch.err :
               Last 4096 bytes of stderr :
               Error: Could not find or load main class org.apache.hadoop.mapreduce.v2.app.MRAppMaster
               Please check whether your etc/hadoop/mapred-site.xml contains the below configuration:
               <property>
               <name>yarn.app.mapreduce.am.env</name>
               <value>HADOOP_MAPRED_HOME=${full path of your hadoop distribution directory}</value>
               </property>
               <property>
               <name>mapreduce.map.env</name>
               <value>HADOOP_MAPRED_HOME=${full path of your hadoop distribution directory}</value>
               </property>
               <property>
               <name>mapreduce.reduce.env</name>
               <value>HADOOP_MAPRED_HOME=${full path of your hadoop distribution directory}</value>
               </property>
               [2019-02-20 16:37:05.291]Container exited with a non-zero exit code 1. Error file: prelaunch.err.
```

Figure 5-16. *This MRAppMaster is one of the most common MapReduce errors you will find when starting out with PolyBase and Hadoop*

Assuming both of these configuration files are correct, the third place to look is yarn-site.xml on the Hadoop side. For my Hortonworks Data Platform 3.0 installation, I needed to modify the yarn.application.classpath configuration setting to contain the value in Listing 5-5.

Listing 5-5. You might need to replace your `yarn.application.classpath` setting with this if you use the Hortonworks Data Platform distribution of Hadoop and receive MRAppMaster errors

```
$HADOOP_CONF_DIR, {{hadoop_home}}/hadoop/*, {{hadoop_home}}/hadoop/lib/*,
{{hadoop_home}}/hadoop-hdfs/*, {{hadoop_home}}/hadoop-hdfs/lib/*, {{hadoop_
home}}/hadoop-yarn/*, {{hadoop_home}}/hadoop-yarn/lib/*, {{hadoop_home}}/
hadoop-mapreduce/*, {{hadoop_home}}/hadoop-mapreduce/lib/*
```

Finally, if all else fails, do what the error message says and ensure that your `mapred-site.xml` on the Hadoop side contains the configuration settings in the error message.

This advice applies to general pushdown failures, but you might run into an error in SQL Server 2016 or SQL Server 2017 when trying to perform predicate pushdown against an ORC file sitting on a Hadoop server with Hive 3. This particular error message has you go to the job history service in Hadoop, where you will see a series of errors like the one in Figure 5-17.

```
Error: java.lang.IllegalArgumentException: Unrecognized Hadoop major version number: 3.1.1.3.0.1.0-187 at
org.apache.hadoop.hive.shims.ShimLoader.getMajorVersion(ShimLoader.java:174) at
org.apache.hadoop.hive.shims.ShimLoader.loadShims(ShimLoader.java:139) at
org.apache.hadoop.hive.shims.ShimLoader.getHadoopShims(ShimLoader.java:100) at org.apache.hadoop.hive.conf.HiveConf$ConfVars.<clinit>
(HiveConf.java:368) at org.apache.hadoop.hive.ql.io.orc.RecordReaderImpl.<init>(RecordReaderImpl.java:195) at
org.apache.hadoop.hive.ql.io.orc.ReaderImpl.rowsOptions(ReaderImpl.java:539) at com.microsoft.pp.converter.ORCFileToPaxBlockConverter.<init>
(ORCFileToPaxBlockConverter.java:95) at
com.microsoft.polybase.storage.input.ORCFileToPaxBlockInputFormat$OrcFileToPaxBlockRecordReader.initialize(ORCFileToPaxBlockInputFormat.java:64)
at org.apache.hadoop.mapred.MapTask$NewTrackingRecordReader.initialize(MapTask.java:560) at
org.apache.hadoop.mapred.MapTask.runNewMapper(MapTask.java:798) at org.apache.hadoop.mapred.MapTask.run(MapTask.java:347) at
org.apache.hadoop.mapred.YarnChild$2.run(YarnChild.java:174) at java.security.AccessController.doPrivileged(Native Method) at
javax.security.auth.Subject.doAs(Subject.java:422) at org.apache.hadoop.security.UserGroupInformation.doAs(UserGroupInformation.java:1730) at
org.apache.hadoop.mapred.YarnChild.main(YarnChild.java:168)
```

Figure 5-17. *The Hive shim code fails to recognize this version of Hadoop. This is due to an outdated configuration in the calling code*

This error message, `Unrecognized Hadoop major version number`, stems from a configuration change in Apache Hive between Hadoop major versions 2 and 3. If your Hadoop cluster is running Hortonworks Data Platform 2.x or Cloudera Distribution of Hadoop 5.x, you will not see this error; you need to have Hortonworks Data Platform 3.x or Cloudera Distribution of Hadoop 6.x to see it.

To fix this error, ensure that you have the latest update for your version of SQL Server. SQL Server 2019 supports Hive 3 out of the box, but SQL Servers 2016 and 2017 RTM did not.

Errors with Scale-Out Groups

PolyBase Scale-Out Groups offer an added level of complexity for administration. In this section, we will look at a general troubleshooting process for diagnosing Scale-Out Group issues as well as two common issues relating to Scale-Out Groups.

Diagnosing Scale-Out Group Problems

The first thing to do when diagnosing a problem with Scale-Out Groups is to run the query in Listing 5-6, which checks the set of attached compute nodes, against your PolyBase control node.

Listing 5-6. Check the dm_exec_compute_nodes DMV to make sure all of your compute and control nodes are configured correctly

```
SELECT
    n.compute_node_id,
    n.type,
    n.name,
    n.address
FROM sys.dm_exec_compute_nodes n;
GO
```

In Figure 5-18, we can see that I have a connection with SQLCOMPUTE2 but no connection with SQLCOMPUTE1. If I am missing a node which I know has successfully connected before, the first thing I check is to ensure that the PolyBase Data Movement Service is running on my missing compute node. I can enable this easily with PowerShell by running the code in Listing 5-7 for the machine in question.

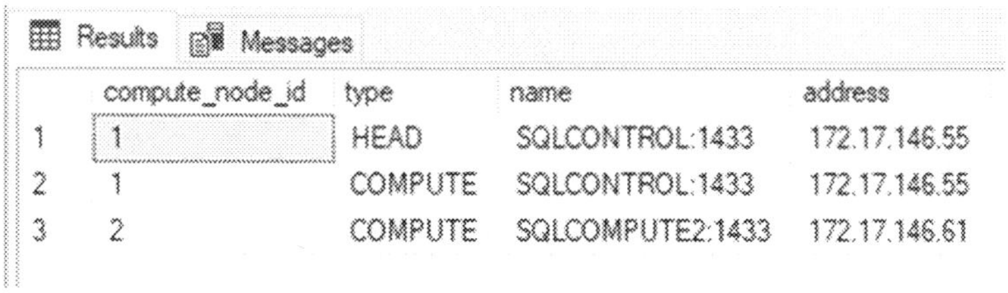

	compute_node_id	type	name	address
1	1	HEAD	SQLCONTROL:1433	172.17.146.55
2	1	COMPUTE	SQLCONTROL:1433	172.17.146.55
3	2	COMPUTE	SQLCOMPUTE2:1433	172.17.146.61

Figure 5-18. *One PolyBase compute node is available, but the other is missing*

Listing 5-7. Start the PolyBase data movement service using PowerShell. You could alternately run `Start-Service` when directly connected to the remote machine

```
Get-Service -Name SQLPBDMS -ComputerName SQLCOMPUTE1 | Set-Service
-Status Running
```

If the issue was due to the service being off, the PolyBase compute node should be able to rejoin the Scale-Out Group within a minute or two, and you will see it when running Listing 5-3.

In the event that you see errors when using a Scale-Out Group and the troubleshooting techniques in this chapter have not helped, try taking the compute nodes out of the Scale-Out Group using the `sp_polybase_leave_group` stored procedure until you have just the head node. If your query still fails, you will know it is an issue with the query and not your Scale-Out Group. If your query succeeds, the cause might be one of the following.

Differing Configuration Settings

The most common issue when working with Scale-Out Groups is when nodes have different configuration settings. When working with several compute nodes, it can be easy to forget to copy over a `yarn-site.xml` configuration change to one of them, especially if you do it by hand.

Change tracking processes are critical here, particularly if you have more than two or three compute nodes. Even minor changes in configuration files, such as setting the maximum Java VM size, might lead to failures. Review all of the SQL Server–side XML configuration files to ensure they are consistent across compute nodes.

Kerberos Misconfiguration

If you have Kerberos enabled, ensure that all compute nodes have the same Kerberos configuration settings. If you have an inconsistent configuration, you might see strange errors on the head node which do not look related to Kerberos at all. Only when looking at the logs on the compute node will you find the root cause.

Patch All Nodes Consistently

A PolyBase Scale-Out Group can include SQL Server instances with different patch levels—for example, a head node running SQL Server 2017 CU6 and compute nodes running SQL Server 2017 CU4. This can potentially lead to errors if the PolyBase binaries differ between these patch levels. Ensure that your compute nodes are on the same build of SQL Server as your head node.

Conclusion

In this chapter, we took a look at some of the classes of errors you can run into while working with PolyBase. Due to the complicated natures of SQL Server and Hadoop, you can expect strange integration issues to pop up. You might also need to dig through PolyBase and Hadoop logs to find the real error. Once you do, one of the most common root causes of errors is an incorrect configuration setting. Ensuring that your configuration is correct will help you avoid wasting quite as much time on nebulous errors between complicated systems.

Reiterating the note in the introduction to this chapter, having a good Hadoop administrator available is critical if you are not one yourself. A good SQL Server database administrator can troubleshoot practically any Azure Blob Storage problem—most commonly, these will be misconfigured SQL Servers or incorrect permissions—but Hadoop is orders of magnitude more complicated.

In the next chapter, we will begin our look at SQL Server 2019's extended PolyBase functionality and connect to our first PolyBase V2 destination: another SQL Server instance.

CHAPTER 6

Integrating with SQL Server

The first five chapters of this book have focused on PolyBase V1: that version of PolyBase which was available in SQL Servers 2016 and 2017. As of SQL Server 2019, we are in the realm of PolyBase V2. With it, the purpose of PolyBase shifts from being a Hadoop integration system (with a salutary side effect of being able to connect to Azure Blob Storage) to the linchpin of a data virtualization system. We now have the capability to tie together diverse systems such as Oracle, MongoDB, Cosmos DB, Teradata, Apache Spark, and even other SQL Server instances. The best part is we can continue to use the T-SQL we know and (mostly) love.

Over the next three chapters, we will look at integration with most of these new technologies, including SQL Server in Chapter 6, Oracle and Cosmos DB in Chapter 7, and Apache Spark and Apache Hive in Chapter 8. Each chapter will include a high-level overview of connection options available, common use patterns, and areas where you might run into implementation troubles. Because PolyBase V2 is a new technology, none of these chapters will be as comprehensive as our survey on Hadoop in Chapters 3 through 5. As we learn more and the PolyBase engine continues to evolve, there will certainly be more to say about each of these topics. In the meantime, on with the survey.

In this chapter, we will cover using PolyBase to integrate one SQL Server instance with another. We will contrast PolyBase vs. linked servers to ascertain under which circumstances we should use each technology. We will then compare the performance of PolyBase vs. linked servers for SQL Server to SQL Server connections, including a review of execution plans when strategies differ. Finally, we will see what, if any, effect Scale-Out Groups have on performance when connecting to a single SQL Server instance.

K. Feasel, *PolyBase Revealed*, https://doi.org/10.1007/978-1-4842-5461-5_6

Meet the New Boss

To this point, we have covered the four key components to PolyBase functionality: an optional Database Scoped Credential, an external data source, an external file format, and an external table. When working with Azure Blob Storage or Hadoop, you still need these components. When working with one of the new V2 integrations, however, the rules change a bit. First, external file formats are no longer necessary, as we are dealing with either structured data sets—such as SQL Server or Oracle tables—or data sets which return data as JSON. The second change is inside the declaration of an external data source.

Creating an External Data Source

Listing 6-1 shows an example of an external data source connecting to Azure Blob storage.

Listing 6-1. Create an external data source to Azure Blob Storage

```
IF NOT EXISTS
(
    SELECT 1
    FROM sys.external_data_sources e
    WHERE
        e.name = N'AzureNCPopBlob'
)
BEGIN
    CREATE EXTERNAL DATA SOURCE AzureNCPopBlob WITH
    (
        TYPE = HADOOP,
        LOCATION = 'wasbs://ncpop@cspolybaseblob.blob.core.windows.net',
        CREDENTIAL = AzureStorageCredential
    );
END
GO
```

Listing 6-2, meanwhile, shows us how to create an external data source to a SQL Server instance named SQLWIN10. For the sake of completeness, this also includes the operation to create a Database Scoped Credential.

Listing 6-2. Create a database scoped credential and external data source to SQL Server

```
IF NOT EXISTS
(
    SELECT 1
    FROM sys.database_scoped_credentials dsc
    WHERE
        dsc.name = N'SqlWin10Credentials'
)
BEGIN
    CREATE DATABASE SCOPED CREDENTIAL SqlWin10Credentials
    WITH IDENTITY = 'PolyBaseUser', Secret = '<<Some Password>>';
END
GO
IF NOT EXISTS
(
    SELECT 1
    FROM sys.external_data_sources e
    WHERE
        e.name = N'SQLWIN10'
)
BEGIN
    CREATE EXTERNAL DATA SOURCE SQLWIN10 WITH
    (
        LOCATION = 'sqlserver://SQLWIN10',
        PUSHDOWN = ON,
        CREDENTIAL = SqlWin10Credentials
    );
END
GO
```

The biggest obvious difference is the removal of the TYPE parameter. Instead, the PolyBase engine is able to understand based on the protocol in the LOCATION parameter that our destination is a SQL Server instance, so type is redundant.

Another difference between V1 and V2 is that you now have the option to enable or disable predicate pushdown. I would recommend enabling it by default unless you have a strong reason to disable it.

Creating an External Table

Without the need for an external file format, we can jump straight from creating an external data source to creating an external table. The definition for creating an external table is similar to the format in PolyBase V1, as we can see in Listing 6-3. Here we will connect to the dbo.CityPopulationCenter table from Chapter 2, which contains nine rows.

Listing 6-3. Create an external table against a SQL Server data source

```
CREATE EXTERNAL TABLE [dbo].[CityPopulationCenter]
(
    [CityName] [varchar](120) NOT NULL,
    [PopulationCenterName] [varchar](30) NOT NULL
)
WITH
(
    LOCATION = 'PolyBaseRevealed.dbo.CityPopulationCenter',
    DATA_SOURCE = SQLWIN10
);
```

The key difference between this external table and the external tables we have seen before is that the LOCATION parameter contains a three-part naming scheme for our external table's location on our external data source. The CityPopulationCenter table lives in the PolyBaseRevealed database in the dbo schema, and we need to include all three parts, not just the two-part name we would use within a database. As we can see in Figure 6-1, we query the table like we would any other external or local table; at that point, this is just another table in the database.

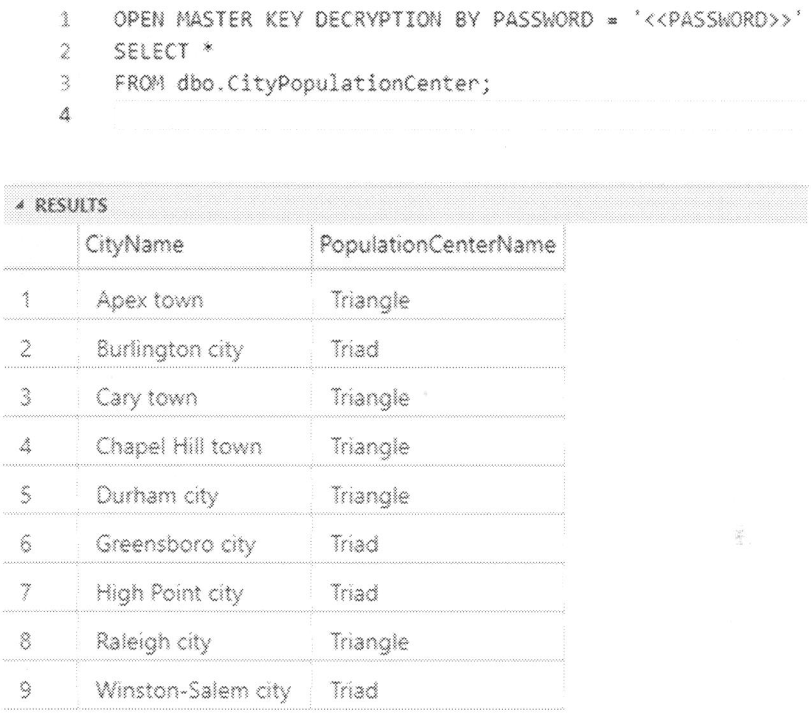

```
1    OPEN MASTER KEY DECRYPTION BY PASSWORD = '<<PASSWORD>>'
2    SELECT *
3    FROM dbo.CityPopulationCenter;
4
```

▲ RESULTS

	CityName	PopulationCenterName
1	Apex town	Triangle
2	Burlington city	Triad
3	Cary town	Triangle
4	Chapel Hill town	Triangle
5	Durham city	Triangle
6	Greensboro city	Triad
7	High Point city	Triad
8	Raleigh city	Triangle
9	Winston-Salem city	Triad

Figure 6-1. *After decrypting the master key, we can query this external table*

Note   Upon running a PolyBase query in a new session, whether that is to create an external object or querying an external table, you might need to open the master key. Doing this requires the CONTROL permission on the database.

One difference here between PolyBase V1 and PolyBase V2 is that the PolyBase engine will proactively attempt to connect to this SQL Server data source and will not let you create an external table against an invalid destination. Figure 6-2 shows the results of an attempt to create an external table against a SQL Server instance which does not exist.

```
Msg 105082, Level 16, State 1, Line 40
105082;Generic ODBC error: [Microsoft][ODBC Driver 17 for SQL Server]Named Pipes Provider:
    Could not open a connection to SQL Server [53].
Additional error <2>: ErrorMsg: [Microsoft][ODBC Driver 17 for SQL Server]
    Login timeout expired, SqlState: HYT00, NativeError: 0
Additional error <3>: ErrorMsg: [Microsoft][ODBC Driver 17 for SQL Server]
    Invalid connection string attribute, SqlState: 01S00, NativeError: 0
Additional error <4>: ErrorMsg: [Microsoft][ODBC Driver 17 for SQL Server]
    A network-related or instance-specific error has occurred while
    establishing a connection to SQL Server. Server is not found or not accessible.
    Check if instance name is correct and if SQL Server
    is configured to, SqlState: 08001, NativeError: 53 .
```

Figure 6-2. *This error happens when trying to create a table against an invalid external data source*

If you attempt to create an external table but the remote table does not exist, you will receive an error like the one in Figure 6-3.

```
Msg 2706, Level 16, State 1, Line 40
Table '"Scratch"."dbo"."CityPopulationCenter2"' does not exist.
```

Figure 6-3. *The remote table must exist in order to create an external table against it*

Now that we have an idea of how to create links to SQL Server, it makes sense to compare this method to the method already in place for cross-server connections: linked servers.

PolyBase vs. Linked Servers

Linked servers are a classic technique database administrators and developers can use to query another server's data from the local server. On the plus side, there is extensive OLEDB driver support, and linked servers can reach out to technologies like Oracle, Apache Hive, other SQL Server instances, and even Excel. On the minus side, linked servers have an oft-deserved reputation for bringing over too much data from the remote server during queries and a somewhat undeserved reputation for being a security issue. Still, introducing the idea of an alternative for linked servers should excite many a DBA. Here is where I have mixed news for you: PolyBase can be superior to linked servers in some circumstances, but you will not want to replace all of your linked servers with external tables, as there are some cases where linked servers will be superior. Instead, think of these as two complementary technologies with considerable overlap.

Contrasting PolyBase and Linked Servers

There are a few factors which can help you choose between linked servers and SQL Server to SQL Server PolyBase, including scope, intent, scale-out requirements, and data sizes. Table 6-1 provides a summary of these differences, and the following sections cover each difference in detail.

Table 6-1. *A comparison between PolyBase external tables and linked servers*

	PolyBase External Table	Linked Server
Object scope	Database level, focusing on a single table	Instance level
Operational intent	Read-only	Read and write
Scale-out	Able to use Scale-Out Groups	No scale-out capabilities
Expected data size	Large tables with analytic workloads	OLTP-style workloads querying a small number of rows

Object Scopes

Linked servers are scoped at the instance level, which means that when you create a linked server, any database on that instance has access to the linked server. Furthermore, on the remote side, linked servers allow you to query any table or view on any database where the remote login has rights. The advantage to the linked server model is its flexibility: you can use linked servers for any number of queries across an indefinite number of remote tables or views. The biggest disadvantage of this approach is that it promotes the idea that perhaps you **ought** to make that cross-server join of two very large tables.

By contrast, PolyBase requires more deliberation: a database administrator or developer needs to create the external table link on a table-by-table or view-by-view basis before anybody can use it. This additional effort should make the creator think about whether a cross-server link is really necessary and can provide a bit of extra documentation about which tables the staff intend to use for cross-server queries. The downside to this is, if you have a large number of tables to query, it means writing a large

157

number of external table definitions and also maintaining these definitions across table changes. This makes PolyBase a better choice for more stable data models and linked servers for more dynamic data models.

Operational Intent

Linked servers allow for reads as well as inserts, updates, and deletes. With PolyBase V1, we were able to read and insert but could not update or delete data. For the PolyBase V2 types, we are able to read but the engine prohibits any data modification, including inserts. If you attempt a data modification statement against a PolyBase V2 external table, you will get an error message similar to that in Figure 6-4.

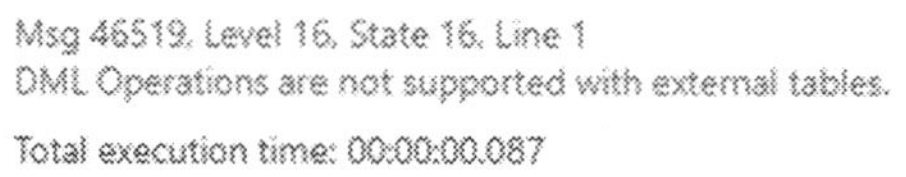

Msg 46519, Level 16, State 16, Line 1
DML Operations are not supported with external tables.

Total execution time: 00:00:00.087

Figure 6-4. *PolyBase V2 does not support any data modification, including insertion*

Linked servers are the more flexible option here.

Scale-Out Capabilities

Linked servers offer no ability to scale out. One SQL Server instance may read from one SQL Server instance. If you experience performance problems, there is no way to add additional SQL Server instances to the mix to share the load. PolyBase, meanwhile, offers Scale-Out Groups for cases when three or four servers are better than one. In this regard, PolyBase is strictly superior.

Data Sizes

Tying in with scale-out capabilities, linked servers and PolyBase have different expectations for ideal data size. If you intend to pull back one row or a few rows from a small table, linked servers will generally be a superior option because there are fewer moving parts. As you get more complicated queries with larger data sets, PolyBase tends to do at least as well and often better.

Over the rest of this chapter, we will test the performance of PolyBase vs. linked servers in several scenarios to see when PolyBase succeeds and when linked servers come out ahead.

Testing a Large Table

Our first scenario looks at testing a large table: the New York City parking violations data set. One way to create this data set on SQL Server is to follow the instructions in Chapter 3 to load the data set in Hadoop (or alternatively, blob storage), create an external table linking to this data, and then insert and run the command in Listing 6-4 to insert the contents of this data set into a new SQL Server table.

Listing 6-4. This script is one way to migrate parking violations data to a local SQL Server instance

```
USE [PolyBaseRevealed]
GO
SELECT *
INTO dbo.ParkingViolationsLocal
FROM dbo.ParkingViolations;
```

Note   You can also use other techniques to load this data, including loading the text files into SQL Server using SQL Server Integration Services.

This data set includes approximately 33 million records, making it much larger than the ideal size for a linked server and in the ballpark for what you would want with PolyBase.

In this case, I loaded the data set onto a server named SQLCONTROL. From the machine named SQLWIN10, I prepared an external table. Listing 6-5 includes each step: creating a Database Scoped Credential, followed by an external data source, and then an external table to round things out.

Listing 6-5. Create a PolyBase link from SQLWIN10 to SQLCONTROL's parking violations data. Note that the full external table script will be available in the accompanying code repository

```
IF NOT EXISTS
(
    SELECT 1
    FROM sys.database_scoped_credentials dsc
    WHERE
        dsc.name = N'SqlControlCredentials'
)
BEGIN
    CREATE DATABASE SCOPED CREDENTIAL SqlControlCredentials
    WITH IDENTITY = 'PolyBaseUser', Secret = '<<Some Password>>';
END
GO
IF NOT EXISTS
(
    SELECT 1
    FROM sys.external_data_sources e
    WHERE
        e.name = N'SQLCONTROL'
)
BEGIN
    CREATE EXTERNAL DATA SOURCE SQLCONTROL WITH
    (
        LOCATION = 'sqlserver://SQLCONTROL',
        PUSHDOWN = ON,
        CREDENTIAL = SqlControlCredentials
    );
END
GO
CREATE EXTERNAL TABLE [dbo].[ParkingViolationsSQLControl]
(
    [SummonsNumber] [varchar](50) NULL,
    -- Remaining columns...
```

```
    [DoubleParkingViolation] [varchar](50) NULL
)
WITH
(
    LOCATION = 'PolyBaseRevealed.dbo.ParkingViolationsLocal',
    DATA_SOURCE = SQLCONTROL
);
GO
```

Next, we will need to create a linked server. Listing 6-6 uses the same PolyBaseUser login to connect the SQLWIN10 instance to SQLCONTROL.

Listing 6-6. Create a linked server connection from SQLWIN10 to SQLCONTROL

```
USE [master]
GO
EXEC master.dbo.sp_addlinkedserver @server = N'SQLCONTROL',
@srvproduct=N'SQL Server'
EXEC master.dbo.sp_addlinkedsrvlogin @rmtsrvname=N'SQLCONTROL',
@useself=N'False',@locallogin=NULL,@rmtuser=N'PolyBaseUser',
@rmtpassword='########'
EXEC master.dbo.sp_serveroption @server=N'SQLCONTROL', @optname=N'collation
compatible', @optvalue=N'false'
EXEC master.dbo.sp_serveroption @server=N'SQLCONTROL', @optname=N'data
access', @optvalue=N'true'
EXEC master.dbo.sp_serveroption @server=N'SQLCONTROL', @optname=N'dist',
@optvalue=N'false'
EXEC master.dbo.sp_serveroption @server=N'SQLCONTROL', @optname=N'pub',
@optvalue=N'false'
EXEC master.dbo.sp_serveroption @server=N'SQLCONTROL', @optname=N'rpc',
@optvalue=N'false'
EXEC master.dbo.sp_serveroption @server=N'SQLCONTROL', @optname=N'rpc out',
@optvalue=N'false'
EXEC master.dbo.sp_serveroption @server=N'SQLCONTROL', @optname=N'sub',
@optvalue=N'false'
EXEC master.dbo.sp_serveroption @server=N'SQLCONTROL', @optname=N'connect
timeout', @optvalue=N'0'
```

```
EXEC master.dbo.sp_serveroption @server=N'SQLCONTROL', @optname=N'collation
name', @optvalue=null
EXEC master.dbo.sp_serveroption @server=N'SQLCONTROL', @optname=N'lazy
schema validation', @optvalue=N'false'
EXEC master.dbo.sp_serveroption @server=N'SQLCONTROL', @optname=N'query
timeout', @optvalue=N'0'
EXEC master.dbo.sp_serveroption @server=N'SQLCONTROL', @optname=N'use
remote collation', @optvalue=N'true'
EXEC master.dbo.sp_serveroption @server=N'SQLCONTROL', @optname=N'remote
proc transaction promotion', @optvalue=N'true'
GO
```

Now that we have a data source and an external table on one side and a linked server on the other side, we can try several operations. Before jumping into queries, it is important to note that the parking violations table is a heap with no nonclustered indexes, so we will not be able to take advantage of indexing for fast lookups for these initial queries.

Top Ten Rows

This first query is a simple one: retrieve the top ten rows from our parking violations data set. The ideal operation here is to begin streaming rows from SQLCONTROL and stopping after ten records. This should be a fast operation. Listing 6-7 provides the two sample queries.

Listing 6-7. Query ten rows from the parking violations data set using PolyBase and then a linked server

```
USE [PolyBaseRevealed]
GO
SELECT TOP(10) *
FROM dbo.ParkingViolationsSQLControl;

SELECT TOP(10) *
FROM [SQLCONTROL].PolyBaseRevealed.dbo.ParkingViolationsLocal;
```

The two operations take approximately the same amount of time: 279 milliseconds for the external table and 254 milliseconds for the linked server. The execution plans both end up looking like the one in Figure 6-5, with a remote query returning ten rows.

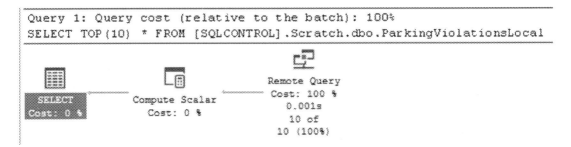

Figure 6-5. *Both queries have approximately the same execution plan, at least at this level of abstraction*

This execution plan is particularly interesting for PolyBase in part for what we do not see: streaming all of the data over from our remote instance to our local instance and then filtering locally. With Hadoop and Azure Blob Storage, we would need to stream all of the data over to our local SQL Server instance before seeing anything unless we created a MapReduce job against a Hadoop cluster. With an external table pointing at another SQL Server instance, we can already see a positive difference.

Finding Ohio Plates

The second query we will look at focuses on locating only those vehicles registered in the state of Ohio. There are relatively few such vehicles in the data set, but because we lack any indexes, this will necessitate a table scan. Listing 6-8 shows the dual queries.

Listing 6-8. Two competing queries to view vehicles registered in Ohio whose drivers received parking tickets

```
USE [PolyBaseRevealed]
GO
SELECT COUNT(*)
FROM dbo.ParkingViolationsSQLControl
WHERE
```

```
    RegistrationState = 'OH';

SELECT COUNT(*)
FROM SQLCONTROL.PolyBaseRevealed.dbo.ParkingViolationsLocal
WHERE
    RegistrationState = 'OH';
```

The interesting question is whether this will require streaming the data over via the PolyBase Data Movement Service or if we are able to push down the registration state predicate, perform the filter on our remote server, and stream only the relevant results. Figure 6-6 shows the execution plans for these two queries.

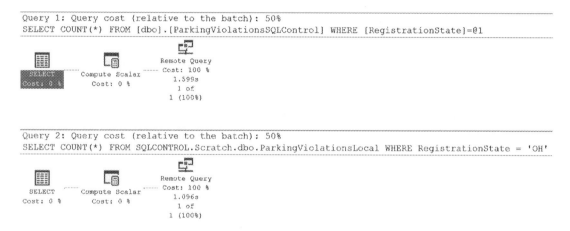

Figure 6-6. *Both methods leave the heavy lifting to the remote server*

Once more, the execution plan shape looks nearly identical. Furthermore, both operations take approximately the same amount of time: 1.6 seconds for the external table and 1.1 seconds for the linked server. When watching the network with Wireshark, I confirmed that PolyBase does not stream all of the data over, but instead pushes down the string predicate.

At this point, it makes sense to reiterate that for SQL Server, we were able to push down a string predicate. This is something you cannot do as part of a MapReduce job on Hadoop but can do here. This tells us that SQL Server to SQL Server PolyBase connections will allow for more complicated predicates than SQL Server to Hadoop connections, and these complicated predicates will be important as we get to more complicated queries like the ones in the following.

Joining Local and Remote Tables

Instead of querying strictly against our external table, this time we will create a temporary table on SQLWIN10 and then join it to the parking violations data set. We will include all results in Ohio as well as Kentucky. Listing 6-9 contains the code needed for this query.

Listing 6-9. Create a local table and join it to our remote tables to perform a filter

```
CREATE TABLE #RegistrationStates
(
    RegistrationState VARCHAR(30)
);
INSERT INTO #RegistrationStates(RegistrationState)
VALUES('OH'),('KY');
SELECT COUNT(*)
FROM PolyBaseRevealed.dbo.ParkingViolationsSQLControl p
    INNER JOIN #RegistrationStates r
        ON p.RegistrationState = r.RegistrationState;

SELECT COUNT(*)
FROM SQLCONTROL.PolyBaseRevealed.dbo.ParkingViolationsLocal p
    INNER JOIN #RegistrationStates r
        ON p.RegistrationState = r.RegistrationState;
```

This results in the first major difference between PolyBase and linked servers: the PolyBase operation took 17.4 seconds to complete, but the linked server took 35.1 seconds to complete. Figure 6-7 helps us see why the linked server is slower.

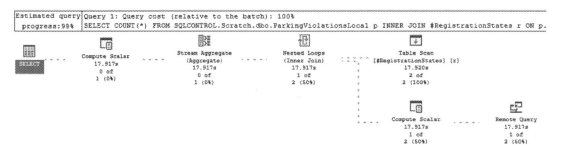

Figure 6-7. *This linked server execution plan shows two separate remote query scans*

The linked server execution plan performs one table scan for each row in the local table. Each table scan takes approximately 17–18 seconds, so the two scans add up to approximately 35 seconds. By contrast, the PolyBase execution plan pulls back 166 pre-aggregated rows, as we can see in Figure 6-8.

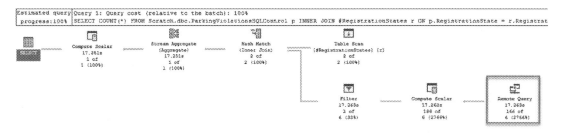

Figure 6-8. *The external table execution plan returns 166 rows from its remote query*

Figure 6-9 helps us unravel the mystery of why we see the number 166.

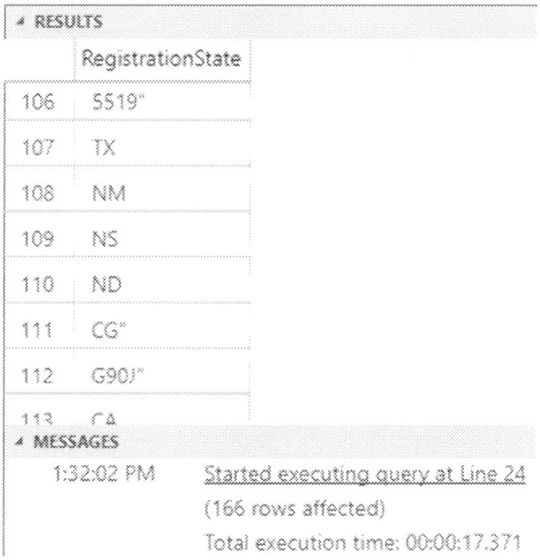

Figure 6-9. *There are 166 distinct values for RegistrationState in the remote table*

There are 166 separate results for registration states, so the PolyBase engine asked the remote SQL Server instance to return the count of rows by registration state for all records in the table and then ship those partial aggregates over the wire to our local SQL Server instance. From there, the database engine performed a simple filter operation to retrieve the two rows we needed, sum the partial aggregates together, and return the total to us. This execution plan happens to be more efficient because our remote SQL Server instance needed to scan all of the rows anyhow.

Adding an Index

Scanning large heap tables is hopefully not a core part of your SQL Server data access strategy. To deal with a more realistic scenario, we can add an index to the remote parking violations table such as the one in Listing 6-10.

Listing 6-10. This covering index should speed up our queries

```
USE [PolyBaseRevealed]
GO
IF NOT EXISTS
(
    SELECT 1
```

```
    FROM sys.indexes i
    WHERE
        i.name = N'IX_ParkingViolationsLocal_VehicleYear_RegistrationState'
)
BEGIN
    CREATE NONCLUSTERED INDEX [IX_ParkingViolationsLocal_VehicleYear_
    RegistrationState] ON [dbo].[ParkingViolationsLocal]
    (
        [VehicleYear] ASC,
        [RegistrationState] ASC
    )
    INCLUDE
    (
        [VehicleBodyType],
        [VehicleMake]
    ) WITH (DATA_COMPRESSION = PAGE);
END
GO
```

With this index, we can use a more complicated query which looks for vehicles with Ohio or Kentucky plates and model years between 2005 and 2008. Listing 6-11 gives us the relevant queries.

Listing 6-11. A more realistic aggregation of our parking violations data includes local and remote tables

```
CREATE TABLE #RegistrationStates
(
    RegistrationState VARCHAR(30)
);
INSERT INTO #RegistrationStates(RegistrationState)
VALUES('OH'),('KY');

SELECT
    p.VehicleBodyType,
    p.VehicleMake,
    COUNT(*)
```

```
FROM PolyBaseRevealed.dbo.ParkingViolationsSQLControl p
    INNER JOIN #RegistrationStates r
        ON p.RegistrationState = r.RegistrationState
WHERE
    p.VehicleYear IN ('2005', '2006', '2007', '2008')
GROUP BY
    p.VehicleBodyType,
    p.VehicleMake;

SELECT
    p.VehicleBodyType,
    p.VehicleMake,
    COUNT(*)
FROM SQLCONTROL.PolyBaseRevealed.dbo.ParkingViolationsLocal p
    INNER JOIN #RegistrationStates r
        ON p.RegistrationState = r.RegistrationState
WHERE
    p.VehicleYear IN ('2005', '2006', '2007', '2008')
GROUP BY
    p.VehicleBodyType,
    p.VehicleMake;
```

Running this query takes PolyBase 14.4 seconds but only 250 milliseconds for a linked server. Figure 6-10 shows us the execution plan our external table query uses.

Figure 6-10. *Solving this query requires streaming millions of rows to our local SQL Server instance, at least based on this execution plan*

We pull back 5.5 million rows, which happens to be the number of records with model year between 2005 and 2008. The PolyBase engine pushes down the predicate on year but not state, so it streams back all of the data for those four model years and then joins to the local registration state temp table to return the 2315 rows needed to satisfy this query. Figure 6-11 shows the linked server query, which immediately retrieves just the 2315 records.

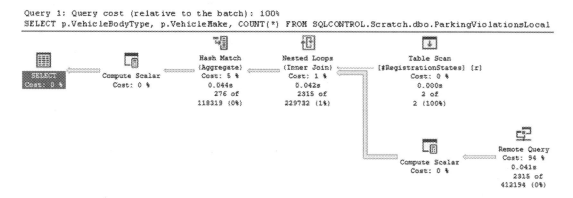

Figure 6-11. *The linked server query makes full use of the remote table's index and returns just the necessary data*

The key problem is that the PolyBase engine believes it will get back only 10,809 records, and so it would be cheaper to stream that data over. When we get back a much larger number, it ruins the plan quality, and we end up waiting unnecessarily long.

When we see this problem on a regular table, a common solution is to create table statistics, which provide the database optimizer with additional information about the distribution of data for selected columns on the table. We can do the same with external tables.

Adding Statistics to External Tables

Chapter 11 will contain a fuller discussion of statistics in PolyBase. For now, let us create a new statistic on the external table against our key fields: vehicle year, registration date, vehicle body type, and vehicle make. Listing 6-12 does exactly that.

Listing 6-12. Creating statistics on an external table. This should run on the server with the external table, not on the remote server where the external table points

```
IF NOT EXISTS
(
    SELECT *
    FROM sys.stats s
    WHERE
        s.name = N'sParkingViolationsSQLControl_VehicleYear_
        RegistrationState'
)
BEGIN
    CREATE STATISTICS [sParkingViolationsSQLControl_VehicleYear_
    RegistrationState] ON dbo.ParkingViolationsSQLControl
    (
        VehicleYear,
        RegistrationState,
        VehicleBodyType,
        VehicleMake
    ) WITH FULLSCAN;
END
GO
```

After creating statistics on the table, we get back 16,924 records, a much better result than before. Now, instead of 14.4 seconds, it takes only 778 milliseconds. This is still worse than the 250 milliseconds for a linked server, but that difference is typically negligible.

Querying Big States

So far, we have looked at parking violations among people with Ohio and Kentucky tags. I chose those states on purpose: my expectation was that there would be relatively few vehicles with those two states' tags in the New York City parking violations data set, an expectation which comports with reality. Now it would behoove us to look at a much larger percentage of the record set. To do this, I have a new registration states table which contains New York, Connecticut, New Jersey, and Pennsylvania as the four states. My expectation here is that these four states are four of the largest in the data set due to New York City's proximity to (or, in the case of New York, existence within) each state. To narrow down the selection a bit, I also added in a filter on vehicle year between 2013 and 2017. Listing 6-13 shows these new queries.

Listing 6-13. Testing queries against retrieving a much larger percentage of total rows

```
CREATE TABLE #RegistrationStates
(
    RegistrationState VARCHAR(30)
);
INSERT INTO #RegistrationStates(RegistrationState)
VALUES('NY'),('CT'),('NJ'),('PA');

SELECT
    p.VehicleBodyType,
    p.VehicleMake,
    p.VehicleYear,
    p.RegistrationState,
    COUNT(*)
FROM PolyBaseRevealed.dbo.ParkingViolationsSQLControl p
    INNER JOIN #RegistrationStates r
        ON p.RegistrationState = r.RegistrationState
WHERE
    p.VehicleYear IN ('2013', '2014', '2015', '2016', '2017')
GROUP BY
    p.VehicleBodyType,
    p.VehicleMake,
    p.VehicleYear,
    p.RegistrationState;

SELECT
    p.VehicleBodyType,
    p.VehicleMake,
    p.VehicleYear,
```

```
    p.RegistrationState,
    COUNT(*)
FROM SQLCONTROL.PolyBaseRevealed.dbo.ParkingViolationsLocal p
    INNER JOIN #RegistrationStates r
        ON p.RegistrationState = r.RegistrationState
WHERE
    p.VehicleYear IN ('2013', '2014', '2015', '2016', '2017')
GROUP BY
    p.VehicleBodyType,
    p.VehicleMake,
    p.VehicleYear,
    p.RegistrationState;
```

This time around, the external table took 1.7 seconds to finish, but the linked server required 66.1 seconds, an enormous difference. Figure 6-12 shows us the execution plan for the linked server query.

Figure 6-12. *This linked server query streams a large percentage of the total number of rows over*

We can see that the linked server expected 1 million rows but ended up streaming 8.8 million rows over the wire over the course of four nested loop joins. This is a woefully inefficient execution plan. Contrast that with Figure 6-13, the external table execution plan.

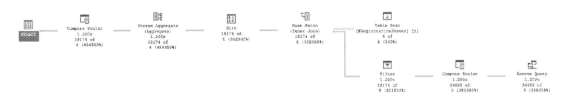

Figure 6-13. *The external table query streams a smaller number of pre-aggregated rows*

With this plan, we can see that the PolyBase engine requests 34,658 partially aggregated rows. The number 34,658 is the cross product of vehicle body types, vehicle makes, vehicle years, and registration states, which the PolyBase data movement service moves over into a temporary table on our local SQL Server instance. From there, the local database engine joins together the registration states temp table with our partially aggregated data set and returns the 18,174 results.

For these large aggregation operations, PolyBase seems to be at least as good as linked servers and can be significantly better. Now let's look at an even larger table and see how PolyBase fares vs. linked servers.

Testing a Very Large Table

A table with 33 million rows is a good start, but that might not be enough to test Scale-Out Groups effectively. Therefore, I have created a table with 400 million rows, this time on SQLWIN10. The schema is fairly straightforward, as you can see in Listing 6-14, which covers the external table. The actual table itself has the same set of columns and data types, but also contains a clustered columnstore index.

Listing 6-14. The MoleCrusher external table. Review the accompanying code repository for the base table and a way to generate arbitrary data to run your own queries

```
CREATE EXTERNAL TABLE [dbo].[MoleCrusherSqlWin10]
(
    [RunID] [int] NOT NULL,
    [CustomerID] [int] NOT NULL,
    [RunStart] [datetime2](0) NOT NULL,
    [NumberOfSecondsInRun] [decimal](6, 2) NOT NULL,
    [NumberOfSecondsBeforeNextRunBegins] [decimal](6, 2) NOT NULL,
    [MolesWhacked] [int] NOT NULL
)
WITH
(
```

```
        LOCATION = 'PolyBaseRevealed.dbo.MoleCrusher',
        DATA_SOURCE = SQLWIN10
)
GO
```

The query in Listing 6-15 looks for customers with at least 260 attempts, summing up the total number of seconds spent and number of moles hit per customer.

Listing 6-15. A query against the `MoleCrusher` table on `SQLWIN10`. The linked server version is similar enough that we can skip it at this point

```
SELECT
    mc.CustomerID,
    SUM(mc.MolesWhacked) AS MolesWhacked,
    SUM(mc.NumberOfSecondsInRun) AS NumberOfSecondsInRun,
    COUNT(1) AS NumberOfAttempts
FROM dbo.MoleCrusherSqlWin10 mc
WHERE
    mc.RunStart > '2019-01-01'
GROUP BY
    mc.CustomerID
HAVING
    COUNT(1) > 260
ORDER BY
    MolesWhacked DESC;
```

The query performance is mixed for PolyBase with respect to linked servers. The linked server took approximately 31 seconds to run this query on my hardware with little else running concurrently. A single-node PolyBase instance with no statistics took approximately 40 seconds. Adding external table statistics on the combination of `RunStart`, `CustomerID`, `MolesWhacked`, and `NumberOfSecondsInRun` knocked the time down to 25 seconds. From there, adding two additional nodes in the Scale-Out Group took the query down to 19 seconds. All of these times are marginally worse than running the query locally with no data transfer, but a Scale-Out Group with appropriate statistics gets the closest to the edge.

Additional PolyBase Notes

As we wrap up our survey of SQL Server to SQL Server PolyBase, here are a few notes aside from a comparison to linked server performance which might help you determine if external tables are right for your circumstances.

PolyBase Supports Views

It is possible to create an external table which actually queries a remote view. Listing 6-16 includes the syntax to create a view on SQLWIN10.

Listing 6-16. A simple view off of the dbo.MoleCrusher table

```
CREATE VIEW dbo.vMoleCrusher AS
SELECT * FROM dbo.MoleCrusher;
```

Then, we can create an external table on SQLCONTROL which references this view, which we see in Listing 6-17.

Listing 6-17. Creating an external table which reads from a remote view

```
IF (OBJECT_ID('dbo.vMoleCrusherSqlWin10') IS NULL)
BEGIN
    CREATE EXTERNAL TABLE [dbo].[vMoleCrusherSqlWin10]
    (
        [RunID] [int] NOT NULL,
        [CustomerID] [int] NOT NULL,
        [RunStart] [datetime2](0) NOT NULL,
        [NumberOfSecondsInRun] [decimal](6, 2) NOT NULL,
        [NumberOfSecondsBeforeNextRunBegins] [decimal](6, 2) NOT NULL,
        [MolesWhacked] [int] NOT NULL
    )
    WITH
    (
        LOCATION = 'PolyBaseRevealed.dbo.vMoleCrusher',
```

```
        DATA_SOURCE = SQLWIN10
    );
END
GO
```

Finally, we can write a query which references the view, such as the one in Listing 6-18.

Listing 6-18. Query a view via an external table

```
SELECT
    mc.CustomerID,
    SUM(mc.MolesWhacked) AS MolesWhacked,
    SUM(mc.NumberOfSecondsInRun) AS NumberOfSecondsInRun,
    COUNT(1) AS NumberOfAttempts
FROM dbo.vMoleCrusherSqlWin10 mc
WHERE
    mc.RunStart > '2019-01-01'
GROUP BY
    mc.CustomerID
HAVING
    COUNT(1) > 260
ORDER BY
    MolesWhacked DESC;
```

This view works the same way as a table and comes with the normal set of caveats when dealing with views, particularly that nested views can lead to a deterioration in performance. Keeping these caveats in mind, however, views are an excellent method for shielding your external tables from changes. Creating a view which represents your underlying remote table decouples your local database from your remote database and allows us to change tables in the remote database without having to worry about modifying external tables on the local database. For example, we could split a remote table into two or three tables, but need not change our external table definition if it references a view which combines the remote tables together. Furthermore, we can use views to predefine how the remote table ought to look—for example, we might put together the query needed to populate a dimension table and expose that as a view, to which our external table will point.

Chained External Tables Not Supported

One idea which might sound promising (or horrifying, depending upon your perspective) would be to create an external table against an external table. For example, we have an external table on SQLCONTROL called dbo.MoleCrusherSqlWin10 which reaches out to SQLWIN10. If we have another SQL Server instance—which we'll call SQLEXTERNAL for the purposes of giving it a name—we can create an external table on it which queries the external table on SQLCONTROL. Conceptually, this chain could stretch indefinitely and possibly even circle back on itself, with an external table on SQLWIN10 which reads the external table on SQLEXTERNAL which reads the external table on SQLCONTROL which reads the original table on SQLWIN10.

Fortunately, for those of us who don't like database designs out of M.C. Escher paintings, this scenario is impossible. It is possible to create an external table which references another external table, but if you attempt to query the table at the far end of the chain, you will see an error like in Figure 6-14.

```
Msg 7320, Level 16, State 110, Line 3
Cannot execute the query "Remote Query" against OLE DB provider "SQLNCLI11" for linked server "(null)".
105082;Generic ODBC error: [Microsoft][ODBC Driver 17 for SQL Server][SQL Server]
    Access to the remote server is denied because no login-mapping exists. .
```

Figure 6-14. *It is not possible to create chains of external tables. Thank goodness*

External Table Security

In this section, we will look at several considerations when dealing with securing external tables.

Rights for Remote Queries

One technique for testing user accounts is to run EXECUTE AS USER='UserName' as a sysadmin or other high-privilege user. This typically allows you to run queries with the permission set of a different user account. It is not possible to do this when querying external tables, however; if you attempt to execute as another user and query data from an external table, you will end up with an error message like Figure 6-15.

```
◢ MESSAGES
    6:09:45 PM      Started executing query at Line 1
                    Commands completed successfully.
    6:09:45 PM      Started executing query at Line 2
                    Msg 15274, Level 16, State 1, Line 2
                    Access to the remote server is denied because the current security context is not trusted.

                    Total execution time: 00:00:00.013
```

Figure 6-15. *Attempting to query a remote table while impersonating another account leads to this error*

Instead of executing as a user, you should log in as the user and execute the query directly. You could also make the database trustworthy, but that comes with its own pains and security risks. A full reckoning of those risks is outside the scope of this book, so if you decide to make a database trustworthy, make sure you understand the potential consequences before acting.

When connecting directly as the user, you might get an error like that in Figure 6-16.

```
◢ MESSAGES
    6:16:04 PM      Started executing query at Line 1
                    Commands completed successfully.
    6:16:04 PM      Started executing query at Line 2
                    Msg 7416, Level 16, State 2, Line 2
                    Access to the remote server is denied because no login-mapping exists.

                    Total execution time: 00:00:00.015
```

Figure 6-16. *When a user lacks relevant permissions, you are liable to see this error*

This error might seem confusing as we do indeed have a login mapping: the Database Scoped Credential. Furthermore, researching this error will bring up posts concerning linked servers, making it tougher to find the real cause.

Heterogeneous Security Models

The security model for external tables differs from that of linked servers. With linked servers, we have a few security options, which you can see in Figure 6-17.

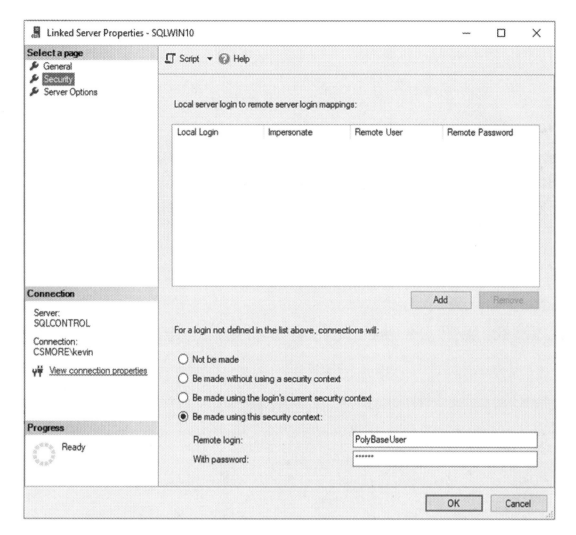

Figure 6-17. *There are several ways to secure a linked server connection, including using a specific login*

In this case, we are using a remote SQL authenticated account to perform remote queries, but we could also use the current login's context or even set up an account-by-account mapping.

PolyBase external tables are more limited in this regard, as we have only the option of using a single SQL authenticated account for any tables stemming from an external data source. If we require additional flexibility, a database administrator can set up multiple external data sources. For example, suppose that there are tables with two levels of sensitivity on a single instance: regular-security tables and high-security tables. One SQL authenticated account might have access to regular-security tables and a different account access to high-security tables. We would then create two Database Scoped Credentials, one for each account, and then tie them to two separate external data sources. Then, we can create external tables against the appropriate external data source.

On the other hand, suppose we have (without loss of generality) a single external data source which provides us the link to multiple external tables, such as `Employee`, `EmployeeSalaryHistory`, and `AnnualGoal`. We might wish to allow everybody access to the `Employee` table, Human Resources staff the right to see data in `EmployeeSalaryHistory`, and HR plus management the right to query `AnnualGoal`.

To do this with linked servers, we would need to grant or deny rights on the remote tables and use linked server mappings to ensure that people in each group get access to the correct data. For PolyBase, we can do this on the external table level. We can grant all logins the right to query the `Employee` external table. Then, we can grant Human Resources staff the right to query `EmployeeSalaryHistory` and optionally deny all other logins `SELECT` access to that table, depending upon whether users have the `db_datareader` built-in database role or some pattern of rights which implicitly grants access to this table. For `AnnualGoal`, we would grant members of Human Resources and members of management rights to query the table and deny or revoke access for everybody else.

In addition to granting or denying access, it might make sense to drop external tables into schemas based on rights. You might have, for example, a `HumanResources` schema which contains local and external tables which only members of the Human Resources group may access. This behavior further promotes the idea that external tables are just like regular tables to the end user, regardless of where the data actually lives.

No Constraints on External Tables

You cannot create any sorts of constraints on external tables. If you attempt to do so on an existing table, you will get an error like that in Figure 6-18.

Started executing query at Line 44
Msg 46518, Level 16, State 2, Line 1
The feature 'ALTER TABLE' is not supported with external tables.

Total execution time: 00:00:00.065

Figure 6-18. *It is not possible to alter an external table*

If you try to create a table with a primary key constraint as part of the initial CREATE EXTERNAL TABLE statement, you get the error in Figure 6-19.

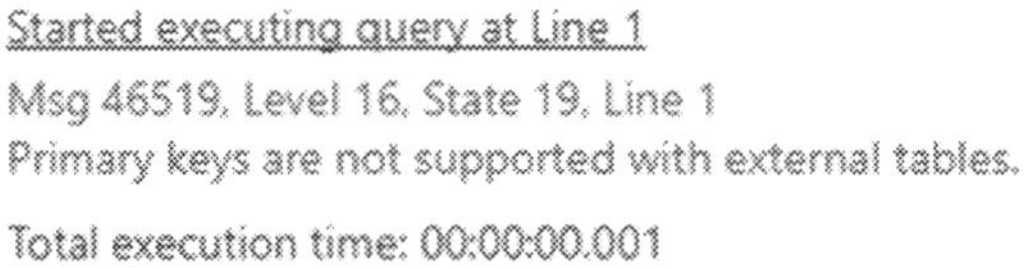

Started executing query at Line 1
Msg 46519, Level 16, State 19, Line 1
Primary keys are not supported with external tables.

Total execution time: 00:00:00.001

Figure 6-19. *External tables do not support key constraints of any sort*

This applies not only to primary key constraints but also to unique keys, foreign keys, check constraints, and default constraints. The only way we may modify external tables is to add statistics. This rule makes sense, as the data does not live in your external table, so your local SQL Server instance will have no control over data modification which might violate your constraints.

Conclusion

In this chapter, we looked at connecting together disparate SQL Server instances using linked servers and PolyBase. Although we might want to use PolyBase as a full replacement for linked servers, its positioning is a bit different than linked servers—whereas linked servers are best for smaller data sets and point lookups, PolyBase tends to work better with larger data sets and analytic queries.

In Chapter 7, we will look at integrating with a couple of unlikely candidates: Oracle and Cosmos DB via a MongoDB connector.

CHAPTER 7

Built-In Integrations: Cosmos DB, Oracle, and More

Integration with SQL Server is one of the most exciting aspects of PolyBase V2, but it is by no means the only one. Microsoft has also provided out-of-the-box support for three major providers: Oracle, MongoDB, and Teradata. Because the mechanisms are the same between these three drivers, we will focus in this chapter on connecting to Microsoft's Cosmos DB using the MongoDB connector rather than performing a deep dive into each provider separately. We will then briefly review integration with Oracle and wrap up this chapter with a note on integration with Teradata.

Integration with Cosmos DB

Cosmos DB is a multimodel cloud database. From its humble origins as a competitor to MongoDB in the document database space, Cosmos DB has expanded to include APIs for SQL, graph (using its Gremlin API), columnar (with its Cassandra API), and key-value (via its Table API) storage.

What makes Cosmos DB a target for us is its support for MongoDB's Binary JSON (BSON) object notation. PolyBase supports integration with MongoDB and converting BSON objects to relational tables. Because Cosmos DB supports the MongoDB API as well, we can convince SQL Server that it is connecting to a regular MongoDB instance while convincing Cosmos DB that our application is just another MongoDB client.

183

The process we will follow is similar to what we have done in prior chapters. Here it is laid out:

- Prepare our external data source with data of interest.

- Create a Database Scoped Credential.

- Create an external data source using the `mongodb` protocol.

- Create an external table.

Just like with SQL Server, we do not need to define an external file format here, as we already have a structured data set in BSON notation. Also, if you would like to play along and have both a MongoDB server and no desire to use Cosmos DB, the steps in SQL Server will be the same. The only major differences will be how you import the data and ensuring that you have the necessary ports open to allow SQL Server to communicate with your MongoDB instance.

Prepare Data in Cosmos DB

Before we use PolyBase to connect SQL Server to Cosmos DB, we will want to create a collection and populate it with data.

Create a Cosmos DB Collection

In this section, we will create a new Cosmos DB account and collection. This does require an Azure account and will cost money. At the lowest end, it will cost approximately 77 cents per day at current prices, though prices are subject to change whether I want them to or not.

First, we need to create an Azure Cosmos DB account. To do that, we will navigate to `https://portal.azure.com` and, after logging in, select the Azure Cosmos DB option on the Azure services list, by typing in "Cosmos DB" in the search box, or selecting Azure Cosmos DB from the Favorites menu on the left. Figure 7-1 shows all three of these options.

Note   If you have not signed up for Azure services before, navigate to `https://azure.microsoft.com/en-us/free/` and you can sign up for a free trial. The work we will do in this chapter around Cosmos DB will fit well within the parameters of the free trial.

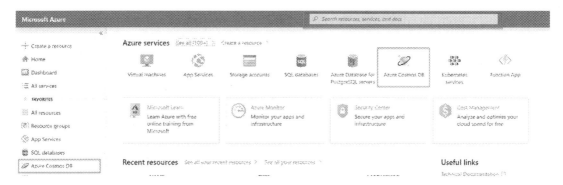

Figure 7-1. *Three options are available to navigate to Cosmos DB*

Once you have navigated to the Cosmos DB blade, click the Add button to create a new Cosmos DB account. You can name your account whatever you would like and place it in whichever zone makes the most sense for you, but be sure to select the "Azure Cosmos DB for Mongo API" option for API. Figure 7-2 shows an example of my `cspolybase` account.

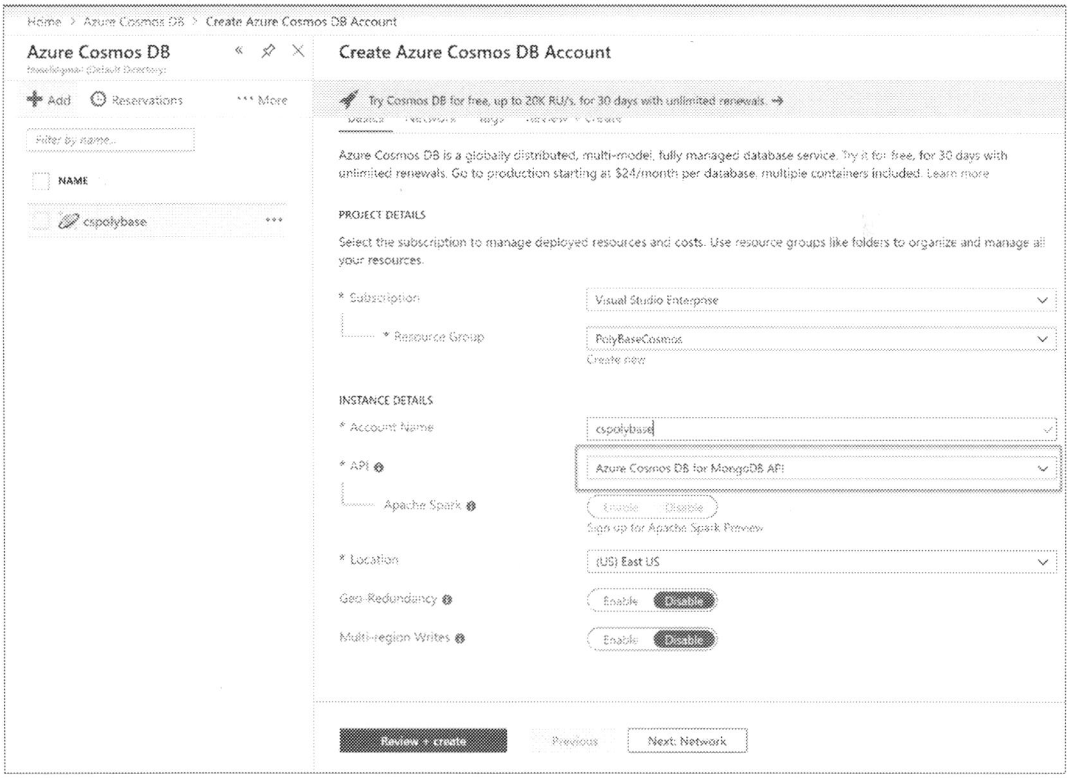

Figure 7-2. *Creating a new Azure Cosmos DB account. Be sure to select the Azure Cosmos DB for MongoDB API*

With an account in place, we can add a new collection. Click the Add Collection button as shown in Figure 7-3. Doing so will bring up a pane.

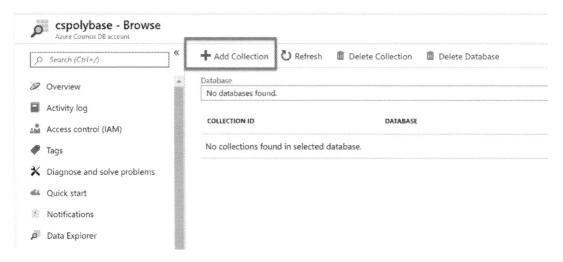

Figure 7-3. *Add a new Cosmos DB collection*

The Add Collection pane will allow you to create a new collection in an existing database or in a new database, as you can see in Figure 7-4. To unpack Cosmos DB terminology, a *database* is a namespace for a number of *containers*. With each API, there is a separate name for what the underlying container is, so for the Cassandra API, the container is called a Table. For the Gremlin API, that container is called a Graph. For the SQL and MongoDB APIs, the underlying container is called a Collection. One of the key differences between a Cosmos DB container and a SQL Server table is that Cosmos DB containers are always independent—there is no notion of foreign key constraints linking together containers like we tie together tables in a relational database model. Another key difference is that Cosmos DB containers have no enforced schema, meaning that one row may have attributes which do not exist in the next.

Caution   If you read the last sentence and became concerned about how SQL Server handles cases where attributes change on a row-by-row basis, you are right! This schema-flexible style works great for Cosmos DB, but we need to define a single schema for SQL Server to work. To do this, we can include every column name which might come back from Cosmos DB. That way, if a column does not appear on a particular record, we get a NULL back in SQL Server for that column.

---

* Database id ⓘ

◉ Create new   ○ Use existing

PolyBaseTest

☐ Provision database throughput ⓘ

* Collection id ⓘ

Volcano

* Storage capacity ⓘ

| Fixed (10 GB) | Unlimited |

* Throughput (400 - 10,000 RU/s) ⓘ

400   ⊖ ⊕

Estimated spend (USD): **$0.032 hourly / $0.77 daily** (1 region x
400RU/s x $0.00008/RU)

Choose unlimited storage capacity for more than 10,000 RU/s.

Figure 7-4. *Create a new collection to store volcano data*

Create a database named PolyBaseTest and a collection named Volcano. To
minimize costs, we will use a fixed maximum size of 10GB and 400 Request Units (RUs)
per second. Request Units allow you to define how much data you want Cosmos DB
to be able to send per second. Although it does not tie exactly to a throughput in bytes
per second, there are calculators (such as the one Microsoft hosts at https://cosmos.
azure.com/capacitycalculator) to estimate the number of Request Units needed to
perform actions. To give you an idea here, it costs 1 Request Unit to read a document of
up to 1KB or to read 1KB from a larger document.

With all of these pieces in place, we can begin loading data.

Load Data into Cosmos DB

Microsoft has a Data Explorer tool built into the Azure Portal. This Data Explorer
tool includes a friendly method for creating data for every API *except* our MongoDB
API. Without a built-in method for loading data, we will need to build and deploy
something on our own which does this.

In the code for Chapter 7, there is a zip file called CosmosMongo.zip. It contains a
Visual Studio solution which itself includes a simple class library and a test project. In
the app.config file for the test project, fill in the username, host, and password files with

the data in the Connection String settings page. Figure 7-5 shows an example of where you can find your username, host, port, and password data. Save this data somewhere useful, as we will also need it later when connecting SQL Server to Cosmos DB.

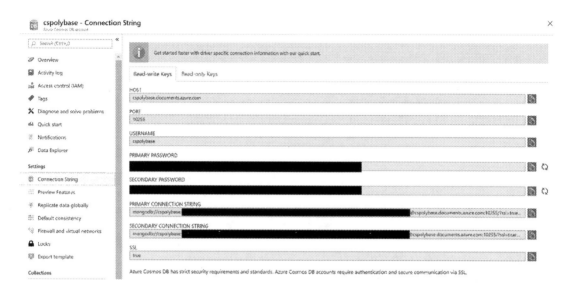

Figure 7-5. *The Connection String settings page has your host, port, username, and password settings, as well as the ability to reset passwords as needed. Copy this information as you will need it a couple of times in this chapter*

Once these values are properly configured, run the `CreateVolcano()` test method from the Visual Studio Test Explorer. To open up the Test Explorer, open the `LoadVolcanoData.cs` file in the `MongoPusher` test project. From there, navigate to Test ➤ Windows ➤ Test Explorer, as in Figure 7-6.

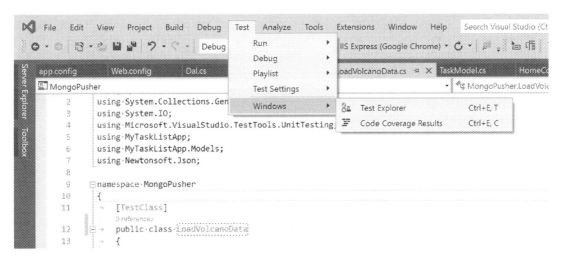

Figure 7-6. *Navigate to the Test Explorer in Visual Studio*

In the Test Explorer, drill down to the test named CreateVolcano, right-click that test, and select Run Selected Tests. Assuming your credentials are configured appropriately, this test will add a single volcano into the Volcano collection on the PolyBaseTest database. You can confirm that the test was successful by navigating to the Data Explorer in Cosmos DB and drilling down from the PolyBaseTest database into the Volcano collection and then the Documents section. You should see a single document populated with the data from our test. Figure 7-7 shows an example of the Data Explorer results.

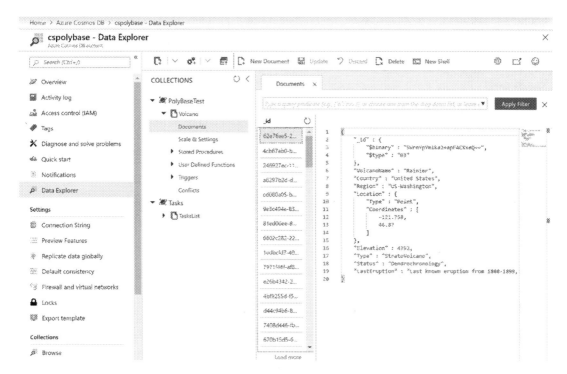

Figure 7-7. *One of many volcanoes*

Now that we know we can successfully load data into Cosmos DB using the MongoDB API, right-click and run the LoadVolcanoes test. This will take a moment, but when it is complete, you will have a new collection of volcanoes similar to Figure 7-7. With this data and our Cosmos DB credentials in place, we can move over to SQL Server to continue the process.

Create a Database Scoped Credential

Cosmos DB requires authentication for all database connections, so we will need to create a Database Scoped Credential on the SQL Server side. Listing 7-1 shows the code necessary to do this.

Listing 7-1. Create a Database Scoped Credential to authenticate against
Cosmos DB

```
IF NOT EXISTS
(
    SELECT 1
    FROM sys.database_scoped_credentials dsc
    WHERE
        dsc.name = N'CosmosCredential'
)
BEGIN
    CREATE DATABASE SCOPED CREDENTIAL CosmosCredential
    WITH IDENTITY = '<Your User>', Secret = '<Your PWD>';
END
GO
```

Note   Listing 7-1 assumes that you have already created a database master
key. If you have been following other examples so far, you likely have created a
database master key, but if you have not, you can create one by executing CREATE
MASTER KEY ENCRYPTION BY PASSWORD = '<Your password here>';

For our Database Scoped Credential, we will use the username field in Cosmos DB
as our identity and either the primary or secondary password as our secret.

With a Database Scoped Credential in place, we can move to the next step: creating
an external data source.

Create an External Data Source

We can create an external data source to Cosmos DB or MongoDB just as we did in
Chapter 6 with connecting to a remote SQL Server instance. The only difference is that
for MongoDB and Cosmos DB, we will connect on the mongodb protocol. Listing 7-2
shows an example of creating an external data source to Cosmos DB.

Listing 7-2. Create a new external data source going out to Cosmos DB

```
IF NOT EXISTS
(
    SELECT 1
    FROM sys.external_data_sources ds
    WHERE
        ds.name = N'CosmosDB'
)
BEGIN
    CREATE EXTERNAL DATA SOURCE CosmosDB WITH
    (
        LOCATION = 'mongodb://cspolybase.documents.azure.com:10255',
        CONNECTION_OPTIONS = 'ssl=true',
        CREDENTIAL = CosmosCredential,
        PUSHDOWN = ON
    );
END
GO
```

Other than the protocol change, external data sources are pretty straightforward. Where things begin to differ considerably, however, are external tables.

Create an External Table

MongoDB and Cosmos DB in its Mongo mode are document databases, meaning that we store data in a structured format—usually JSON or Binary JSON (BSON)—but that the structure can differ considerably from document to document. Within a document, you also have the ability to add nested structures: arrays and lists. These nested structures do not play nicely with relational databases, which want atomic rather than nested values, so we need to have a way to translate documents into consistent, atomic values. This is where the PolyBase engine steps in and *flattens* our data.

Flattening Data

There are several rules around flattening document data either with MongoDB or Cosmos DB, which you can find on Microsoft Docs at `https://docs.microsoft.`

com/en-us/sql/relational-databases/polybase/polybase-configure-mongodb?view=sqlallproducts-allversions#flattening. In this section, we will review briefly those rules, particularly as they pertain to our volcano data set.

First, review Figure 7-7 to understand the JSON structure for our volcano data set. In it, we have a built-in identifier called _id and several top-level attributes which fit regular data types. For the purpose of creating an external table, PolyBase will translate those columns directly to a tabular data structure. This leaves the Location object, which is a nested, unordered set of attributes inside our volcano object. Inside this, we have two pieces of information: an attribute called Type and an array called Coordinates. The PolyBase engine will treat these two differently. For Type, we will get back a column named Location_Type—that is, a name in the format Object_Attribute.

The Coordinates array behaves quite differently, however. Here, the PolyBase engine names our new column Volcano_Coordinates, that is, Collection_Attribute. The engine then explodes out the Coordinates array and returns one row per array element. For our scenario, where we have X and Y coordinates, we will get back two rows: one with our volcano attributes and the X coordinate and one with our volcano attributes and the Y coordinate. Figure 7-8 shows what this will look like once we have loaded our data.

_id	VolcanoName	Country	Region	Location_Type	Elevation	Type	Status	LastEruption	Volcano_Coordinates
1	E56AE762-8EC8-8A4E-86F9-...	Rainier	United States	US-Washington	Point	4392	StratoVolcano	Dendrochronology	Last known eruption from 18...	121.758
2	E56AE762-9626-8A4E-86F9-...	Rainier	United States	US-Washington	Point	4392	StratoVolcano	Dendrochronology	Last known eruption from 18...	46.87
3	BE74IB4C-1A8A-8A0E-8DFC-...	Abu	Japan	Honshu-Japan	Point	571	Shield volcano	Holocene	Unknown	131.6
4	B07A86AC-1A8A-8A0E-8DFC-...	Abu	Japan	Honshu-Japan	Point	571	Shield volcano	Holocene	Unknown	34.1
5	EC276824-C611-DA6E-B87C-...	Acamarachi	Chile	Chile-N	Point	6046	Stratovolcano	Holocene	Unknown	-67.62
6	EC276824-C611-DA6E-B87C-...	Acamarachi	Chile	Chile-N	Point	6046	Stratovolcano	Holocene	Unknown	23.3
7	2D7829A6-0400-4A8C-8C42...	Acatenango	Guatemala	Guatemala	Point	3976	Stratovolcano	Historical	Last known eruption in 1964...	90.876
8	2D7829A6-0400-4A8C-8C42...	Acatenango	Guatemala	Guatemala	Point	3976	Stratovolcano	Historical	Last known eruption in 1964	14.501
9	050A08CD-458C-8A87-0CBE...	Acigol-Nevsehir	Turkey	Turkey	Point	1689	Maar	Holocene	Undated, but probable Holoc...	34.52
10	050A09CD-4EEE-8A87-0C9E...	Acigol-Nevsehir	Turkey	Turkey	Point	1689	Maar	Holocene	Undated, but probable Holoc...	38.57

Figure 7-8. *Two rows come back for each volcano, one tied to each coordinate in the pair*

With a single array, this result is not terrible, but because the number of rows is the cross product of all array elements, it can explode quickly. For example, if we have a coordinates array with X and Y values, an array with eruption probabilities for each of the past 5 years, and an array of the number of people who climbed the volcano per year over the past 8 years, we will have $2 * 5 * 8 = 320$ rows returned *per object*. In other words, if your Cosmos DB documents have multiple arrays, you probably do not want to bring them into PolyBase as is; instead, you will likely want to flatten out the arrays yourself first to prevent unexpectedly large row counts and to define array values. In our simple example, we have latitude and longitude expressed as array elements, but in Figure 7-8, we lose this important distinction as both join to form a generic volcano coordinate column.

Creating the Table

Now that we have a clearer understanding of what PolyBase is doing to documents in MongoDB or Cosmos DB, we can create an external table which allows us to see our Cosmos DB data in SQL Server. Listing 7-3 provides the script to create an external table for our Cosmos DB data.

Listing 7-3. Create an external table which connects to our volcano collection in Cosmos DB

```
IF NOT EXISTS
(
    SELECT 1
    FROM sys.external_tables t
    WHERE
        t.name = N'Volcano'
)
BEGIN
    CREATE EXTERNAL TABLE dbo.Volcano
    (
        _id NVARCHAR(100) NOT NULL,
        VolcanoName NVARCHAR(100) NOT NULL,
        Country NVARCHAR(100) NULL,
        Region NVARCHAR(100) NULL,
        Location_Type NVARCHAR(100) NULL,
        Elevation INT NULL,
        Type NVARCHAR(100) NULL,
        Status NVARCHAR(200) NULL,
        LastEruption NVARCHAR(300) NULL,
        [Volcano_Coordinates] FLOAT(53)
    )
    WITH
    (
```

```
        LOCATION='PolyBaseTest.Volcano',
        DATA_SOURCE = CosmosDB
    );
END
GO
```

With that table in place, we can try out a few queries.

Note   If you are familiar with SQL Server's FOR JSON and OPENJSON functionality, which has been available in the product since SQL Server 2016, PolyBase behaves quite differently. You do not have direct control over the JSON or BSON itself; instead, you provide a table structure which ought to fit, and PolyBase translates the input data to fit your table structure.

Querying Cosmos DB

Because we have an array, a simple SELECT * query will return each volcano twice, once with the first coordinate and once with the second. If we want to avoid that, we can perform a distinct query, ignoring the location type and coordinates. Listing 7-4 provides an example of such a query.

Listing 7-4. Ignore coordinates and return just volcano names and nonrepeated details

```
SELECT DISTINCT
    v.VolcanoName,
    v.Country,
    v.Region,
    v.Elevation,
    v.Type,
    v.Status,
    v.LastEruption
FROM dbo.Volcano v;
```

This is much closer to what we would expect to get, with one row per volcano. But if we want to bring back in coordinates, we can use the STRING_AGG() function in SQL Server to create a comma-separated list of coordinates for each volcano. Listing 7-5 shows the query.

Listing 7-5. Load volcano data into a temp table and then aggregate the information to return a single row per volcano

```
SELECT *
INTO #Volcanoes
FROM dbo.Volcano;

SELECT
    v.VolcanoName,
    v.Country,
    v.Region,
    v.Location_Type AS LocationType,
    STRING_AGG(v.Volcano_Coordinates, ',') AS Coordinates,
    v.Elevation,
    v.Type,
    v.Status,
    v.LastEruption
FROM #Volcanoes v
GROUP BY
    v.VolcanoName,
    v.Country,
    v.Region,
    v.Location_Type,
    v.Elevation,
    v.Type,
    v.Status,
    v.LastEruption
ORDER BY
    v.Elevation ASC;
```

Figure 7-9 shows the results of this query.

	VolcanoName	Country	Region	LocationType	Coordinates	Elevation	Type	Status	LastEruption
1	Arshan	China	China-E	Point	120.7,47.5	NULL	Cinder cones	Radiocarbon	Last known eruption B.C. (Ho...
2	Forecast Seamount	United States	Mariana Is-C Pacific	Point	143.917,13.4	NULL	Submarine volcano	Fumarolic	Undated, but probable Holoc...
3	Hainan Dao	China	SE Asia	Point	110.1,19.7	NULL	Pyroclastic cones	Historical	Last known eruption from 19...
4	In Ezzane Volc Field	Algeria	Africa-N	Point	10.833,23	NULL	Volcanic field	Holocene?	Uncertain Holocene eruption
5	Manda Gargori	Ethiopia	Ethiopia	Point	41.483,11.75	NULL	Fissure vents	Anthropology	Undated, but probable Holoc...
6	Río Murta	Chile	Chile-S	Point	-72.667,-46.167	NULL	Pyroclastic cones	Holocene?	Uncertain Holocene eruption
7	Tin Zaouatene Volc Field	Mali	Africa-N	Point	2.833,19.833	NULL	Volcanic field	Holocene	Undated, but probable Holoc...
8	Unnamed	Argentina	Argentina	Point	-68.267,-25.1	NULL	Pyroclastic cone	Holocene?	Uncertain Holocene eruption
9	Unnamed	Iran	Iran	Point	45.567,39.25	NULL	Volcanic field	Holocene	Undated, but probable Holoc...
10	Unnamed	Pacific Ocean	Pacific-E	Point	-103.583,10.733	NULL	Submarine volcano	Historical	Last known eruption in 1964 ...

Figure 7-9. *We now get back one row per volcano and a list of coordinates*

Now we have a query which is functionally similar to the original documents.

Caution   In the event that you have several arrays, this query will not return the original set but will include duplicates. For example, if we have coordinates as a two-element array and number of visitors as a five-element array, we will get back ten rows, so STRING_AGG( ) will show each coordinate five times. If we can guarantee that the array values will be unique, we can potentially get around this issue, but at the cost of a more complex query. And if array values are not guaranteed to be unique for an object, our job becomes all the more difficult.

Considerations When Using Cosmos DB

There are two major considerations when thinking about accessing Cosmos DB from PolyBase: cost and data shape. In this section, we will cover each in order.

Cost Considerations

Cosmos DB charges you for throughput, meaning you pay for the amount of data you wish to retrieve per second. Metaphorically, you are paying for the diameter of a pipe—at lower prices, the pipe is narrower and less data can flow through, but as you pay more, the diameter increases and you can get more results faster.

With this in mind, remember that Cosmos DB is one of the more expensive Azure services, and if you are using Cosmos DB as part of a regular application, you only have a limited amount of throughput available. There is no direct way within SQL Server to throttle a Cosmos DB query, so a big `SELECT *` operation might end up using your entire Resource Unit allotment and starve out other application queries. Even with predicate pushdown, Cosmos DB queries can get expensive.

Data Shape Considerations

In the realm of data shape, we have two things to keep in mind: mixed structure and arrays.

Mixed Structure

One of the biggest benefits of document databases is its inherent lack of cross-document structure, meaning that the first document might contain seven attributes and the next document might contain five of those seven plus three additional attributes. This flexibility can be useful in complex web applications. It does make life more difficult when using PolyBase, however, as we need data to come back as atomic attributes following the same data shape. If an attribute is missing from a document, PolyBase reads the value as NULL, so this means that you will need the full combination of all values in the document. When dealing with changes in document structure over time, this may mean a fairly large number of attributes and a somewhat sparse result set. This behavior only applies to attributes which you include in the external table definition: if you do not include the attribute as a column in your external table definition, the PolyBase engine will ignore it on any documents which do contain the attribute. This combination of behaviors is a polite alternative to failure as your document data model evolves.

Dealing with Arrays

In the section "Querying Cosmos DB," we walked through one way of dealing with a single array and pointed out the risks of flattening multiple arrays: a Cartesian product of all array components, which can lead to an absurd number of rows.

In the event that these are independent arrays which you can query separately, one solution is to create multiple external tables, one per array. By doing this, we can include common non-array attributes across each of the tables while keeping the arrays as separate tables, limiting the number of "duplicate" rows.

This approach also highlights the power of creativity when converting from nonrelational objects to relational data: there are multiple ways to view a thing, and sometimes multiple views are better than one. We may store different sets of attributes in documents within a single collection, but we do not need to replicate that faithfully in PolyBase external tables. Figure 7-10 shows an example of this philosophy.

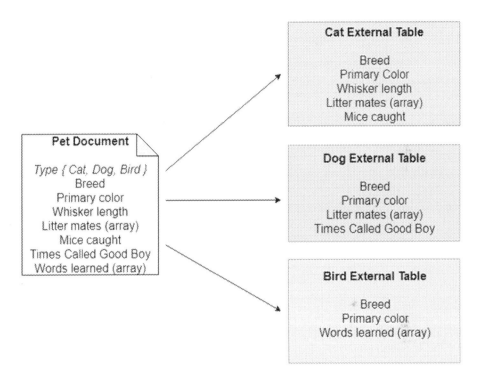

Figure 7-10. *A Cosmos DB document might include a wide range of attributes which we can best represent as multiple external tables*

In this scenario, we have a Pet container which contains important attributes about a variety of pets. Each document will have some subset of these attributes. Some of these attributes will be common across all pets, such as breed and primary color. Others will be specific to a particular type of pet, such as the set of words a pet bird might learn to mimic. Instead of trying to cram the nonrelational document form into a single table, creating three separate external tables against the same collection will make it easier for users to understand how best to query this data.

One Potential Use Case

Given the preceding considerations, one good use case for pulling data from Cosmos DB might be as an occasional ETL service. Suppose you have a "proper" collection with arrays, nested objects, and optional attributes; you might use that to serve data on a web site. If you want that data in SQL Server, it could make sense to use a tool like Azure Data Factory or Azure Databricks to translate the document-centric data into a more relational-friendly shape by removing arrays, preflattening objects, collapsing names of attributes which have changed over time, and removing attributes which you do not need in the database. That could feed into a different collection which you read with PolyBase.

Further, to reduce costs, it could make sense to move this data into SQL Server, using PolyBase as an Extract-Load-Transform (ELT) tool rather than a true data virtualization tool. This would reduce the load on Cosmos DB and allow you to keep service at a lower number of Request Units per Second (RU/s).

You can, of course, still use Cosmos DB (or MongoDB) as an external data source in a true data virtualization scenario, but if you do, be sure to understand the cost considerations.

Speaking of expensive products, let's take a look at Oracle.

Integration with Oracle

PolyBase will allow you to connect to Oracle versions 11g and later. For this example, we will connect to an Oracle Express 18c database. For instructions on how to create a Docker container running Oracle Express, check out the GitHub repository at `https://github.com/fuzziebrain/docker-oracle-xe`.

Note   If you would prefer to install Oracle Express directly, there is a good tutorial on PolyBase and Oracle 11g from Rajendra Gupta at SQL Shack, which you can access at `www.sqlshack.com/enhanced-polybase-sql-2019-external-tables-for-oracle-db/`. The Oracle web site has additional documentation on installing Oracle Express Edition on Windows at `https://docs.oracle.com/en/database/oracle/oracle-database/18/xeinw/`.

Just as before, we first need to create a Database Scoped Credential and then an external data source. Listing 7-6 walks us through these steps.

Listing 7-6. Create a Database Scoped Credential and external data source

```
IF NOT EXISTS
(
    SELECT 1
    FROM sys.database_scoped_credentials dsc
    WHERE
        dsc.name = N'OracleCredential'
)
BEGIN
    CREATE DATABASE SCOPED CREDENTIAL OracleCredential
    WITH IDENTITY = '<Your User>', Secret = '<Your PWD>';
END
GO

IF NOT EXISTS
(
    SELECT 1
    FROM sys.external_data_sources ds
    WHERE
        ds.name = N'Oracle'
)
BEGIN
    CREATE EXTERNAL DATA SOURCE Oracle WITH
    (
        LOCATION = 'oracle://SQLWIN10:1521',
        CREDENTIAL = OracleCredential,
        PUSHDOWN = ON
    );
END
GO
```

Once you have the source in place, you can create an external table to query data. Listing 7-7 shows how to create an external table for the EMPLOYEES sample table.

Listing 7-7. Create an external table to retrieve employee information

```
IF NOT EXISTS
(
    SELECT 1
    FROM sys.external_tables t
    WHERE
        t.name = N'Employees'
)
BEGIN
    CREATE EXTERNAL TABLE Employees
    (
        EMPLOYEE_ID DECIMAL(38),
        FIRST_NAME VARCHAR(100),
        LAST_NAME VARCHAR(100),
        EMAIL VARCHAR(255),
        PHONE_NUMBER VARCHAR(20),
        HIRE_DATE DATE,
        JOB_ID VARCHAR(10),
        SALARY DECIMAL(38,16),
        COMMISSION_PCT DECIMAL(2,2),
        MANAGER_ID DECIMAL(38)
    )
    WITH
    (
        LOCATION = '[XE].[HR].[EMPLOYEES]',
        DATA_SOURCE = Oracle
    );
END
GO
```

Once you have created an external table, querying is the same as any other table we have dealt with thus far. I would like to cover a couple of errors you might experience when trying to create an external table.

Common Oracle Errors

If you receive an error with ORA-12203, this is an indication that the machine running SQL Server cannot reach your Oracle database. The most common solutions are to check the hostname and port to ensure that your hostname is reachable and you have the correct TSN listener port, which is 1521 by default. In my case, I needed to set up an entry in my /etc/hosts file to route traffic to Oracle, as the Docker container I used for SQL Server did not know about the server named *SQLWIN10* and would try to reach a different IP address altogether.

On a different occasion, I received the error message in Listing 7-8.

Listing 7-8. An error message concerning authentication protocols

```
Msg 105082, Level 16, State 1, Line 1
105082;Generic ODBC error: [Microsoft][ODBC Oracle Wire Protocol driver]
[Oracle]ORA-28040: No matching authentication protocol Additional error
<2>: ErrorMsg: [Microsoft][ODBC Oracle Wire Protocol driver][Oracle]ORA-
28040: No matching authentication protocol, SqlState: HY000, NativeError:
28040 .
```

You might receive this error message because the Oracle driver SQL Server uses for PolyBase is tied to Oracle 11, but Oracle 18c (at least Express Edition) does not by default allow Oracle 11 clients to connect.

The solution here is to navigate to $ORACLE_HOME/network/admin and modify the file named sqlnet.ora to add in the following line: SQLNET.ALLOWED_LOGON_VERSION_SERVER=11. After you do this, you should be able to connect with SQL Server. This change does not require restarting the TSN listener or Oracle database.

Integration with Teradata

In addition to MongoDB, Cosmos DB, and Oracle, PolyBase has built-in support for one additional external data source: Teradata. Setup on the SQL Server side is the same as for Oracle: create a Database Scoped Credential, then create an external data source, and finally create an external table. The only difference between Teradata and Oracle here is the use of the teradata:// protocol rather than the oracle:// protocol.

Caution   My last real Oracle and Teradata experience was from about 2006 or so. For this reason, I judge myself entirely incompetent at comparing native Oracle or Teradata performance vs. performance over external tables and therefore did not include any performance comparisons in this book. I will leave it to practitioners who are far better qualified than I regarding Oracle and Teradata performance optimizations.

Conclusion

In this chapter, we looked at PolyBase options using built-in ODBC drivers, focusing on Cosmos DB (via its MongoDB interface) and Oracle, as well as touching on Teradata. These providers will offer you the best ODBC experience because everything is tested and ready for you to use.

In the next chapter, we will look at how you can integrate with other external data sources such as Apache Spark, Apache Hive, and even Microsoft Excel via third-party ODBC drivers.

CHAPTER 8

Integrating via ODBC

The two prior chapters gave us a taste of the new capabilities in PolyBase with SQL Server 2019. In this chapter, we will go one step further and integrate with several data sources using PolyBase's generic ODBC capabilities. We will first start with a basic flow that we will follow for each driver and ODBC data source. From there, we will survey different data platform technologies to test PolyBase integration capabilities. Although our survey will not be exhaustive, we will cover integrating with three technologies. The first two, Apache Spark and Apache Hive, are critical parts of the greater Hadoop ecosystem. The third, Excel, is critical for business users but might not make sense as a serious PolyBase target. Nonetheless, sometimes it helps to see what kinds of wacky ideas you can bring to fruition. Finally, I will rant a bit about how unnecessarily difficult integrating via ODBC can be.

The Basic Flow

For each of the data storage products in this chapter, we will follow a similar process:

- Obtain and install a third-party ODBC driver for that product.

- Configure an ODBC Data Source Name (DSN) to test the ODBC driver.

- Create a database scoped credential whenever authentication is required.

- Create an external data source, using the `CONNECTION_OPTIONS` parameter either to select the existing DSN or define the necessary configuration parameters.

- Create an external table.

© Kevin Feasel 2020
K. Feasel, *PolyBase Revealed*, https://doi.org/10.1007/978-1-4842-5461-5_8

As we will see throughout this chapter, each one of these steps may cause problems. If you run into problems along the way—particularly if those problems differ from the ones I have experienced—you might want to try a different third-party ODBC driver and test that you can connect to the ODBC data source directly, outside of PolyBase. If you can, the issue might be in the external data source's `CONNECTION_OPTIONS` definition. There is almost no documentation available on Microsoft Docs regarding what these connection options look like, and the reason for that is simple: the ODBC driver itself controls the set of available connection options. This can make troubleshooting difficult, but there is an upside to this: any online resources you can find for that driver are likely to apply to PolyBase connectivity, as this is usually in the realm of the driver rather than the PolyBase engine.

With this preamble completed, let us now integrate with our first data platform technology, Apache Spark.

Integration with Apache Spark

Apache Spark is one of the most exciting technologies in the Hadoop ecosystem. In Chapter 3, we lamented over how slow Hadoop integration via MapReduce jobs is, and Spark is a key reason why our expectations regarding Hadoop performance have changed over the past decade. Spark is a distributed, in-memory clustered computing system which promises performance improvements of 10–100x over MapReduce and in practice can offer 3–30x improvements over MapReduce.[1] Because the remote Hadoop cluster we are using in this chapter has a single node, we will not perform any serious benchmarking of Spark against MapReduce here; our primary concern is to establish a working connection. To do this, we will follow the steps in the basic flow in order.

Obtain and Install a Valid Driver

The cluster we will test against is running the Hortonworks Data Platform (HDP) version 3.0. You can download the Hortonworks Spark ODBC Driver from the Cloudera web site at `https://www.cloudera.com/downloads/hdp.html`.

---

[1]See, for example, Li Liu's 2015 PhD thesis from the University of Delaware (`http://udspace.udel.edu/bitstream/handle/19716/17628/2015_LiuLu_MS.pdf`), pp 23–33.

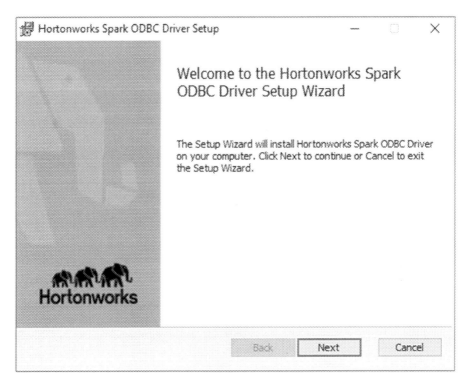

Figure 8-1. *The installer for the Hortonworks Spark ODBC driver*

Installing the Hortonworks Spark ODBC driver is fairly straightforward. Figure 8-1 shows the first screen for the installer wizard.

As an alternative to the Hortonworks Spark ODBC driver, you can obtain a Spark ODBC driver from Databricks, the commercial enterprise behind Apache Spark. You will need to navigate to `https://databricks.com/spark/odbc-driver-download` and fill out a form to get the driver. The ODBC driver comes as an installer, and Figure 8-2 shows the first screen of the Databricks ODBC driver installer.

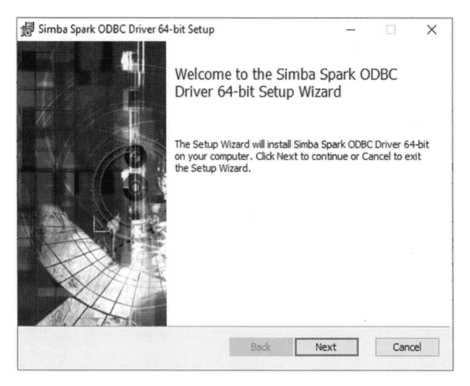

Figure 8-2. *The Databricks ODBC installer for Apache Spark*

Once you have a valid driver, you can test your connection, as we will do in the next section.

Create a Data Source Name

Creating a Data Source Name (DSN) is optional, but it is a good idea to create one at least to test connectivity from Windows to the remote data source. Regardless of the Spark driver you choose, there are a few settings you will want to configure. Figure 8-3 shows the DSN setup screen for the Hortonworks Spark ODBC driver; the Simba Spark ODBC Driver configuration will look similar, with most of the same fields.

Figure 8-3.   *The DSN setup for a Spark cluster*

The Hortonworks Data Platform 3.0 cluster I have configured runs an Apache Thrift server on port 10016 which allows me to integrate with Apache Spark. I do not have Kerberos enabled, though I could change the authentication mechanism to Kerberos if it were. Clicking the "SSL Options" button gives the option to enable or disable SSL connectivity. In my case, my cluster does not have an SSL certificate, and so I have this option disabled. Finally, Figure 8-4 shows the Advanced Options screen, where I have one important change. I need to change the *Default string column length* field to a number smaller than its default. Each field of data type STRING that comes in from Spark will translate to an NVARCHAR or VARCHAR of the given length in SQL Server, so if you set the default to something over 8000, you will get a conversion error.

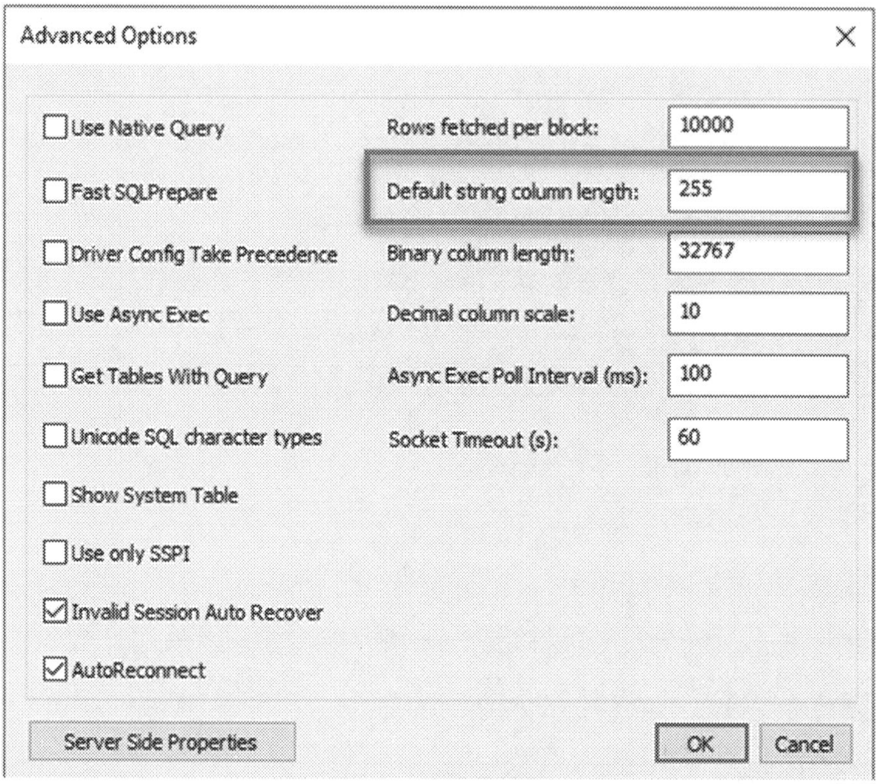

Figure 8-4. *PolyBase will use the driver's default string column length to determine how long each Spark field with a data type of STRING will be*

Once we have these settings configured, we can test the DSN to ensure that it is working as expected. If so, we can continue to the next step.

Create a Database Scoped Credential

For this scenario, we will not use the DSN directly. Therefore, we will need to authenticate against our Apache Spark server using credentials we define in SQL server. To do this, we will create a new Database Scoped Credential called SparkCredential. Listing 8-1 is a script which creates this credential.

Listing 8-1. Create a database scoped credential to access a Spark cluster

```
IF NOT EXISTS
(
    SELECT 1
    FROM sys.database_scoped_credentials dsc
    WHERE
        dsc.name = N'SparkCredential'
)
BEGIN
    CREATE DATABASE SCOPED CREDENTIAL SparkCredential
    WITH IDENTITY = '<Your User>', Secret = '<Your PWD>';
END
GO
```

With this credential in place, we can create an external data source using it.

Create an External Data Source

Our external data source will include a new parameter, CONNECTION_OPTIONS. In this parameter, we define the necessary configuration settings for the ODBC driver we will use. Listing 8-2 contains the code to connect to our Spark cluster over port 10016.

Listing 8-2. Create an external data source to access a Spark cluster

```
IF NOT EXISTS
(
    SELECT 1
    FROM sys.external_data_sources ds
    WHERE
        ds.name = N'ClusterinoSpark'
)
BEGIN
    CREATE EXTERNAL DATA SOURCE ClusterinoSpark WITH
    (
        LOCATION = 'odbc://clusterino:10016',
```

```
        CONNECTION_OPTIONS = 'Driver={Hortonworks Spark ODBC Driver};
        Host = clusterino; Port = 10016; Database = default; ServerNode =
        clusterino:10016',
        CREDENTIAL = SparkCredential,
        PUSHDOWN = ON
    );
END
GO
```

Let's cover those connection options in a bit more detail. First, notice the duplication of clusterino and 10016: we define this host and port in the LOCATION parameter, then again for Host, then for Port, and finally for ServerNode. PolyBase uses the ServerNode parameter and Spark the Host and Port. We also need to specify the name of the driver we would like to use, similar to creating a linked server.

With an external data source in place, we can jump directly to the external table. We are able to avoid creating an external file format because our Spark data is stored in a table and therefore is accessible as a structured data set rather than an unstructured collection of files in HDFS.

Create an External Table, Take 1

For our first attempt, we will load North Carolina population information onto the Spark cluster. This is a rather small data file but serves as a simple functional test.

Populate a Spark Table

Listing 8-3 contains Scala code necessary to load the North Carolina population data set from HDFS (refer back to Chapter 3 for this) and write to Spark as a table in ORC format. I ran this in Apache Zeppelin, which comes with the Hortonworks Data Platform distribution of Hadoop, but you can execute this code however you choose, whether that be via spark-shell, a Spark job, or a Zeppelin notebook.

Listing 8-3. Import population data into Spark

```
val ncPop = spark.read.format("CSV").option("header","true").load("hdfs://
clusterino/PolyBaseData/NorthCarolinaPopulation.csv")
```

```
ncPop.write.format("orc").saveAsTable("NorthCarolinaPopulation")
```

Change the load function to point to the appropriate location, and we can create an external table against NorthCarolinaPopulation. Listing 8-4 contains the create script.

Listing 8-4. Create an external table

```
IF NOT EXISTS
(
    SELECT 1
    FROM sys.external_tables t
    WHERE
        t.name = N'NorthCarolinaPopulationSpark'
)
BEGIN
    CREATE EXTERNAL TABLE dbo.NorthCarolinaPopulationSpark
    (
        SUMLEV NVARCHAR(255),
        COUNTY NVARCHAR(255),
        PLACE NVARCHAR(255),
        PRIMGEO_FLAG NVARCHAR(255),
        NAME NVARCHAR(255),
        POPTYPE NVARCHAR(255),
        YEAR NVARCHAR(255),
        POPULATION NVARCHAR(255)
    )
    WITH
    (
        LOCATION = 'NorthCarolinaPopulation',
        DATA_SOURCE = ClusterinoSpark
    );
END
GO
```

Note that all of the data types in Listing 8-4 are NVARCHAR(255). This is because we set the default string length to 255 characters, and by default, all columns on CSV files are converted to STRING data types in Spark DataFrames unless you configure the `inferSchema` parameter on load. If we try to use a data type on our external table definition which does not directly convert to the remote table, we will receive an error like that in Figure 8-5.

```
Started executing query at Line 40
Msg 105083, Level 16, State 1, Line 1
105083:The following columns in the user defined schema are incompatible with
 the external table schema for table 'NorthCarolinaPopulationSparkT2':
user defined column type: ([SUMLEV] INT) vs. detected external table column
type: ([SUMLEV] NVARCHAR(255)
```

Figure 8-5. *Msg 105083 tells us our external table creation script has an improper data type, specifically for the SUMLEV column*

The error message includes the entire definition, so look for any type mismatches if you receive this error and fix them on the creation script.

Suppose, however, that we would like to use the correct data types on our external table. In that case, we need to build a Spark table which uses the appropriate data types.

Create an External Table, Take 2

Going back to Spark, we will run a new command to create a table called `NorthCarolinaPopulationTyped`. This table will remove any records where the population is non-numeric and then convert each column to the correct data type. Listing 8-5 contains the Scala script, which runs a Spark SQL query to perform data conversions and then writes the results out to a new table.

Listing 8-5. Create a Spark table with appropriate data types

```
import org.apache.spark.sql.functions._

spark.sql("""
    SELECT
        INT(SUMLEV) AS SummaryLevel,
        INT(COUNTY) AS CountyID,
        INT(PLACE) AS PlaceID,
        BOOLEAN(PRIMGEO_FLAG) AS IsPrimaryGeography,
        NAME AS Name,
```

```
        POPTYPE AS PopulationType,
        INT(YEAR) AS Year,
        INT(POPULATION) AS Population
    FROM NorthCarolinaPopulation
    WHERE
        POPULATION <> 'A'
""")
    .write.format("orc").saveAsTable("NorthCarolinaPopulationTyped")
```

With this table in place, we can return to SQL Server and create a new external table, one which fits the source data a bit better. Listing 8-6 shows the fruits of our labor.

Listing 8-6. Create an external table. Again

```
IF NOT EXISTS
(
    SELECT 1
    FROM sys.external_tables t
    WHERE
        t.name = N'NorthCarolinaPopulationTypedSpark'
)
BEGIN
    CREATE EXTERNAL TABLE dbo.NorthCarolinaPopulationTypedSpark
    (
        SummaryLevel INT,
        CountyID INT,
        PlaceID INT,
        IsPrimaryGeography BIT,
        Name NVARCHAR(255),
        PopulationType NVARCHAR(255),
        Year INT,
        Population INT
    )
    WITH
    (
```

```
        LOCATION = 'NorthCarolinaPopulationTyped',
        DATA_SOURCE = ClusterinoSpark
    );
END
GO
```

Now the table has meaningful data types, and we can write queries like the one in Listing 8-7 to filter on the table as though it were a regular SQL Server table.

Listing 8-7. Querying the typed Spark external table

```
SELECT
    ncp.Name,
    ncp.PopulationType,
    ncp.Population
FROM dbo.NorthCarolinaPopulationTypedSpark ncp
    INNER JOIN dbo.CityPopulationCenter cpc
        ON ncp.Name = cpc.CityName
WHERE
    ncp.PopulationType = 'CENSUSPOP'
    AND ncp.Year = 2010
    AND ncp.IsPrimaryGeography = 0;
```

This provides us the T-SQL development plane for our coding needs and opens up the possibility of predicate pushdown of numeric features. The downside to this approach is that it also precludes us from using Spark SQL–specific functionality, such as Spark user–defined functions. If you need this kind of functionality, the best bet is still to access a Spark cluster with native code via `spark-shell`, a Spark application, or a Zeppelin or Jupyter notebook.

With Apache Spark successfully handled, we can move on to the next Hadoop ecosystem product, Apache Hive.

Integration with Apache Hive

Prior to Apache Spark's ascendance, Apache Hive was the premier technology in the Hadoop ecosystem. Hive offers the ability to write SQL against data in HDFS, making it an easy way to get started with Hadoop. The process for connecting to Hive is similar to that for Spark: obtain drivers and then create external resources in SQL Server.

Obtain and Install a Valid Driver

Several ODBC drivers for Apache Hive are available, but not all will work. In this section, we will cover one of the working drivers: the Cloudera ODBC Driver for Apache Hive.

Note   During the research portion of this chapter, I investigated four separate drivers. The Cloudera ODBC Driver for Apache Hive version 2.6.4 and Progress Software's DataDirect 8.0 Apache Hive Wire Protocol worked successfully. The Microsoft Hive ODBC Driver, intended for interaction with Microsoft's HDInsight product, does not appear to connect to a server running HiveServer 2. The CData ODBC Driver for Apache Hive might connect though something in my setup gave me a null pointer exception. Your outcomes may differ from mine, of course, so I would not necessarily proscribe against the other two drivers, but I did want to share my experiences.

Obtain the Cloudera ODBC Driver for Apache Hive from Cloudera's web site (`www.cloudera.com/downloads.html`) and navigate to *Hive ODBC Driver Downloads*. In Figure 8-6, you can see the versions available. Be sure to download version 2.6.4 or later.

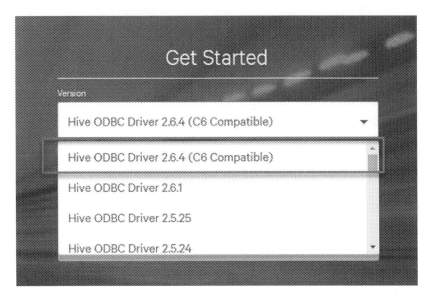

Figure 8-6. *Download the Hive ODBC Driver version 2.6.4 or later*

If you try to use a version of the Hive ODBC Driver prior to 2.6.4, you may end up with the error message in Figure 8-7.

Started executing query at Line 17
Msg 105082, Level 16, State 1, Line 1
105082:Generic ODBC error: [Cloudera][Support] (30030) Error while calling function %1% [%2%: %3%].
Check that the operation is supported and the function is implemented. .

Figure 8-7. *A rather generic error in a generic ODBC driver*

Installation of the Cloudera ODBC Driver for Apache Hive is straightforward: follow the wizard prompts and the installer takes care of the rest.

Create a Data Source Name

Once you have installed the Cloudera ODBC Driver for Apache Hive, you can open the 64-bit ODBC Data Sources either through searching on the start menu or by running odbcad32.exe. Then, create a new ODBC data source by clicking the Add button. Figure 8-8 shows the 64-bit ODBC Data Source Administrator.

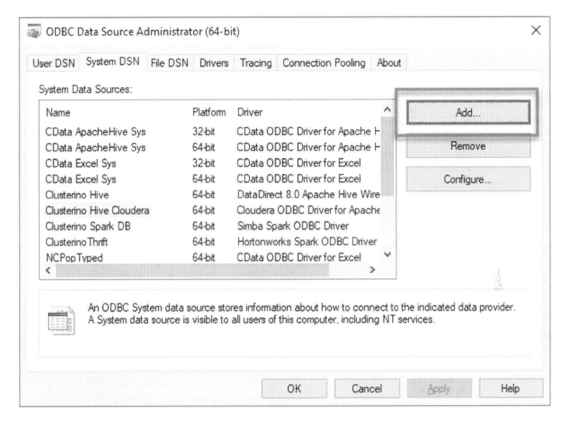

Figure 8-8. *Create a new ODBC data source*

From there, select `Cloudera ODBC Driver for Apache Hive` as the driver and click the `Finish` button. This will bring you to a data source configuration screen like in Figure 8-9.

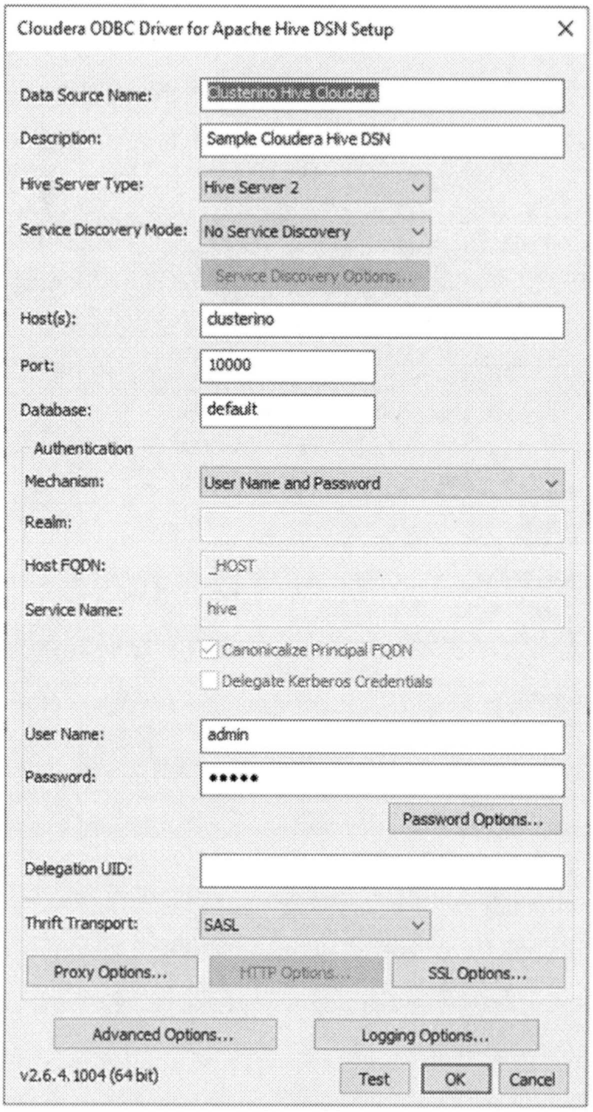

Figure 8-9. *Create a new Data Source Name to connect to Apache Hive*

Be sure to configure *Advanced Options* and *SSL Options* like in the Spark example, changing the default string column length to 255 characters in Advanced Options and configuring SSL to match your Hadoop cluster settings. With this DSN in place, we will be able to connect to Hive. Test your setup to ensure that everything is working as expected, and if so, we can continue on to the next step in the process.

Create a Database Scoped Credential

The process to create a database scoped credential is the same as we've seen a few times already, and if you have both Spark and Hive running on the same Hadoop cluster, you may be able to reuse your Spark credentials. Assuming this is a new setup, I will create a new Database Scoped Credential in Listing 8-8.

Listing 8-8. Create a new Database Scoped Credential for Hive access

```
IF NOT EXISTS
(
    SELECT 1
    FROM sys.database_scoped_credentials dsc
    WHERE
        dsc.name = N'HiveCredential'
)
BEGIN
    CREATE DATABASE SCOPED CREDENTIAL HiveCredential
    WITH IDENTITY = '<Your User>', Secret = '<Your PWD>';
END
GO
```

With a credential in place, we can move to the next step: creating an external data source.

Create an External Data Source

In the case of Apache Hive, I found it easiest to define the external data source off of the DSN, although you can specify the connection options individually as well. Listing 8-9 shows how to create an external data source for Hive.

Listing 8-9. Create an external data source for Apache Hive

```
IF NOT EXISTS
(
    SELECT 1
    FROM sys.external_data_sources ds
    WHERE
```

```
        ds.name = N'ClusterinoHive'
)
BEGIN
    CREATE EXTERNAL DATA SOURCE ClusterinoHive WITH
    (
        LOCATION = 'odbc://clusterino:10000',
        CONNECTION_OPTIONS = 'Driver={Cloudera ODBC Driver for
        Apache Hive}; DSN = Clusterino Hive Cloudera; ServerNode =
        clusterino:10000', CREDENTIAL = HiveCredential,
        PUSHDOWN = ON
    );
END
GO
```

After creating the data source, we can easily create an external table.

Create an External Table

Creating an external table for Apache Hive is the same as Spark. Listing 8-10 shows the necessary code.

Listing 8-10. Create an external table for Hive

```
IF NOT EXISTS
(
    SELECT 1
    FROM sys.external_tables t
    WHERE
        t.name = N'NorthCarolinaPopulationHive'
)
BEGIN
    CREATE EXTERNAL TABLE dbo.NorthCarolinaPopulationHive
    (
        SummaryLevel INT,
        CountyID INT,
        PlaceID INT,
        IsPrimaryGeography BIT,
```

```
        Name NVARCHAR(255),
        PopulationType NVARCHAR(255),
        Year INT,
        Population INT
    )
    WITH
    (
        LOCATION = 'northcarolinapopulation',
        DATA_SOURCE = ClusterinoHive
    );
END
GO
```

This assumes that there is a Hive table named northcarolinapopulation, so you will need to create this first if you are trying it out on your own.

Now that we have Spark and Hive working, let's round out this chapter with a third technology, Microsoft Excel.

Integration with Microsoft Excel

When you think of "big data" technologies, Excel should probably be at the bottom of your list. Nonetheless, we can still use an Excel ODBC driver to read data from a spreadsheet using PolyBase. The spreadsheet will need to be in a tabular format, meaning that we have columns starting from the top left of the spreadsheet like when importing a CSV file.

The natural driver for this would be the driver installed through the Microsoft Access 2016 Runtime, but if you install this driver and attempt to create an external table, you will see an error like the one in Figure 8-10.

Started executing query at Line 7
Msg 105082, Level 16, State 1, Line 1
105082;Generic ODBC error: [Microsoft][ODBC Excel Driver]Optional feature not implemented .

Total execution time: 00:00:00.853

Figure 8-10. *The Microsoft Access 2016 Runtime ODBC Excel driver will not work with PolyBase*

There is a third-party driver from a company named CData which does work with PolyBase. A 30-day trial of the driver is available on CData's web site at `https://www.cdata.com/drivers/excel/download/odbc/`.

With this driver, the first step is to create a DSN and link it to an Excel file, like in Figure 8-11.

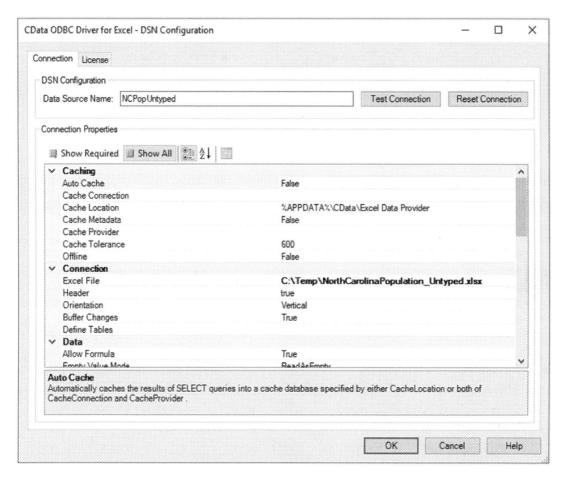

Figure 8-11. *Create a data source to an Excel spreadsheet*

With this data source in place, we can continue to the next step: creating an external data source.

Create an External Data Source

In the prior examples, we created a Database Scoped Credential, but that is not necessary for an Excel spreadsheet, so we can jump straight to the data source. Listing 8-11 includes the T-SQL code necessary for this.

Listing 8-11. Create an external data source

```
IF NOT EXISTS
(
    SELECT 1
    FROM sys.external_data_sources ds
    WHERE
        ds.name = N'NorthCarolinaPopulationExcelUntyped'
)
BEGIN
    CREATE EXTERNAL DATA SOURCE NorthCarolinaPopulationExcelUntyped WITH
    (
        LOCATION = 'odbc://noplace',
        CONNECTION_OPTIONS = 'Driver={CData Excel Source};
        DSN=NCPopUntyped'
    );
END
GO
```

Note here that in the CONNECTION_OPTIONS section, we specify a DSN rather than filling in all of the details. In addition, the LOCATION parameter does not need to be set to a real value so long as we use a DSN.

Create an External Table, Take 1

By default, string columns in Excel will translate to NVARCHAR(4000) columns in SQL Server, so we need to represent that in the code in Listing 8-12.

Listing 8-12. Create an external table with max-width string columns

```
IF NOT EXISTS
(
```

```
    SELECT 1
    FROM sys.external_tables t
    WHERE
        t.name = N'NorthCarolinaPopulationExcelUntyped'
)
BEGIN
    drop  EXTERNAL TABLE dbo.NorthCarolinaPopulationExcelUntyped
    CREATE EXTERNAL TABLE dbo.NorthCarolinaPopulationExcelUntyped
    (
        RowID INT,
        SUMLEV NVARCHAR(4000),
        COUNTY NVARCHAR(4000),
        PLACE NVARCHAR(4000),
        PRIMGEO_FLAG NVARCHAR(4000),
        NAME NVARCHAR(4000),
        POPTYPE NVARCHAR(4000),
        YEAR NVARCHAR(4000),
        POPULATION NVARCHAR(4000)
    )
    WITH
    (
        LOCATION = 'NorthCarolinaPopulation',
        DATA_SOURCE = NorthCarolinaPopulationExcelUntyped
    );
END
GO
```

The RowID column is something which the CData driver adds on automatically, and if you try to leave it off or forget it, the PolyBase engine will complain about a column mismatch.

All of this looks great, at least until you try to query the table. Querying a single column like SUMLEV works okay, but once I got up to five columns, I received the error in Figure 8-12, telling me that there was not enough buffer space for a row.

Started executing query at Line 47
Msg 7320, Level 16, State 110, Line 1
Cannot execute the query "Remote Query" against OLE DB provider "SQLNCLI11" for linked server "(null)".
105082;Generic ODBC error: COdbcReadConnection::ReadBuffer: not enough buffer space for one row

Figure 8-12. *We have run out of buffer space for a single row*

This looks like a bad situation, but there is one setting we can change to give us a bit more room in the buffer. Figure 8-13 shows the setting for maximum column size. Reducing that to a number which we know is sufficient will allow us to include more columns in our query.

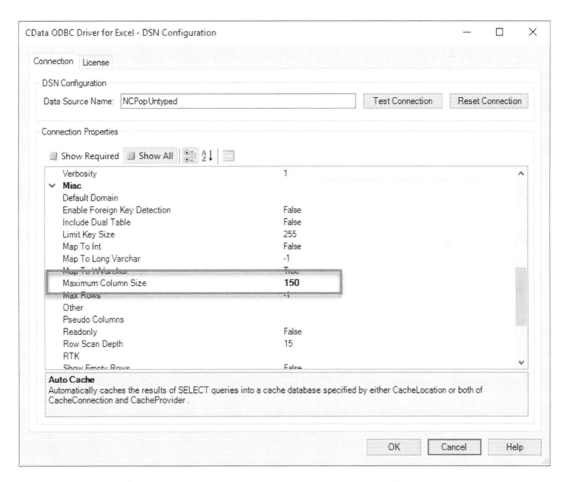

Figure 8-13. *Reducing the maximum column size in the driver*

With this change in place, we can successfully query the data in Excel. But we can do one better.

Create an External Table, Take 2

By default, all columns in Excel are typed as General, which the CData driver converts to text. If we explicitly type the columns in our Excel spreadsheet, we can use the appropriate data types. For example, we can convert the SUMLEV column to a column named SummaryLevel with a Number data type. Figure 8-14 shows an example of this.

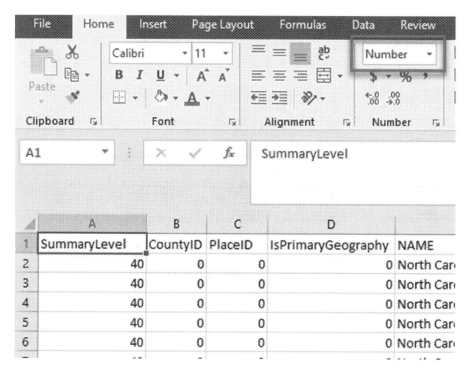

Figure 8-14. *Setting the data type for each column in Excel, starting with summary level*

With this work done, we can create a new external table which uses a more reasonable data type. Listing 8-13 shows us what this new external table looks like after we have created a new DSN called NCPopTyped to point to the typed Excel spreadsheet.

Listing 8-13. Create an external data source and external table for a typed spreadsheet

```
IF NOT EXISTS
(
    SELECT 1
    FROM sys.external_data_sources ds
    WHERE
        ds.name = N'NorthCarolinaPopulationExcelTyped'
)
BEGIN
    CREATE EXTERNAL DATA SOURCE NorthCarolinaPopulationExcelTyped WITH
    (
        LOCATION = 'odbc://clusterino',
        CONNECTION_OPTIONS = 'Driver={CData Excel Source}; DSN=NCPopTyped'
    );
END
GO

IF NOT EXISTS
(
    SELECT 1
    FROM sys.external_tables t
    WHERE
        t.name = N'NorthCarolinaPopulationExcelTyped'
)
BEGIN
    CREATE EXTERNAL TABLE dbo.NorthCarolinaPopulationExcelTyped
    (
        RowID INT,
        SummaryLevel FLOAT(53),
        CountyID FLOAT(53),
        PlaceID FLOAT(53),
        IsPrimaryGeography FLOAT(53),
        Name NVARCHAR(4000),
        PopulationType NVARCHAR(4000),
```

```
        Year FLOAT(53),
        Population FLOAT(53)
    )
    WITH
    (
        LOCATION = 'NorthCarolinaPopulation',
        DATA_SOURCE = NorthCarolinaPopulationExcelTyped
    );
END
```

These data types may look a bit odd—using float instead of an integer type is sure to raise suspicions—but they do the job.

An Extended Note on Driver Support

Before wrapping up this chapter, I would like to offer an extended note (aka. rant) on driver support, joining together my experiences working with Spark, Hive, and Excel. In all three cases, I noticed that different third-party ODBC drivers worked to differing degrees of success. In each case, the Microsoft driver ended up failing: those were the Microsoft Hive ODBC Driver and the Microsoft Access 2016 Runtime. "Direct" third-party drivers provided mixed success. For example, I was able to use the Hortonworks Spark ODBC driver, but their Hive ODBC driver would return the strange error message in Figure 8-7. With third-party paid drivers, I also experienced mixed success. Whereas the CData Excel driver worked perfectly, the CData Hive driver would not connect to my cluster, and I had to use a driver from Progress Software.

The moral of this story is to try different drivers and that your choice of driver may affect more than you'd think. If you experience failure with one driver, try out a couple more and see if you get the same error message. Versions of drivers can also cause problems: older versions of the Cloudera Hive ODBC driver failed, though version 2.6.4 worked successfully against my HDP cluster.

In the end, we can use PolyBase with various ODBC drivers to access data sources of all sorts, but some drivers are more finicky than others. Furthermore, PolyBase seems to bring out the worst in drivers, causing failure even when the driver tests successfully in the ODBC Data Sources application.

Conclusion

In this chapter, we looked at ways to connect to three external data sources lacking "built-in" support: Apache Spark, Apache Hive, and Microsoft Excel. With a working ODBC driver and a bit of fiddling, you will find that other external data sources are also accessible as long as they offer ODBC drivers for connectivity.

In the next chapter, we will leave the world of on-premises SQL Server and move into Azure Synapse Analytics. Given PolyBase's status with Azure Synapse Analytics as the preferred method for data ingestion, we will see some of the investments the Azure Synapse Analytics team has put into PolyBase which have not yet reached the on-premises world.

CHAPTER 9

PolyBase in Azure Synapse Analytics

After having looked at the plethora of new data sources available to us with PolyBase V2, we will change our focus in this chapter to look at how PolyBase works for ETL in Azure Synapse Analytics. We will start with an overview of the PolyBase surface area and see how Azure Synapse Analytics muddies the waters with respect to functionality. Next, we will create a new Azure Synapse Analytics database. Then, we will use PolyBase to read data from Azure Blob Storage into Azure Synapse Analytics and look at a couple tips for speeding up data loads. After that, we will dive into some of the special benefits available when using PolyBase on Azure Synapse Analytics.

A Different Breed of PolyBase

Throughout this book, I have referred to "PolyBase V1" as the version of PolyBase available on-premises in SQL Server 2017 and "PolyBase V2" as the version of PolyBase available on-premises in SQL Server 2019. There is a third breed of PolyBase which does not neatly fit into the V1 vs. V2 construct: the version of PolyBase available on Azure Synapse Analytics.

Note　In the course of writing this book, Microsoft has changed Azure SQL Data Warehouse, renaming SQL Data Warehouse to Azure Synapse Analytics SQL Pools. Throughout this book, I will use "Azure Synapse Analytics" and "Azure Synapse Analytics SQL Pools" interchangably. This product is under active development and will include support for Spark clusters and more. Instructions in this chapter are liable to change as a result of this development.

© Kevin Feasel 2020

K. Feasel, *PolyBase Revealed*, https://doi.org/10.1007/978-1-4842-5461-5_9

This version of PolyBase is, in many ways, a superset of PolyBase V1. For example, it uses the same concepts of external data sources, external file formats, and external tables, and it allows you to retrieve data from Azure Blob Storage efficiently. It does lack one key feature which is available in PolyBase V1 on-premises: you cannot connect to a Hadoop cluster and execute MapReduce jobs from Azure Synapse Analytics.

Setting aside that restriction, Azure Synapse Analytics's version of PolyBase has several features which are not available in on-premises PolyBase, either in V1 or in V2. Two of the features that we will look at in more detail later on in the chapter are rejected row locations and defining the first record in a file. The former allows us to define an Azure Blob Storage location for where you would like to store detailed information on why the PolyBase engine rejects particular rows, and the latter gives us the ability to skip header rows rather than seeing them show up in the rejected row list. In addition to these, PolyBase on Azure Synapse Analytics supports row lengths of 1 MB, whereas the on-premises version supports a maximum length of 32 KB.

The chart in Figure 9-1 is my attempt at summarizing the differences between these versions, with an emphasis on functionality available only in Azure Synapse Analytics. For brevity's sake, I do not include all V2 data sources.

	SQL Server 2017	SQL Server 2019	Azure SQL DW
Query Hadoop	✔	✔	✘
Query Azure Blob Storage	✔	✔	✔
Query Azure Data Lake Store	✘	✘	✔
Query SQL Server	✘	✔	✘
Query via ODBC	✘	✔	✘
Rejected row locations	✘	✘	✔
First row on file format	✘	✘	✔
CTAS / CETAS	✘	✘	✔
Managed Identities support	✘	✘	✔

Figure 9-1. *A feature comparison chart for PolyBase between SQL Server 2017 (V1), SQL Server 2019 (V2), and Azure Synapse Analytics (formerly known as Azure SQL Data Warehouse)*

With this feature set difference in mind, let's create an Azure Synapse Analytics SQL Pool and use PolyBase to shuffle data around.

Creating an Azure Synapse Analytics SQL Pool

Azure Synapse Analytics is one of the most expensive resources available on Azure. Before we get started, make sure you can absorb the expense, whether through a free trial, Azure credits, a company willing to invest in Azure, or deep pockets. If you perform the activities in this chapter in one fell swoop, your bill will likely be in the range of several dollars, but even leaving Azure Synapse Analytics on for a weekend might leave you with an uncomfortably large bill. With this in mind, let us continue creating an Azure Synapse Analytics SQL pool.

In the Azure portal, search for "SQL data warehouse" to find the *SQL data warehouses* service. Figure 9-2 shows an example of this search.

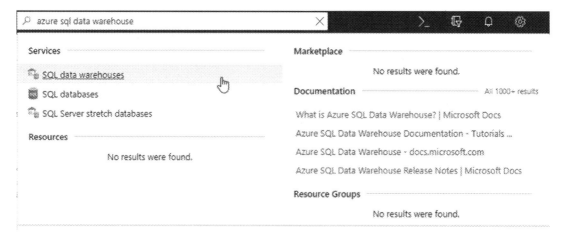

Figure 9-2. *Selecting the Azure Synapse Analytics service*

Inside this service, you will be prompted to create a new SQL data warehouse if you do not already have one, as you can see in Figure 9-3. Click the *Create SQL data warehouses* button to continue.

No SQL data warehouses to display

Try changing your filters if you don't see what you're looking for

Create SQL data warehouses

Figure 9-3. *Create a new SQL data warehouse*

From there, you will need to fill out server and database details. Figure 9-4 shows an example of the type of information you will need.

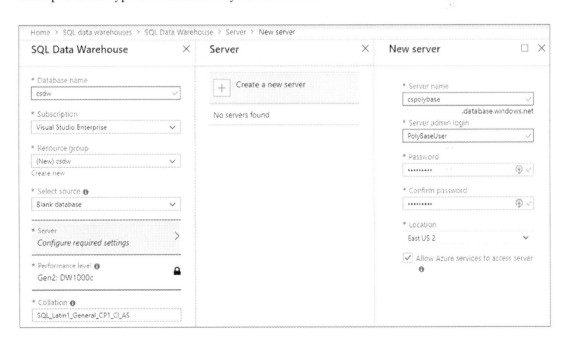

Figure 9-4. *Sample settings for a SQL data warehouse. Note that the images in this section may change as Azure Synapse Analytics evolves*

Azure charges you differently for SQL data warehouses depending upon which generation of Azure Synapse Analytics you are using. In Generation 1, they measured compute in Data Warehouse Units (DWUs), which serve as a combination of storage, network, and compute power. In Generation 2, they now measure it in terms of compute

237

Data Warehouse Units (cDWUs). In both generations, you pay for storage and compute separately, so if your warehouse only needs to serve queries for a portion of the day, you can pause the warehouse during periods of non-use and save on compute costs during those times.

Once you have configured your warehouse and it is up and running, navigate to the *Firewalls and virtual networks* security setting and add your client IP address in order to be able to connect to your warehouse. Figure 9-5 walks you through the steps.

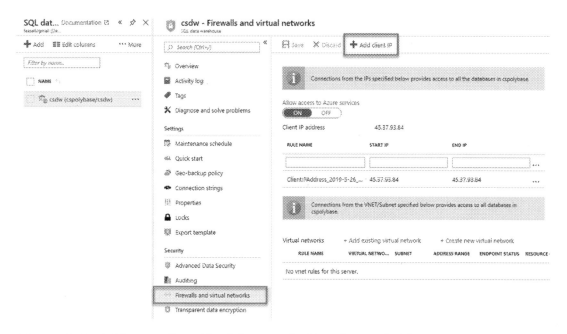

Figure 9-5. *Add your client IP address to the list of IPs valid for connection*

Once you have done this, you can connect to the warehouse using SQL Server Management Studio and SQL Server Authentication. Figure 9-6 provides an example of connecting to the `cspolybase` server.

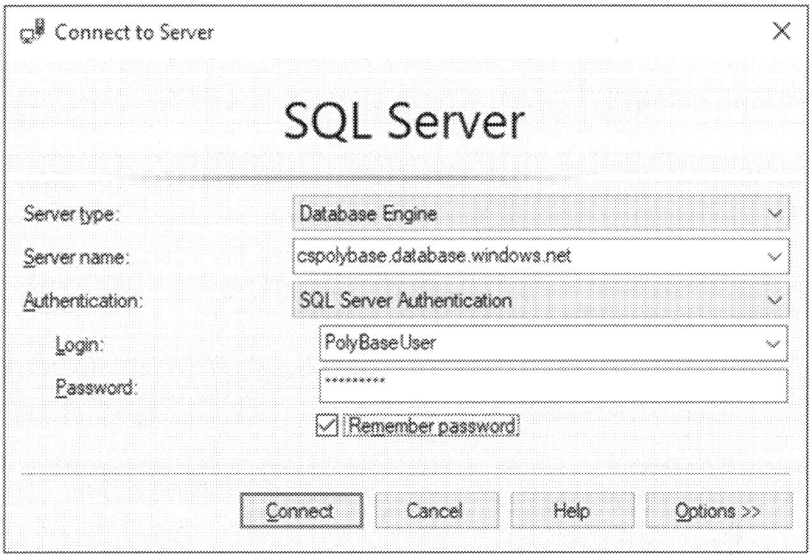

Figure 9-6. *Connecting to an Azure Synapse Analytics server*

Once connected, you will see your database.

Loading Data into Azure Synapse Analytics

Now that we have our database created, we can work to load some data into it. In this section, I will load New York City taxi ride data, following along with the demo on Microsoft Docs.[1] The first step is to create a data loader account. Creating a separate account for ETL work is usually a good idea regardless of your platform, but it becomes critical for Azure Synapse Analytics because you can put the account into a static resource class, giving it a fixed maximum percentage of total resources. In Listing 9-1, we will create the DataLoaderRC60 login in the master database.

Listing 9-1. Creating a data loader login. Note that this must be in the master database and you cannot switch databases directly from a query window

```
CREATE LOGIN DataLoaderRC60 WITH PASSWORD = '<Your Password>';
CREATE USER DataLoaderRC60 FOR LOGIN DataLoaderRC60;
GO
```

---

[1]https://docs.microsoft.com/en-us/azure/sql-data-warehouse/
load-data-from-azure-blob-storage-using-polybase

With the login and user created in the master database, we can then open a new query window and execute the following scripts in the user database. Listing 9-2 shows the scripts I ran against csdw, my user database.

Listing 9-2. Preparatory scripts for data loading. These scripts should run against the user database, not master

```
CREATE USER DataLoaderRC60 FOR LOGIN DataLoaderRC60;
GRANT CONTROL ON DATABASE::[csdw] TO DataLoaderRC60;
EXEC sp_addrolemember 'staticrc60', 'DataLoaderRC60';
GO
CREATE MASTER KEY;
GO
```

Unlike the on-premises version of SQL Server, when we run CREATE MASTER KEY, we do not specify a password.

At this point, we have an account we can use to load data from Azure Blob Storage. Open a new connection using this data loader account in SQL Server Management Studio to run the next set of scripts. Listing 9-3 shows the creation of our external data source, one external file format, a schema for external tables, and one external table. For the full set of items, refer to the code samples for this chapter.

Listing 9-3. Create an external data source, one external file format, and one external table

```
CREATE EXTERNAL DATA SOURCE NYTPublic
WITH
(
    TYPE = Hadoop,
    LOCATION = 'wasbs://2013@nytaxiblob.blob.core.windows.net/'
);
GO
CREATE EXTERNAL FILE FORMAT CSV WITH
(
    FORMAT_TYPE = DELIMITEDTEXT,
    FORMAT_OPTIONS
    (
```

```
            FIELD_TERMINATOR = ',',
            STRING_DELIMITER = '',
            DATE_FORMAT = '',
            USE_TYPE_DEFAULT = FALSE
    )
);
GO
CREATE SCHEMA ext;
GO
CREATE EXTERNAL TABLE [ext].[HackneyLicense]
(
    [HackneyLicenseID] int NOT NULL,
    [HackneyLicenseBKey] varchar(50) COLLATE SQL_Latin1_General_CP1_CI_AS
    NOT NULL,
    [HackneyLicenseCode] varchar(50) COLLATE SQL_Latin1_General_CP1_CI_AS
    NULL
)
WITH
(
    LOCATION = 'HackneyLicense',
    DATA_SOURCE = NYTPublic,
    FILE_FORMAT = CSV,
    REJECT_TYPE = value,
    REJECT_VALUE = 0
);
GO
```

These three create statements look quite similar to the examples of connecting to Azure Blob Storage in Chapter 2 with one difference: the external data source does not have a Database Scoped Credential associated with it. You can certainly create one in Azure Synapse Analytics, but this particular storage blob is publicly available and does not require an authorization token.

Once you have loaded all of the external tables, refreshing the tables list should give you a result similar to Figure 9-7.

Figure 9-7. *The complete set of external tables*

In this next section, we will look at ways in which PolyBase for Azure Synapse Analytics differs from the on-premises versions.

PolyBase Differences in Action

This section will look at several of the niceties available in PolyBase for Azure SQL Data Warehouse.

CTAS and Command Progress

The first difference I would like to cover is technically not PolyBase itself, but exposes Azure Synapse Analytics's Parallel Data Warehouse (PDW) roots. Listing 9-4 shows how you can use the CREATE TABLE AS SELECT (CTAS) syntax to create a new table in your SQL Pool based off of the contents of an external table.

Listing 9-4. Creating a new table from a SELECT statement

```
CREATE TABLE [dbo].[Date]
WITH
(
    DISTRIBUTION = ROUND_ROBIN,
    CLUSTERED COLUMNSTORE INDEX
)
AS SELECT * FROM [ext].[Date]
OPTION (LABEL = 'CTAS : Load [dbo].[Date]');
```

This is nice by itself, as it allows us to re-create tables quickly without needing to specify the definition. This is most useful for wide dimension tables. But there is one extra line which makes the operation even nicer: the LABEL. Defining a label allows us to trace the status of a particular external operation by querying the sys.dm_pdw_exec_ requests DMV. Listing 9-5 shows a query which will return the status and gigabytes of data processed for each of our load operations.

Listing 9-5. A status report for each warehouse table load

```
SELECT
    r.command,
    s.request_id,
    r.status,
    count(distinct input_name) as nbr_files,
    sum(s.bytes_processed)/1024/1024/1024.0 as gb_processed
FROM
    sys.dm_pdw_exec_requests r
    INNER JOIN sys.dm_pdw_dms_external_work s
    ON r.request_id = s.request_id
WHERE
    r.[label] IN
    (
        'CTAS : Load [dbo].[Date]',
        'CTAS : Load [dbo].[Geography]',
        'CTAS : Load [dbo].[HackneyLicense]',
        'CTAS : Load [dbo].[Medallion]',
```

```
        'CTAS : Load [dbo].[Time]',
        'CTAS : Load [dbo].[Weather]',
        'CTAS : Load [dbo].[Trip]'
    )
GROUP BY
    r.command,
    s.request_id,
    r.status
ORDER BY
    nbr_files desc,
    gb_processed desc;
GO
```

Running this query will give results like what you see in Figure 9-8, where six of the seven tables have finished and the Trip table has just started processing.

	command	request_id	status	nbr_files	gb_processed
1	CREATE TABLE [dbo].[Weather] WITH (DISTRI...	QID448	Completed	60	0.031250
2	CREATE TABLE [dbo].[Geography] WITH (DIST...	QID435	Completed	60	0.015625
3	CREATE TABLE [dbo].[Time] WITH (DISTRIBU...	QID445	Completed	60	0.005859
4	CREATE TABLE [dbo].[Trip] WITH (DISTRIBUT...	QID472	Running	60	0.000000
5	CREATE TABLE [dbo].[HackneyLicense] WITH (...	QID439	Completed	52	0.001953
6	CREATE TABLE [dbo].[Date] WITH (DISTRIBU...	QID407	Completed	28	0.000976
7	CREATE TABLE [dbo].[Medallion] WITH (DISTR...	QID442	Completed	18	0.000000

Figure 9-8. *Tracking the status of warehouse table loads*

In a regular production environment, you might also include or at least filter by submit_time or start_time, which show when a particular request was submitted and when work began, respectively.

Rejected Row Location

Few things in PolyBase are more frustrating than loading a million (or billion) row table and finding out that ten records will not display. A major part of the pain is just how little information bubbles to the surface. This is where the rejected row location parameter on external tables becomes important. Listing 9-6 shows the creation of a table for North Carolina population, similar to the external table in Chapter 2 but with one additional parameter: rejected row location.

Listing 9-6. An external table with a rejected row location

```
CREATE EXTERNAL TABLE dbo.NorthCarolinaPopulation
(
    SumLev INT NOT NULL,
    County INT NOT NULL,
    Place INT NOT NULL,
    IsPrimaryGeography BIT NOT NULL,
    [Name] VARCHAR(120) NOT NULL,
    PopulationType VARCHAR(20) NOT NULL,
    Year INT NOT NULL,
    Population INT NOT NULL
)
WITH
(
    LOCATION = N'Census/NorthCarolinaPopulation.csv',
    DATA_SOURCE = AzureNCPopBlob,
    FILE_FORMAT = CSV,
    REJECT_TYPE = VALUE,
    REJECT_VALUE = 5,
    REJECTED_ROW_LOCATION = 'Reject/NorthCarolinaPopulation'
);
GO
```

If we query this table, we will get back all of the viable rows, but as we saw in Chapter 2, there are a few rows whose summary level is non-numeric, and PolyBase therefore rejects the rows. Back in Chapter 2, we looked through the data set in Excel, but the rejected row location parameter gives us a much better solution.

Figure 9-9 shows an example of one rejected row file. We wrote to the Reject/ NorthCarolinaPopulation storage blob, and our PolyBase-driven SQL query created a new _rejectedrows folder with the time of our query.

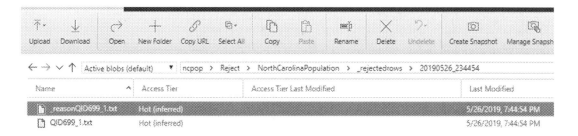

Figure 9-9. *A rejected row file in Azure Blob Storage*

Opening up the file gives us the following results:

```
Location: /Census/NorthCarolinaPopulation.csv Column ordinal: 1, Expected
data type: INT NOT NULL, Offending value: SUMLEV  (Column Conversion
Error), Error: Error converting data type NVARCHAR to INT., Reject file
location: /Reject/NorthCarolinaPopulation/_rejectedrows/20190526_234454/
QID699_1.txt
Location: /Census/NorthCarolinaPopulation.csv Column ordinal: 8, Expected
data type: INT NOT NULL, Offending value: A  (Column Conversion Error),
Error: Error converting data type NVARCHAR to INT., Reject file location:
/Reject/NorthCarolinaPopulation/_rejectedrows/20190526_234454/QID699_1.txt
Location: /Census/NorthCarolinaPopulation.csv Column ordinal: 8, Expected
data type: INT NOT NULL, Offending value: A  (Column Conversion Error),
Error: Error converting data type NVARCHAR to INT., Reject file location:
/Reject/NorthCarolinaPopulation/_rejectedrows/20190526_234454/QID699_1.txt
Location: /Census/NorthCarolinaPopulation.csv Column ordinal: 8, Expected
data type: INT NOT NULL, Offending value: A  (Column Conversion Error),
Error: Error converting data type NVARCHAR to INT., Reject file location:
/Reject/NorthCarolinaPopulation/_rejectedrows/20190526_234454/QID699_1.txt
```

We can see four total errors, one for the header (SUMLEV) and three rows with the character A instead of a number. Although this does not tell us exactly which record numbers failed, it does at least give us the values so we can investigate further.

Combining this with the next technique will further reduce the number of false positive rejections.

Defining the First Row

With the on-premises versions of PolyBase, we have needed to use the REJECT_VALUE parameter on external tables to deal with file headers. PolyBase for Azure Synapse Analytics gives us a parameter on the external file format which lets us deal with this: FIRST_ROW. Listing 9-7 shows an example of a CSV-based external file format which starts on the second row, ignoring the first row as a header.

Listing 9-7. Create an external file format which ignores the first row

```
CREATE EXTERNAL FILE FORMAT CSVRow2 WITH
(
    FORMAT_TYPE = DELIMITEDTEXT,
    FORMAT_OPTIONS
    (
        FIELD_TERMINATOR = ',',
        STRING_DELIMITER = '',
        DATE_FORMAT = '',
        USE_TYPE_DEFAULT = FALSE,
        FIRST_ROW = 2
    )
);
```

If we re-create the North Carolina population external table based on this external file format, the rejected row file will contain only the following three rows:

```
Location: /Census/NorthCarolinaPopulation.csv Column ordinal: 8, Expected
data type: INT NOT NULL, Offending value: A  (Column Conversion Error),
Error: Error converting data type NVARCHAR to INT., Reject file location:
/Reject/NorthCarolinaPopulation/_rejectedrows/20190526_235653/QID778_1.txt
Location: /Census/NorthCarolinaPopulation.csv Column ordinal: 8, Expected
data type: INT NOT NULL, Offending value: A  (Column Conversion Error),
Error: Error converting data type NVARCHAR to INT., Reject file location:
/Reject/NorthCarolinaPopulation/_rejectedrows/20190526_235653/QID778_1.txt
Location: /Census/NorthCarolinaPopulation.csv Column ordinal: 8, Expected
data type: INT NOT NULL, Offending value: A  (Column Conversion Error),
Error: Error converting data type NVARCHAR to INT., Reject file location:
/Reject/NorthCarolinaPopulation/_rejectedrows/20190526_235653/QID778_1.txt
```

Our three rows with bad data still exist, but we no longer get an error concerning SUMLEV.

Next up, we will look at a nice way to move data from Azure Synapse Analytics into Azure Blob Storage.

The CETAS Statement

PolyBase on Azure Synapse Analytics has another trick for us: the CREATE EXTERNAL TABLE AS SELECT (CETAS) statement. This gives us the ability to create an external table in a storage blob in just a few lines of code. Listing 9-8 shows how we can migrate data from the Time table back to our ncpop storage blob with a minimum of fuss.

Listing 9-8. Move data from a table into Azure Blob Storage with the CETAS syntax

```
CREATE EXTERNAL TABLE ext.PolyBaseTime
WITH
(
    LOCATION = '/Taxi/Time',
    DATA_SOURCE = AzureNCPopBlob,
    FILE_FORMAT = CSV
)
AS
SELECT *
FROM dbo.Time;
```

Figure 9-10 shows the results of this operation.

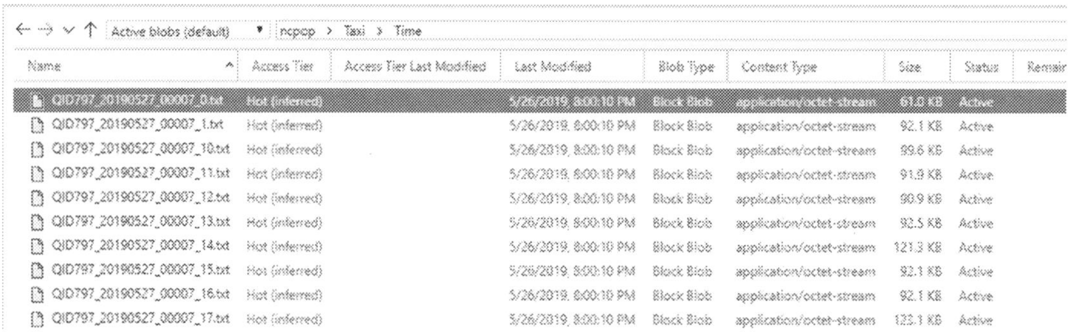

Figure 9-10. We have migrated the contents of dbo.Time into Azure Blob Storage

For data warehouses which only need to run occasionally—such as at month end or quarter end—we can move our data onto less expensive storage blobs and save even more money. Even when the warehouse should stay up 24/7, this still gives us a great technique for making data available to other services like on-premises SQL Servers. Natively querying Azure Synapse Analytics through PolyBase from an on-premises server would be great, but because that is not possible, this is a reasonable second-best alternative.

Additional Functionality

Azure Synapse Analytics's version of PolyBase does have one unique data source which you cannot connect to from on-premises: Azure Data Lake Store. This is true both for Generation 1 and Generation 2 of Azure Data Lake Store. PolyBase supports read and write scenarios, making it a good technique for moving data from a data lake into a data warehouse.

With Azure Data Lake Store, there is the ability to use Managed Identities for Azure Resources, which works with Azure Active Directory and removes the need for including the secret in your Database Scoped Credential. Listing 9-9 shows an example of creating a Managed Identities for Azure Resources Database Scoped Credential. Note that you must use `Managed Service Identity` as the identity for this to work.

Listing 9-9. Create a Managed Identity for Azure Resources Database Scoped Credential

```
CREATE DATABASE SCOPED CREDENTIAL ManagedIdentity WITH IDENTITY = 'Managed
Service Identity';
```

Conclusion

In this chapter, we took a look at Azure Synapse Analytics and contrasted its version of PolyBase to the versions available in SQL Server 2017 and SQL Server 2019. We can see that within the paradigm of PolyBase V1 and V2, the version in Azure Synapse Analytics does not fit cleanly: it has more functionality in some areas than PolyBase V2 (such as connectivity to Azure Data Lake Store) but lags behind PolyBase V1 in its support for Hadoop and V2 in its support for other data sources. In the next chapter, we will return to on-premises PolyBase and dive into the PolyBase-specific Dynamic Management Views available to us.

CHAPTER 10

Examining PolyBase via Dynamic Management Views

So far in this book, we have looked at what it takes to get PolyBase up and running on a machine, as well as steps to integrate with a variety of sources. In this chapter, we will dig into the Dynamic Management Views (DMVs) which provide us insights into what, exactly, is going on when we run a remote query through PolyBase. The first part of this chapter will cover the importance of DMVs for management. From there, we will look at each of the DMVs SQL Server exposes in turn. The final part of this chapter will review the information we can learn from DMVs when executing a variety of remote queries.

Dynamic Management Views

The term *Dynamic Management Views* (or DMVs) refers to a set of views or functions which provide us with metadata and metrics in order to diagnose issues in SQL Server. These have been a part of the database administrator's toolbelt since SQL Server 2005, and each subsequent version of SQL Server has added new DMVs.

Each Dynamic Management View exists in the `sys` schema, making it easier to find them. Most DMVs behave like tables or views, meaning you query or filter the DMV as you would a normal table, with all of the classic rules around clauses, joins, and SQL behavior intact. Some DMVs take optional or required parameters—these are *Dynamic Management Functions* (DMFs). Although we can use DMFs to diagnose issues with PolyBase, none of the PolyBase-specific DMVs in this chapter are functions; they are all views.

251

© Kevin Feasel 2020
K. Feasel, *PolyBase Revealed*, https://doi.org/10.1007/978-1-4842-5461-5_10

Note   Many of the Dynamic Management Views we will look at in this chapter are general-purpose DMVs, meaning that you can use them for non-PolyBase queries. Our focus for this chapter is on the PolyBase-specific DMVs as opposed to a general-purpose review of all of the useful Dynamic Management Views.

PolyBase Dynamic Management Views

There are 13 Dynamic Management Views available in SQL Server 2019 which relate to PolyBase. In this section, we will review each of these at a high level, starting with basic metadata resources, followed by the DMVs which help with service and node setup, and finishing with DMVs for query troubleshooting.

Note   If you are using SQL Server 2016 or 2017, most of the Dynamic Management Views will be available to you as well.

Metadata Resources

There are three DMVs which provide us basic metadata: `sys.external_tables`, `sys.external_data_sources`, and `sys.external_file_formats`. Each of these DMVs does exactly what you would expect, returning information for each of the three key PolyBase resources.

These three DMVs are database-specific Dynamic Management Views, meaning that you must be connected to the appropriate database to get back results. For example, if we have created an external data source on the `PolyBaseRevealed` database, querying `sys.external_data_sources` from `master` will not return any results. With that in mind, let's look at each DMV in turn.

External Data Sources

The `sys.external_data_sources` DMV shows metadata for each external data source we have created. Figure 10-1 shows the results of querying this DMV.

	data_source_id	name	location	type	type_desc	resource_manager_location	credential_id	connection_options	pushdown
1	65536	AzureNCPopBlob	wasbs://ncpop@cspolybaseblob.blob.core...	0	HADOOP	NULL	65536	NULL	ON
2	65539	AzureVisitsBlob	wasbs://visits@cspolybaseblob.blob.core...	0	HADOOP	NULL	65536	NULL	ON
3	65542	Clusterino	hdfs://clusterino:8020	0	HADOOP	clusterino:8050	5	NULL	ON
4	65543	SandboxHDP	hdfs://sandbox-hdp.hortonworks.com:8020	0	HADOOP	sandbox-hdp.hortonworks.com...	5	NULL	ON
5	65544	SQLCONTROL	sqlserver://SQLCONTROL	6	NONE	NULL	65537	NULL	ON
6	65546	ClusterinoSpark	odbc://clusterino:10016	6	NONE	NULL	65538	Driver={Hortonworks Spark ODB...	ON
7	65552	NorthCarolinaPopulationExcelTyped	odbc://clusterino	6	NONE	NULL	0	Driver={CData Excel Source}, ...	ON
8	65568	ClusterinoSparkDE	odbc://clusterino:10016	6	NONE	NULL	65538	Driver={Simba Spark ODBC Driv...	ON
9	65575	ClusterinoHive	odbc://clusterino:10000	6	NONE	NULL	65540	Driver={Cloudera ODBC Driver ...	ON
10	65578	NorthCarolinaPopulationExcelUntyped	odbc://noplace	6	NONE	NULL	0	Driver={CData Excel Source}, ...	ON

Figure 10-1. *The external data sources Dynamic Management View*

This DMV returns one row per external data source, including the name we have given each DMV and its location. PolyBase V1 data sources will have a `wasb[s]` or `hdfs` location prefix, and V2 will include something else, such as `mongodb`, `sqlserver`, or `odbc`. The `type` and `type_desc` columns will also help you differentiate between V1 and V2 data sources.

From there, we see the rest of the settings we have chosen throughout this book, including the resource manager (YARN) location, Database Scoped Credentials, connection options for V2 queries, and whether we want to enable predicate pushdown. Note that just because the `pushdown` column is set to "ON" does not mean that predicate pushdown is possible—Azure Blob Storage does not allow predicate pushdown, for example.

External File Formats

The `sys.external_file_formats` DMV includes metadata for each unique file format in your database. Figure 10-2 shows some of the external file formats we have created throughout this book.

	file_format_id	name	format_type	field_terminator	string_delimiter	date_format	use_type_default	serde_method	row_terminator	encoding	data_compression	first_row
1	65538	CsvFileFormat	DELIMITEDTEXT	,	"		1	NULL	\n	UTF8	NULL	NULL
2	65539	OrcFileFormat	ORC	NULL			0	NULL	NULL	NULL	org.apache.hadoop.io.compress...	NULL
3	65540	TsvFileFormat	DELIMITEDTEXT	\t	^		1	NULL	\n	UTF8	NULL	NULL

Figure 10-2. *The external file formats Dynamic Management View*

This view shows each of the most important settings for an external file, be it a delimited file, ORC, or Parquet. Most of the columns pertain to delimited files, including field terminator, string delimiter, date format, row terminator, encoding, and first row (only for Azure Synapse Analytics). The serializer-deserializer (SerDe) method is specific to ORC and Parquet, in the event that we use a different serialization method from the default to load these files. We can also include the data compression format, which is nice for metadata purposes but not required to process gzipped files.

External Tables

The sys.external_tables DMV is considerably wider than the other two DMVs in this set. First, this DMV inherits several columns from sys.objects, including object ID, principal ID, schema ID, parent object ID, type, type description, creation date, modification date, and flags telling us basic internal details around the table, including whether this is a Microsoft-shipped table and the largest column ID used. These fields are quite useful and appear on all tables, not just external tables.

After that block, we get to the PolyBase-specific columns. Figure 10-3 shows a combination of regular table columns plus external table columns.

object_id	name	schema_id	schema_name	type	data_source_id	file_format_id	location	reject_type	reject_value	reject_sample_value
1	1589680701	FireIncidents	1	dbo	U	65542	65540	/PolyBaseData/Fire_Incidents.tsv	VALUE	5000	NULL
2	1061578820	NorthCarolinaPopulation	1	dbo	U	65536	65838	Census/NorthCarolinaPopulation.csv	VALUE	5	NULL
3	2002106173	NorthCarolinaPopulationExcel...	1	dbo	U	65552	0	NorthCarolinaPopulation	NULL	0	NULL
4	342623551	NorthCarolinaPopulationExcel...	1	dbo	U	65576	0	NorthCarolinaPopulation	NULL	0	NULL
5	1618104005	NorthCarolinaPopulationSpark	1	dbo	U	65548	0	NorthCarolinaPopulation	NULL	0	NULL
6	1634104862	NorthCarolinaPopulationTyped...	1	dbo	U	65548	0	NorthCarolinaPopulationTyped	NULL	0	NULL
7	1389578276	ParkingViolations	1	dbo	U	65542	65538	/ PolyBaseData/NYCParkingTickets/	VALUE	5000	NULL
8	1173579219	ParkingViolations2016	1	dbo	U	65542	65538	/ PolyBaseData/NYCParkingTickets/Park...	VALUE	5000	NULL
9	1845381613	ParkingViolationsNum	1	dbo	U	65542	65838	/PolyBaseData/NYCParkingTickets/	VALUE	50000	NULL

Figure 10-3. *Selected columns from the external tables Dynamic Management View*

The useful external table columns include external data source and external file format IDs, allowing us to tie these three tables together. For PolyBase V2 tables, the file format ID will be 0, as we do not use external file formats for these data sources.

Aside from our join criteria, we can learn a few more things from this metadata, including the location where our external data resides as well as properties around rejection. Row rejection is a PolyBase V1–specific concept, so we can see that the value is NULL for V2 tables. This is in line with the fact that we did not specify rejection criteria when creating external tables in Chapters 6 through 8. Finally, the rejected row location column (not included in Figure 10-3) only works for Azure Synapse Analytics and includes the location of the blob where we may find rejected row information. See Chapter 9 for more information on this.

Service and Node Resources

The next batch of DMVs is instance-level DMVs, meaning you can run them and get the same results on any database in the instance. These DMVs provide us important information around compute node and data movement service status.

Compute Nodes

First up is the sys.dm_exec_compute_nodes DMV. This simple DMV returns one row for the head node and one row for each PolyBase compute node, including the server name and port, as well as its IP address. If you have a standalone installation of PolyBase, you will get two rows back: one for the head and one for the local instance's compute node. If you are using a scale-out cluster, you will get back the two rows in a standalone installation as well as one row for each scale-out compute node you have in the cluster. Note that this includes nodes which happen to be offline at the time. Figure 10-4 takes us through the compute node DMV.

	compute_node_id	type	name	address
1	1	HEAD	SQLCONTROL:1433	192.168.100.236
2	1	COMPUTE	SQLCONTROL:1433	192.168.100.236
3	2	COMPUTE	SQLCOMPUTE1:1433	192.168.100.237
4	3	COMPUTE	SQLCOMPUTE2:1433	192.168.100.238

Figure 10-4. *The compute node Dynamic Management View*

Compute Node Status and Errors

The next two Dynamic Management Views give us information regarding the status of each compute node, including high-level measures and errors from each node, respectively.

The sys.dm_exec_compute_node_status DMV connects to each compute node in order to determine if it is available. It retrieves server-level information such as allocated and available memory (in bytes), process and total CPU utilization (in ticks), the last communication time per node, and the latest error to have occurred as well. Figure 10-5 shows an example of some of the columns in this DMV.

	compute_node_id	process_id	process_name	allocated_memory	available_memory	process_cpu_usage	total_cpu_usage
1	1	4236	Engine	607158272	1718181888	0	0
2	1	4216	DMS	607293440	1718194176	0	0
3	2	3840	DMS	586158080	1276952576	0	0
4	3	3888	DMS	602890240	1280618496	0	0

Figure 10-5. *The compute node status Dynamic Management View*

Some of the columns in this DMV were originally intended for Parallel Data
Warehouse and will not show values in the on-premises product. These columns include
process_cpu_usage, total_cpu_usage, and total_elapsed_time.

When it comes to errors, however, we can see the value of all of the columns while
on-premises by querying sys.dm_exec_compute_node_errors. This DMV holds a history
of error messages and is a good place to look when troubleshooting failures on a system.
Figure 10-6 shows an example of the most important compute node error columns.

	error_id	source	type	create_time	compute_node_id	execution_id	details
18	631ff492-c3cc-4935-ab74-f29e...	DMEngine	DistributorInstrumentation:P...	2019-06-18 12:21:46.477	1	QID727	System.Data.SqlClient.SqlException{26:
19	75021a3e-3254-4657-acde-df27...	DMEngine	DistributorInstrumentation:P...	2019-06-18 12:21:46.477	1	QID727	System.Data.SqlClient.SqlException{26:
20	13c77dec-24a4-4710-8812-915f...	DMEngine	DistributorInstrumentation:P...	2019-06-18 12:21:46.477	1	QID727	System.Data.SqlClient.SqlException{26:
21	4079c4c8-7a27-4651-8753-0d6d...	DMEngine	SqlDistributorInstrumentatio...	2019-06-18 12:21:46.477	1	QID727	System.Data.SqlClient.SqlException{39:
22	c3a72184-a0f8-45a7-9626-fcc9...	DMEngine	DistributorInstrumentation:P...	2019-06-18 12:21:46.477	1	QID727	System.Data.SqlClient.SqlException{26:
23	043ef6c7-0977-4278-93ef-7b71...	DMEngine	SqlDistributorInstrumentatio...	2019-06-18 12:21:46.477	1	QID727	System.Data.SqlClient.SqlException{26:
24	c46e3255-ecb5-46bb-b4a7-e91f...	DMEngine	SqlDistributorInstrumentatio...	2019-06-18 12:21:46.463	1	QID727	System.Data.SqlClient.SqlException{26:
25	02c4d3ff-ddc3-4916-aa01-961b...	DMEngine	SqlDistributorInstrumentatio...	2019-06-18 12:21:46.463	1	QID727	System.Data.SqlClient.SqlException{26:
26	7aa18c1c-42c0-4da7-8189-9f4d...	DMEngine	SqlDistributorInstrumentatio...	2019-06-18 12:21:46.463	1	QID727	System.Data.SqlClient.SqlException{26:
27	b6292463-ea19-4258-a8a3-9b81...	Dms	ControlChannel:ErrorEvent	2019-05-31 09:18:51.247	2	NULL	System.IO.IOException: Unable to read
28	aeeab218-2a1f-458e-84d7-d7b8...	Dms	CreditFeedbackReceiver:Error...	2019-05-31 09:18:51.247	2	NULL	System.IO.IOException: Unable to read
29	323662ee-04ca-418a-b782-4f64...	Dms	DataChannelReceiver:ErrorEve...	2019-05-31 09:18:51.233	2	NULL	System.IO.IOException: Unable to read

Figure 10-6. *The compute node errors Dynamic Management View*

Unlike other Dynamic Management Views, the ID column on this DMV is a Guid;
that way, we can easily combine errors from multiple compute nodes. The remaining
columns give us some flavor of what is happening, including the source of the error (the
PolyBase Engine or Data Movement Service), the type of error returned, the compute
node responsible for the error, an execution ID if this happened during a user query, and
some details covering the error itself. We can combine this with the tools and techniques
in Chapter 5 to diagnose PolyBase issues.

In addition to its unique ID data type, the data in sys.dm_exec_compute_node_
errors will persist even after we restart the SQL Server services. Most Dynamic
Management Views—for example, wait stat measures—reset when the database engine
restarts, but compute node errors will stick around.

Data Movement Service Views

There are two views which help us diagnose issues with the PolyBase Data Movement Service. The first of these is sys.dm_exec_dms_services. This view returns one row per compute node—including one row for the head instance's compute node—and the status for each of these nodes. Figure 10-7 shows the output of this DMV.

	dms_core_id	compute_node_id	status
1	1	1	Ready
2	2	2	Ready
3	3	3	Ready

Figure 10-7. *The Data Movement Service Dynamic Management View*

We also have the ability to see the outputs of data movement service operations using the sys.dm_exec_dms_workers DMV. This gives us one row for each execution ID and execution step and includes performance measures, including bytes and rows, total elapsed time, CPU utilization time, and more. Figure 10-8 shows a sample of some of the DMS worker columns.

	execution_id	step_index	compute_node_id	bytes_per_sec	bytes_processed	rows_processed	total_elapsed_time	cpu_time	query_time
1	QID643	3	1	14970	936	4	93	312500	31
2	QID646	3	1	3180000	3108	4	31	0	0
3	QID739	3	1	417702903	32634000	3528	93	468750	0
4	QID649	3	1	296957673	32477548	3502	125	156250	0
5	QID742	3	1	9406	294	3	62	156250	16
6	QID745	3	1	294000	294	3	46	0	0
7	QID748	3	1	27508667	859398	35	46	0	16
8	QID652	3	1	519573431	32477548	3502	78	312500	16
9	QID655	3	1	4817171	75276	9	46	156250	0

Figure 10-8. *The Data Movement Service workers Dynamic Management View*

To clear up potential confusion, the total elapsed time and query time values are in milliseconds, whereas CPU time is in ticks, where 10,000 ticks add up to a millisecond. Therefore, to get a clearer measure across the board, we want to divide the CPU time column by 10,000 to get a better picture of just how much CPU time we are actually using in relation to total elapsed time.

In addition to these measures, we are also able to see the source SQL query for these operations, as well as the error ID if an operation fails. Unlike the compute node errors DMV, the DMS workers Dynamic Management View resets every time you restart the PolyBase engine service.

Resources for Troubleshooting Queries

The final five Dynamic Management Views help us learn more about the SQL queries users run on our instances. Like the server and node resource DMVs we just looked at, these are all instance-level DMVs, meaning we will get the same results when running in any database. These views break down into two types, based on their names: external work and distributed requests. The external work results reset each time we restart the PolyBase engine, whereas the distributed requests DMVs persist even after service restarts.

External Work

First up in our set of views is sys.dm_exec_external_work. This Dynamic Management View returns one row for each of the last 1000 PolyBase queries we have run since the last time the PolyBase engine started, as well as any active queries currently running. Figure 10-9 shows an example of this DMV in action.

	execution_id	step_index	dms_step_index	type	input_name	read_location	read_command	bytes_processed
1	QID2148	6	4	ODBC Data Split	sqlserver://sqlcontrol/Scrat...	NULL	SELECT "PersonID","FirstName...	972
2	QID2153	5	0	File Split	/Census/NorthCarolinaPopulat...	0	NULL	729253
3	QID2179	5	0	File Split	/Census/NorthCarolinaPopulat...	0	NULL	729253
4	QID2184	5	0	File Split	/Census/NorthCarolinaPopulat...	0	NULL	729253

Figure 10-9. *The external work Dynamic Management View*

This DMV contains information on the current status of each execution, including the latest step for each compute node and Data Movement Service step. We can see the type of operation, which is "File Split" for PolyBase V1 queries and "ODBC Data Split" for PolyBase V2 queries. The input name tells us which file, folder, or table we are reading—for the SQL Server example on the first line, the input name is sqlserver://sqlcontrol/PolyBaseRevealed.dbo.Person. If we are reading from a file, the read_location field gives us the starting offset from 0 bytes. In the three cases in Figure 10-9, we read the file starting from the beginning. We can see the actual ODBC command next in the read_command column, which is a new field for SQL Server 2019. Finally, there are some columns containing top-level metrics, including bytes processed, file length (when reading files), start and end dates, the total elapsed time in milliseconds, and the status of each request. This status will be one of the following values: Pending, Processing, Done, Failed, or Aborted.

External Operations

If you perform a predicate pushdown operation against a Hadoop cluster, the sys. dm_exec_external_operations Dynamic Management View will give you a rundown of these pushdown operations. Figure 10-10 shows an example of a pushdown MapReduce job which failed—we can see that the map and reduce progress values are both at 0%.

	execution_id	step_index	operation_type	operation_name	map_progress	reduce_progress
1	QID2260	1	External Hadoop Operation	job_1560175666474_0001	0	0

Figure 10-10. *The external operations Dynamic Management View*

This Dynamic Management View pairs well with the next view, distributed requests.

Distributed Requests

The sys.dm_exec_distributed_requests view returns one line per distributed operation. It provides us with one extremely helpful piece of information: a SQL handle, which we can use to return query text or an execution plan for our PolyBase queries. Figure 10-11 shows several rows from this table, including QID2260, which failed in the prior figure.

	sql_handle	execution_id	status	error_id	start_time	end_time	total_elapsed_time
1.	NULL	QID2259	Completed	NULL	2019-06-10 15:38:12.887	2019-06-10 15:38:12.887	0
1.	0x0200000095118016D8F50B26AB...	QID2260	Failed	e1d48976-509a-4bb1-9488-0884f1e4621c	2019-06-10 15:38:12.927	2019-06-10 15:38:22.283	9338
1.	NULL	QID2261	Completed	NULL	2019-06-10 15:38:14.820	2019-06-10 15:38:14.828	8
2.	NULL	QID2262	Completed	NULL	2019-06-10 15:38:14.830	2019-06-10 15:38:14.830	0

Figure 10-11. *The distributed requests Dynamic Management View*

Taking the plan handle from our distributed requests view, we can derive the base query using the sys.dm_exec_sql_text() Dynamic Management Function, as in Listing 10-1. This will return basic statistics as well as the query text wherever we have query text.

Listing 10-1. Query the distributed results DMV and tie each execution to a specific SQL query

```
SELECT
    r.execution_id,
    r.status,
    r.error_id,
    r.start_time,
    r.end_time,
    r.total_elapsed_time,
    t.text
FROM sys.dm_exec_distributed_requests r
    CROSS APPLY sys.dm_exec_sql_text(r.sql_handle) t
ORDER BY
    r.end_time DESC;
```

Distributed Request Steps

The sys.dm_exec_distributed_request_steps view returns one row per execution ID and step. It is particularly useful when you already know an execution ID and want to understand what happened at each step along the way. Figure 10-12 gives us a glimpse at some of the most important columns here.

	execution_id	step_index	operation_type	distribution_type	location_type	status	total_elapsed_time	row_count	command
1	QID2148	0	RandomIDOperation	Unspecified	Head	Complete	0	-1	TEMP_ID_2
2	QID2148	1	OnOperation	AllDistributions	Compute	Complete	156	-1	CREATE TABLE [tempdb].[dbo]...
3	QID2148	2	OnOperation	AllDistributions	Compute	Complete	0	-1	EXEC [tempdb].[sys].[sp_adde...
4	QID2148	3	OnOperation	AllDistributions	Compute	Complete	15	-1	UPDATE STATISTICS [tempdb].[...
5	QID2148	4	OnOperation	AllDistributions	Compute	Complete	16	-1	CREATE STATISTICS [PersonID]...
6	QID2148	5	MultiStreamOperation	Unspecified	Head	Complete	233	-1	NULL
7	QID2148	6	ExternalGenericRoundRobinOpe...	Unspecified	DMS	Complete	238	3	SELECT [T1_1].[PersonID] AS ...
8	QID2148	7	StreamingReturnOperation	Unspecified	DMS	Complete	68	3	SELECT [T1_1].[PersonID] AS ...
9	QID2148	8	OnOperation	AllDistributions	Compute	Complete	15	-1	DROP TABLE [tempdb].[dbo].[T...

Figure 10-12. *The distributed request steps Dynamic Management View*

We will cover the specific execution steps later in this chapter; for now, we can see that each step is an operation which occurs on a location and may have a distribution. We can see the total elapsed time, number of rows returned, and even a version of the SQL run in each step.

Distributed SQL Requests

The sys.dm_exec_distributed_sql_requests Dynamic Management View is our final DMV of note. It contains one row per SQL-related step on each compute node and for each distribution. Figure 10-13 shows an example of this for execution ID QID2148.

	execution_id	step_index	compute_node_id	distribution_id	status	total_elapsed_time	row_count	spid	command
1	QID2148	1	1	1	Complete	15	-1	141	CREATE TABLE [tempdb].[dbo].[QTa
2	QID2148	1	1	2	Complete	15	-1	143	CREATE TABLE [tempdb].[dbo].[QTa
3	QID2148	1	1	5	Complete	15	-1	142	CREATE TABLE [tempdb].[dbo].[QTa
4	QID2148	1	1	4	Complete	15	-1	148	CREATE TABLE [tempdb].[dbo].[QTa
5	QID2148	1	1	5	Complete	15	-1	149	CREATE TABLE [tempdb].[dbo].[QTa
6	QID2148	1	1	6	Complete	0	-1	146	CREATE TABLE [tempdb].[dbo].[QTa
7	QID2148	1	1	7	Complete	15	-1	147	CREATE TABLE [tempdb].[dbo].[QTa
8	QID2148	1	1	8	Complete	15	-1	144	CREATE TABLE [tempdb].[dbo].[QTa
9	QID2148	2	1	1	Complete	0	3	152	EXEC [tempdb].[sys].[sp_addexter
10	QID2148	2	1	2	Complete	0	1	153	EXEC [tempdb].[sys].[sp_addexter

Figure 10-13. *The distributed SQL requests Dynamic Management View*

This view makes clear the distributed nature of PolyBase: each distributed request step has eight separate SPIDs running on a single compute node. As with the distributed request steps DMV, we will look at this DMV in some greater detail next.

Understanding PolyBase Queries Through Dynamic Management Views

With our review of the 13 Dynamic Management Views complete, we can now walk through several scenarios and review DMV metadata as a way of understanding what, exactly, is going on with each query. We will start with the PolyBase V1 query types and then move to a selection of PolyBase V2 types.

Blob Storage

Our first candidate is a simple Azure Blob Storage query which reads from dbo. NorthCarolinaPopulation. Listing 10-2 shows our sample code, which returns ten results.

Listing 10-2. Population estimates by year for North Carolina

```
SELECT
    p.PopulationType,
    p.Year,
    SUM(p.Population) AS Population
FROM dbo.NorthCarolinaPopulation p
GROUP BY
    p.PopulationType,
    p.Year
ORDER BY
    p.Year DESC,
    p.PopulationType ASC;
```

After running this query, we can review `sys.dm_exec_external_work` to find our operation, which we see in Figure 10-14.

	execution_id	input_name	read_command	status
1	QID2349	/Census/NorthCarolinaPopulation.csv	NULL	Done
2	QID2346	/Census/NorthCarolinaPopulation.csv	NULL	Done
3	QID2232	/PolyBaseData/NYCParkingTicketsORC/000002_0	NULL	Done
4	QID2232	/PolyBaseData/NYCParkingTicketsORC/000000_0	NULL	Done

Figure 10-14. *Using the external work DMV, we can find our query execution ID*

With this ID in hand, we can analyze our request and its request steps. Figure 10-15 shows the combination of these, and you can follow along using script `04 - Sample Queries.sql` in the accompanying code repository.

	sql_handle	execution_id	status	error_id	start_time	end_time	total_elapsed_time
1	0x0200000025BFE6075DD2344A5B...	QID2349	Completed	NULL	2019-06-10 19:18:52.813	2019-06-10 19:18:53.733	919

	execution_id	step_index	operation_type	distribution_type	location_type	total_elapsed_time	row_count	command
1	QID2349	0	RandomIDOperation	Unspecified	Head	0	-1	TEMP_ID_73
2	QID2349	1	OnOperation	AllDistributions	Compute	33	-1	CREATE TABLE [tempdb].[dbo].[TEMP_ID_7:
3	QID2349	2	OnOperation	AllDistributions	Compute	1	-1	EXEC [tempdb].[sys].[sp_addextendedpro(
4	QID2349	3	OnOperation	AllDistributions	Compute	15	-1	UPDATE STATISTICS [tempdb].[dbo].[TEMP_
5	QID2349	4	MultiStreamOperation	Unspecified	Head	848	-1	NULL
6	QID2349	5	HadoopShuffleOperation	Unspecified	DMS	845	13607	SELECT [T1_1].[PopulationType] AS [Popu
7	QID2349	6	StreamingReturnOperation	Unspecified	DMS	804	18	SELECT [T1_1].[PopulationType] AS [Popu
8	QID2349	7	OnOperation	AllDistributions	Compute	12	-1	DROP TABLE [tempdb].[dbo].[TEMP_ID_73]

Figure 10-15. *Request and request step information for a Blob Storage query. The full script is available in the demo code*

Overall, this query took 919 milliseconds to complete, and it went through eight separate steps. The first step creates the name of our temp table, TEMP_ID_73. This appears to be an incrementing value, and the operation runs on the head node.

The second step has us create a temporary table on each compute node named TEMP_ID_73. The shape of this table is the set of columns that we will need for our query: population type, year, and population. After that, the third step adds an extended property named IS_EXTERNAL_STREAMING_TABLE to each of the temp tables, presumably to make it easier to track which temp tables are used for loading external data. Finally, step 4 runs a statistics update, updating statistics and telling SQL Server that we expect the temp table will have 566 rows.

Our fifth step (i.e., step index 4) runs on the head node once more and is a MultiStreamOperation. There is no official documentation on this step, but it takes up 848 of the 919 total milliseconds of elapsed time and appears to be the operation which causes our compute nodes to do work.

From there, we see a HadoopShuffleOperation on the Data Movement Service. This returns all 13,607 rows in the population table. We can see from the cleaned-up query in Listing 10-3 that this is a simple query of all rows from our population table.

Listing 10-3. The command our HadoopShuffleOperation runs

```
SELECT
    [T1_1].[PopulationType] AS [PopulationType],
    [T1_1].[Year] AS [Year],
    [T1_1].[Population] AS [Population]
FROM [PolyBaseRevealed].[dbo].[NorthCarolinaPopulation] AS T1_1
```

While we shuffle data across our compute nodes' Data Movement Services, the next step runs, a `StreamingReturnOperation`. We can tell these are running concurrently because the shuffle operation takes 845 milliseconds and the streaming return operation 804 milliseconds, yet our entire query finished in under a second. This streaming query, which again runs on each of the compute nodes, queries TEMP_ID_73 and performs the aggregation we requested. Of interest is the fact that this query does not follow exactly the same shape as what we sent the database engine. Listing 10-4 shows a cleaned-up version of this query.

Listing 10-4. A roundabout way of aggregating data

```
SELECT
    [T1_1].[PopulationType] AS [PopulationType],
    [T1_1].[Year] AS [Year],
    [T1_1].[col] AS [col]
FROM (
    SELECT
        SUM([T2_1].[col]) AS [col],
        [T2_1].[PopulationType] AS [PopulationType],
        [T2_1].[Year] AS [Year]
    FROM (
        SELECT
            SUM([T3_1].[Population]) AS [col],
            [T3_1].[PopulationType] AS [PopulationType],
            [T3_1].[Year] AS [Year]
        FROM [tempdb].[dbo].[TEMP_ID_73] AS T3_1
        GROUP BY
            [T3_1].[PopulationType],
            [T3_1].[Year]
    ) AS T2_1
    GROUP BY
        [T2_1].[PopulationType],
        [T2_1].[Year]
) AS T1_1
```

We get back ten rows, which is exactly the number of rows in our result set. Finally, each compute node drops any copies of TEMP_ID_73 as we close up shop on this query.

One thing to note is that these operations are not guaranteed to appear in the same way for every query—for example, there are different DMS operations like `HadoopShuffleOperation`, `HadoopBroadCastOperation`, and `HadoopRoundRobinOperation` available to the Data Movement Service.

Hadoop with Predicate Pushdown

Moving on to our next operation, let us take a look at a MapReduce job using predicate pushdown. In this query, we will look at the number of violations by vehicle year, as in Listing 10-5.

Listing 10-5. Performing a MapReduce job to count violations by vehicle year

```
SELECT
    pv.VehicleYear,
    COUNT(*) AS NumberOfViolations
FROM dbo.ParkingViolations pv
GROUP BY
    pv.VehicleYear
ORDER BY
    pv.VehicleYear DESC
OPTION (FORCE EXTERNALPUSHDOWN);
```

Just as before, we can query the external work DMV to figure out the right execution ID. In this case, Figure 10-16 shows us that there are seven rows covering our latest query.

	execution_id	input_name	read_command	status
1	QID2413	/user/pdw_user/TEMP_DIR/e6a819664b9e49898d7493bddbc10514/Output/part-m-00001.ppax	NULL	Done
2	QID2413	/user/pdw_user/TEMP_DIR/e6a819664b9e49898d7493bddbc10514/Output/part-m-00006.ppax	NULL	Done
3	QID2413	/user/pdw_user/TEMP_DIR/e6a819664b9e49898d7493bddbc10514/Output/part-m-00002.ppax	NULL	Done
4	QID2413	/user/pdw_user/TEMP_DIR/e6a819664b9e49898d7493bddbc10514/Output/part-m-00003.ppax	NULL	Done
5	QID2413	/user/pdw_user/TEMP_DIR/e6a819664b9e49898d7493bddbc10514/Output/part-m-00005.ppax	NULL	Done
6	QID2413	/user/pdw_user/TEMP_DIR/e6a819664b9e49898d7493bddbc10514/Output/part-m-00000.ppax	NULL	Done
7	QID2413	/user/pdw_user/TEMP_DIR/e6a819664b9e49898d7493bddbc10514/Output/part-m-00004.ppax	NULL	Done

Figure 10-16. *This MapReduce job created seven files*

Each of these files is in PPAX format, a proprietary binary format Microsoft uses to move data from MapReduce jobs back to PolyBase. We can also see that the execution ID is QID2413, so away we go. The first stop on this journey is the external operations DMV, where we can learn that our Map operations succeeded and we had no Reduce operations. Figure 10-17 shows those results.

	execution_id	step_index	operation_type	operation_name	map_progress	reduce_progress
1	QID2413	1	External Hadoop Operation	job_1560175666474_0006	1	0

Figure 10-17. *Mapping is complete, but no Reduce operations occurred*

We can confirm this by looking at the MapReduce job history UI on the Hadoop cluster, which is `http://clusterino:19888/jobhistory/` for me. Figure 10-18 shows this output.

									Search:
Name ⬍	User ⬍	Queue ⬍	State ⬍	Maps Total ⬍	Maps Completed ⬍	Reduces Total ⬍	Reduces Completed ⬍	Elapsed Time ⬍
Polybase e6a819664b9e49898d7493bddbc10514	pdw_user	default	SUCCEEDED	7	7	0	0	00hrs, 00mins, 28sec
Name	User	Queue	State	Maps	Maps Comp	Reduces	Reduces Cc	Elapsed

First   Previous   1   Next   Last

Figure 10-18. *Seven Map operations and zero Reduce operations*

When reviewing the distributed request and distributed request steps, we can see in Figure 10-19 that this was a mildly more complicated operation.

	sql_handle	execution_id	status	error_id	start_time	end_time	total_elapsed_time
1	0x02000000b6571881408907178...	QID2413	Completed	NULL	2019-06-18 78:35:24.940	2019-06-18 28:36:05.387	40656

	execution_id	step_index	operation_type	distribution_type	location_type	total_elapsed_time	row_count	command
1	QID2413	0	RandomIDOperation	Unspecified	Head	0	-1	TEMP_ID_2
2	QID2413	1	HadoopJobOperation	Unspecified	Head	37807	-1	NULL
3	QID2413	2	RandomIDOperation	Unspecified	Head	0	-1	TEMP_ID_3
4	QID2413	3	OnOperation	AllDistributions	Compute	389	-1	CREATE TABLE [tempdb].[dbo].[TEMP_ID_3] [VehicleYear] VARCHAR(50) COLLATE SQL_Latin1_General_C...
5	QID2413	4	OnOperation	AllDistributions	Compute	35	-1	EXEC [tempdb].[sys].[sp_addextendedproperty] @name=N'IS_EXTERNAL_STREAMING_TABLE', @value=N'tru...
6	QID2413	5	OnOperation	AllDistributions	Compute	15	-1	UPDATE STATISTICS [tempdb].[dbo].[TEMP_ID_3] WITH ROWCOUNT = 400, PAGECOUNT = 2
7	QID2413	6	OnOperation	AllDistributions	Compute	0	-1	CREATE STATISTICS [partialagg1003] ON [tempdb].[dbo].[TEMP_ID_3] [[partialagg1003]] WITH STATS_...
8	QID2413	7	MultiStreamOperation	Unspecified	Head	2298	-1	NULL
9	QID2413	8	HadoopShuffleOperation	Unspecified	DMS	2234	400	HDFS Import - External Shuffle
10	QID2413	9	StreamingReturnOperation	Unspecified	DMS	1902	182	SELECT [T1_1].[VehicleYear] AS [VehicleYear], [T1_1].[col] AS [col] FROM [SELECT COMPAR...
11	QID2413	10	OnOperation	AllDistributions	Compute	35	-1	DROP TABLE [tempdb].[dbo].[TEMP_ID_3]

Figure 10-19. *The distributed request steps in order*

The shape of this operation has some similarities to our Blob Storage query but a few differences as well. The first step is the same: generate a new temp table name. We then begin a Hadoop job operation on the head node which lasts 37.8 of our 40.7 seconds. This starts the MapReduce process. You can see in Figure 10-18 that the job itself took 28 seconds of that time. While this happened, the RandomIDOperation struck again, generating a new temp table, TEMP_ID_3. The compute nodes use this name to generate a temp table, add an extended property, and update statistics just like the Blob Storage scenario. From there, we see one additional operation: creating statistics on a column called partialagg1003, something we did not see the first time around.

Once the MapReduce job has finished, the head node recognizes this and executes a MultiStreamOperation to inform the compute nodes that they have work to do, specifically a HadoopShuffleOperation to bring in the data from those PPAX files and then a StreamingReturnOperation to retrieve aggregated data from our temp table. Listing 10-6 is a cleaned-up version of this query.

Listing 10-6. The query used to retrieve our results from TEMP_ID_3 tables

```
SELECT
    [T1_1].[VehicleYear] AS [VehicleYear],
    [T1_1].[col] AS [col]
FROM (
    SELECT
        CONVERT (INT, [T2_1].[col], 0) AS [col],
        [T2_1].[VehicleYear] AS [VehicleYear]
    FROM (
        SELECT
            ISNULL([T3_1].[col], CONVERT (BIGINT, 0, 0)) AS [col],
            [T3_1].[VehicleYear] AS [VehicleYear]
        FROM (
            SELECT
                SUM([T4_1].[partialagg1003]) AS [col],
                [T4_1].[VehicleYear] AS [VehicleYear]
            FROM [tempdb].[dbo].[TEMP_ID_3] AS T4_1
            GROUP BY [T4_1].[VehicleYear]
        ) AS T3_1
    ) AS T2_1
) AS T1_1
```

Right at the bottom of this mess is our `partialagg1003` column, which represents a partially aggregated value. In this case, our partial aggregate is in fact the full aggregate, but in more complicated queries, we can see a MapReduce job send us a partial aggregation of data and then perform further aggregation on the SQL Server side, especially non-external table columns are part of our final `GROUP BY` clause.

Finally, we want to be kind and drop `TEMP_ID_3`.

SQL Server

The first PolyBase V2 query we will review will connect to another SQL Server instance. In Listing 10-7, we will connect to the `SQLCONTROL` instance and query parking violations.

Listing 10-7. Query parking violations data from another SQL Server instance

```
SELECT
    pv.FeetFromCurb,
    COUNT(*) AS NumberOfViolations
FROM dbo.ParkingViolationsSQLControl pv
GROUP BY
    pv.FeetFromCurb
ORDER BY
    pv.FeetFromCurb DESC;
```

One immediate difference from the prior entries is evident in Figure 10-20, where we see the `read_command` column on our external work DMV return something other than NULL.

	execution_id	input_name	read_command	status
1	QID2437	sqlserver://sqlcontrol/Scrat...	SELECT [T1_1].[FeetFromCurb] AS [FeetFromCurb], ...	Done
2	QID2413	/user/pdw_user/TEMP_DIR/e6a8...	NULL	Done
3	QID2413	/user/pdw_user/TEMP_DIR/e6a8...	NULL	Done
4	QID2413	/user/pdw_user/TEMP_DIR/e6a8...	NULL	Done
5	QID2413	/user/pdw_user/TEMP_DIR/e6a8...	NULL	Done
6	QID2413	/user/pdw_user/TEMP_DIR/e6a8...	NULL	Done
7	QID2413	/user/pdw_user/TEMP_DIR/e6a8...	NULL	Done
8	QID2413	/user/pdw_user/TEMP_DIR/e6a8...	NULL	Done

Figure 10-20. *The external work DMV has a new column for PolyBase V2*

The other difference comes in Figure 10-21, where we see that there is a new operation type: the ExternalGenericShuffleOperation. We no longer see Hadoop-related operations, which gives us further confirmation that we are no longer in the PolyBase V1 world.

	sql_handle	execution_id	status	error_id	start_time	end_time	total_elapsed_time
1	0x020000003157722C857720246...	QID2437	Completed	NULL	2019-06-11 22:32:18.417	2019-06-11 22:32:37.047	18629

	execution_id	step_index	operation_type	distribution_type	location_type	total_elapsed_time	row_count	command
1	QID2437	0	RandomIDOperation	Unspecified	Head	0	-1	TEMP_ID_11
2	QID2437	1	OnOperation	AllDistributions	Compute	48	-1	CREATE TABLE [tempdb].[dbo].[TEMP_ID_11] (
3	QID2437	2	OnOperation	AllDistributions	Compute	6	-1	EXEC [tempdb].[sys].[sp_addextendedproperti
4	QID2437	3	OnOperation	AllDistributions	Compute	7	-1	UPDATE STATISTICS [tempdb].[dbo].[TEMP_ID_
5	QID2437	4	OnOperation	AllDistributions	Compute	7	-1	CREATE STATISTICS [partialage1002] ON [tem
6	QID2437	5	MultiStreamOperation	Unspecified	Head	18566	-1	NULL
7	QID2437	6	ExternalGenericShuffleOperation	Unspecified	DMS	18563	53	External Shuffle
8	QID2437	7	StreamingReturnOperation	Unspecified	DMS	18501	53	SELECT [T1_1].[FeetFromCurb] AS [FeetFromC
9	QID2437	8	OnOperation	AllDistributions	Compute	1	-1	DROP TABLE [tempdb].[dbo].[TEMP_ID_11]

Figure 10-21. *The steps for a SQL Server to SQL Server PolyBase query*

Cosmos DB

Our next destination is Cosmos DB, where we will perform a simple SELECT * from the Volcano table. Figure 10-22 shows us the external work results, giving us a new execution ID and combination of input name and read command.

	execution_id	input_name	read_command	status
1	QID2454	mongodb://cspolybase.documents.azure.com:10255/PolyBaseTest.Volcano	SELECT "Volcano"."_id" AS "_id", "Volcano...	Done
2	QID2437	sqlserver://sqlcontrol/Scratch.dbo.ParkingViolationsLocal	SELECT [T1_1].[FeetFromCurb] AS [FeetFrom...	Done
3	QID2413	/user/pdw_user/TEMP_DIR/e6a819664b9e49898d7493bddbc10514/Output/par...	NULL	Done
4	QID2413	/user/pdw_user/TEMP_DIR/e6a819664b9e49898d7493bddbc10514/Output/par...	NULL	Done
5	QID2413	/user/pdw_user/TEMP_DIR/e6a819664b9e49898d7493bddbc10514/Output/par...	NULL	Done
6	QID2413	/user/pdw_user/TEMP_DIR/e6a819664b9e49898d7493bddbc10514/Output/par...	NULL	Done
7	QID2413	/user/pdw_user/TEMP_DIR/e6a819664b9e49898d7493bddbc10514/Output/par...	NULL	Done
8	QID2413	/user/pdw_user/TEMP_DIR/e6a819664b9e49898d7493bddbc10514/Output/par...	NULL	Done
9	QID2413	/user/pdw_user/TEMP_DIR/e6a819664b9e49898d7493bddbc10514/Output/par...	NULL	Done

Figure 10-22. *The external work DMV results for a Cosmos DB query*

Figure 10-23 shows us the request steps. Once more, there is a new external operator: ExternalGenericRoundRobinOperation. This operator is the PolyBase V2 version of the Hadoop round robin operator. Otherwise, the flow is the same: the head node creates a new temp table ID, the compute nodes generate these temp tables, the head node rounds up the posse, the data movers query our external data source (this time using a round robin approach) and stream back data, and everybody cleans up and goes home at the end of the shift.

	sql_handle	execution_id	status	error_id	start_time	end_time	total_elapsed_time
1	0x0290000018C6373370EF1E116A6...	QID2454	Completed	NULL	2019-06-11 22:51:19.060	2019-06-11 22:51:21.513	2432

	execution_id	step_index	operation_type	distribution_type	location_type	total_elapsed_time	row_count	command
1	QID2454	0	RandomIDOperation	Unspecified	Head	0	-1	TEMP_ID_15
2	QID2454	1	OnOperation	AllDistributions	Compute	18	-1	CREATE TABLE [tempdb].[dbo].[T...
3	QID2454	2	OnOperation	AllDistributions	Compute	15	-1	EXEC [tempdb].[sys].[sp_addext...
4	QID2454	3	OnOperation	AllDistributions	Compute	0	-1	UPDATE STATISTICS [tempdb].[db...
5	QID2454	4	MultiStreamOperation	Unspecified	Head	2381	-1	NULL
6	QID2454	5	ExternalGenericRoundRobinOperation	Unspecified	DMS	2324	3144	SELECT [T1_1].[_id] AS [_id],
7	QID2454	6	StreamingReturnOperation	Unspecified	DMS	2334	3144	SELECT [T1_1].[_id] AS [_id],
8	QID2454	7	OnOperation	AllDistributions	Compute	14	-1	DROP TABLE [tempdb].[dbo].[TEM...

Figure 10-23. *Reviewing the request steps for a query against Cosmos DB*

Spark

Our final example in this chapter includes a query against a Spark table using a separate ODBC driver. Our query this time will be the same as Listing 10-7, except querying the dbo.ParkingViolationsSpark table instead of a SQL Server–based table. Figure 10-24 shows what is by now a familiar sight: the external work results.

	execution_id	input_name	read_command	status
1	QID2466	odbc://clusterino:10016/NYCParkingTickets	SELECT `T_1`.`feetfromcurb` `feetfromcurb`, `partialagg1003` ...	Done
2	QID2454	mongodb://cspolybase.documents.azure.com:10...	SELECT "Volcano"."_id" AS "_id", "Volcano"."VolcanoName" AS "Vo...	Done
3	QID2437	sqlserver://sqlcontrol/Scratch.dbo.ParkingV...	SELECT [T1_1].[FeetFromCurb] AS [FeetFromCurb], [T1_1].[...	Done
4	QID2413	/user/pdw_user/TEMP_DIR/e6a819664b9e49898d7...	NULL	Done
5	QID2413	/user/pdw_user/TEMP_DIR/e6a819664b9e49898d7...	NULL	Done
6	QID2413	/user/pdw_user/TEMP_DIR/e6a819664b9e49898d7...	NULL	Done
7	QID2413	/user/pdw_user/TEMP_DIR/e6a819664b9e49898d7...	NULL	Done
8	QID2413	/user/pdw_user/TEMP_DIR/e6a819664b9e49898d7...	NULL	Done
9	QID2413	/user/pdw_user/TEMP_DIR/e6a819664b9e49898d7...	NULL	Done
10	QID2413	/user/pdw_user/TEMP_DIR/e6a819664b9e49898d7...	NULL	Done

Figure 10-24. *The external work DMV results for a Spark query*

Also familiar is the output from the distributed request steps DMV: it is the same set of operations as in Figure 10-21, down to using the same external generic shuffle operator. This makes sense, considering that we are requesting exactly the same data in exactly the same way, with the only difference being the data source.

Conclusion

In this chapter, we dove into the PolyBase-specific Dynamic Management Views. After learning the general utility of Dynamic Management Views, we looked at 13 separate DMVs which relate in some fashion to PolyBase. We wrapped up the chapter with a review of five different queries from five different external data sources to understand how the external work, distributed requests, and distributed request steps DMVs display valuable information to help us troubleshoot issues.

In the next chapter, we will look at another tool in the performance tuning arsenal: execution plans.

CHAPTER 11

Query Tuning with Statistics and Execution Plans

There are two key tools for tuning PolyBase queries from within SQL Server: statistics and execution plans. In this chapter, we will see how statistics on external tables can allow SQL Server's query optimizer to make better decisions regarding predicate pushdown and join order. Then, we will dig into execution plans, which will provide us information critical for optimizing query performance.

Statistics in SQL Server

SQL Server's query optimizer makes use of statistics to gain information on the distribution of data for a column or set of columns on a table without needing to scan the entire table. Based on the distribution of data, the optimizer can make an educated guess regarding the best method of retrieving data from the table as well as the order in which to query tables. For example, looking at our data set of 33 million New York City parking tickets, we would like to pull back all records where the ticketed cars had Ohio plates. Intuitively, we would expect that to be some percentage of the 33 million rows—possibly even a small percentage—but with no additional information, we can do little more than make a rough guess. We might assume that vehicle state follows a uniform distribution, meaning that there will be approximately equal numbers of vehicles from Ohio as from any other state. This pushes the problem back one step: now we need to get an idea of how many unique states there are. We, as humans, know that there are 50 states in the United States, so if we assume that any non-US tags are statistical noise, we can now assume that Ohio will have one-fiftieth of the 33 million rows, or approximately 660,000 rows.

K. Feasel, *PolyBase Revealed*, https://doi.org/10.1007/978-1-4842-5461-5_11

We can go further, however. If we could just scan the data one time, getting counts of records by vehicle state, we could change our model from a uniform distribution to a more accurate distribution of data. Performing a simple query like the one in Listing 11-1 will return the total number of entries per vehicle state.

Listing 11-1. Retrieve the count of parking violations by registration state. This uses the parking violations data set directly from SQL Server to make the query faster, but the result would be the same regardless of where this data lived

```
USE PolyBaseRevealed
GO
SELECT
    p.RegistrationState,
    COUNT(*) AS NumberOfEntries
FROM dbo.ParkingViolationsLocal p
GROUP BY
    p.RegistrationState
ORDER BY
    p.RegistrationState;
```

We can see some of the results in Figure 11-1.

	RegistrationState	NumberOfEntries
1...	NF	18
1...	NH	28703
1...	NJ	2975173
1...	NM	9329
1...	NS	2964
1...	NT	12
1...	NV	6761
1...	NY	25934477
1...	OH	76733
1...	OK	63422
1...	ON	17346

Figure 11-1. *Parking violations by registration state*

This figure conclusively proves that a uniform distribution is the wrong choice: New York state is responsible for 26 of 33 million results, whereas Ohio is responsible for only 77,000. This is a tenth of what we originally estimated. Furthermore, if we picked a state like New Mexico or Nevada, we would be off by a factor of 100. Being off like this can lead to the optimizer making poor choices in whether to scan or seek for this data, whether to pull from this table first or wait until other joins have happened first, and what sort of physical join operator to use when retrieving this data. Statistics help the optimizer pick the most appropriate choices given the distribution and density of our data.

With all of these decisions in mind, it makes sense to arm SQL Server with the best information you can give it and that means creating statistics on columns. Whenever you create a nonclustered index on a table, SQL Server automatically creates statistics on that index. You can manually create statistics on one or more columns as well, even if you do not want to create and maintain an index on these columns. Furthermore, if you have auto-create statistics turned on at the database level, SQL Server will create new statistics whenever you query the table with a single-column predicate and there are no statistics for that column—whether due to an index, custom statistics, or prior auto-created statistics.

Maintaining statistics is also important. As the distribution of data changes, current statistics become outdated and less accurate. In our registration state example, suppose a slew of Ohio-tagged vehicles receive tickets, to the point where Ohio jumps from 77,000 or so to 30 million. If we use the outdated statistics which indicated 77,000 entries out of 33 million, the optimizer will likely try to filter this data down early, retrieving only the 77,000 or so entries first and then joining to subsequent tables. In reality, once the query runs, we will quickly (or perhaps slowly, as the case may be) find out that we really need to read approximately 50% of the table's rows, and so there might have been a better strategy for retrieving data. This is where updating statistics becomes important. As the shape of data changes, updating statistics can provide SQL Server relevant information on the current distribution of data. In some cases, outdated statistics might be even worse than no statistics—at least with no statistics, the optimizer can realize its ignorance; with outdated statistics, we might get a false sense of confidence.

Database administrators can manage statistics directly as well as enabling automatic statistics updates for the database. SQL Server's automatic statistics updates are not perfect, but they do provide a safety valve with frequently changing data.

All of this information applies to statistics in general. Now we will move to statistics on external tables.

Statistics on External Tables

When you create an external table using PolyBase, the data lives outside of SQL Server. In spite of that, we can still create statistics on external tables. These statistics are fundamentally the same as statistics on regular tables in terms of how they help the optimizer build superior execution plans, but there are a few differences in how they behave against external tables.

The first key difference is that we cannot automatically create or maintain statistics against external tables. The reasoning behind this is that the PolyBase engine does not have direct knowledge of data changes and—especially with V1 data sources like a Hadoop cluster—external tables can be enormous. In order to create statistics, we will need to pull into SQL Server and subsequently scan some percentage of the external table's data. By default, that percentage is 100%, or a "full scan." We also have the ability to create statistics from a sample of the full table. This is useful when dealing with external tables which contain more data than we have room to hold in SQL Server. The downside to sampling is that the results might not be as accurate as cases in which we perform a full scan. Because the statistics auto-creation process does not know ahead of time how big external tables are (and whether the contents would even fit in tempdb), it leaves to the user the task of creating relevant statistics.

Similarly, SQL Server has no direct way of knowing when rows in an external table change. On regular tables, the database engine can keep track of row insertions, deletions, and modifications and use this information to estimate when it would make sense to update statistics. But for external tables, SQL Server has no mechanism to track these modifications and therefore does not have the information needed to know when it might make sense to update statistics. Therefore, the database engine neither creates nor updates statistics on external tables. Any statistics we want, we will need manually to create and maintain. In the next section, we will see how we can do this using T-SQL.

Managing External Statistics

Creating statistics on external tables uses exactly the same T-SQL as regular tables. Listing 11-2 shows how we can create statistics on an external table, in this case against a data set in Azure Blob Storage. In this example, we will implicitly run a full scan of the data, meaning that we will pull all of the data from Azure Blob Storage into a temporary table on SQL Server, create statistics against that data, and then drop the temporary table.

Caution   I want to reiterate here that creating statistics on an external table means that we need to stream all of our data into a temporary table on our SQL Server instance and then the database engine can create statistics the same way it would for regular tables. If you have 100GB of free disk space and try to pull in a 2TB external table, you cannot create statistics using a full scan of the table; you will run out of disk space before that operation completes. For enormous tables in Hadoop and Azure Blob Storage, we can sample the first X percent of rows, which could be biased if we store all of the data contiguously in one file. For example, if we order the year's data by date in the file, sampling might bias us toward earlier dates and leave the database engine unaware of those later dates because our sampling process never gets that far in the file.

Listing 11-2. Create external statistics based on an implicit full scan

```
CREATE STATISTICS [sNorthCarolinaPopulation_Name] ON [dbo].
[NorthCarolinaPopulation]
(
        [Name]
);
GO
```

This gives us the statistical information in Figure 11-2, which we can see if we execute the command DBCC SHOW_STATISTICS('dbo.NorthCarolinaPopulation', 'sNorthCarolinaPopulation_Year_Name').

	Name	Up...	Rows	Rows Sampled	Steps	Density	Average key length
1	sNorthCarolinaPopulation_Year_Name	J...	13610	13610	8	0.125	19.31962

	All density	Average Length	Columns
1	0.125	4	Year
2	0.0001554726	19.31962	Year, Name

	RANGE_HI_KEY	RANGE_ROWS	EQ_ROWS	DISTINCT_RANGE_ROWS	AVG_RANGE_ROWS
1	2010	0	4083	0	1
2	2011	0	1361	0	1
3	2012	0	1361	0	1
4	2013	0	1361	0	1
5	2014	0	1361	0	1
6	2015	0	1361	0	1
7	2016	0	1361	0	1
8	2017	0	1361	0	1

Figure 11-2. *The output of* DBCC SHOW_STATISTICS *for our external statistics*

We can also use the WITH FULLSCAN parameter to specify that we would like to perform a full scan. If we would prefer instead to create statistics based on a sample of our data, we can do so like in Listing 11-3.

Listing 11-3. Sampling an external table to create statistics

```
CREATE STATISTICS [sNorthCarolinaPopulation_SumLev] ON [dbo].
[NorthCarolinaPopulation]
(
        [SumLev]
) WITH SAMPLE 40 PERCENT;
```

We can additionally create statistics on multiple columns, as we saw in Figure 11-2 with statistics on the Year column and then the Name column.

Updating External Statistics

We know already that we cannot have the SQL Server Database Engine automatically update statistics, so let's try to update external statistics manually. Listing 11-4 shows the command we will run.

Listing 11-4. Updating statistics on an external table—or at least making an attempt

```
UPDATE STATISTICS [dbo].[NorthCarolinaPopulation]
([sNorthCarolinaPopulation_Year_Name]) WITH FULLSCAN;
```

Running this returns the message in Figure 11-3.

```
Started executing query at Line 79
Msg 46519, Level 16, State 21, Line 1
Update Statistics are not supported with external tables.

Total execution time: 00:00:00.001
```

Figure 11-3. *We are not able to update external statistics*

In the event the distribution of your underlying data changes, the only tool at your disposal is to drop and re-create statistics.

Sampling Statistics

Not all external data sources support sampling of statistics. None of the PolyBase V2 sources support sampling. For example, if you attempt to create external statistics with sampling on a table querying SQL Server, you will get the error message in Figure 11-4, indicating that you can only create statistics with full scan for SQL Server external data sources.

```
Started executing query at Line 94
Msg 105071, Level 16, State 1, Line 1
105071;CREATE STATISTICS is only supported with the FULLSCAN option for 'sqlserver' external data sources.
Total execution time: 00:00:00.406
```

Figure 11-4. *Not all data sources support sampled statistics*

You will get the same message with the other V2 sources as well.

The Performance Impact of Statistics

External statistics will not make all queries faster. For example, performing a full scan of an external table by bringing the data into a temporary table and then scanning the temporary table will take the same amount of time regardless of whether the external table has statistics. External statistics can make a difference when they help the optimizer decide whether to push down a predicate or reorder joins to other tables. In order to try out external statistics, we will run the query in Listing 11-5 against an external table with no statistics hosted on Apache Spark.

Listing 11-5. Query parking violations data against Apache Spark

```
SELECT
    p.RegistrationState,
    p.VehicleMake,
    COUNT(1) AS NumberOfRows
FROM dbo.ParkingViolationsSpark p
WHERE
    p.VehicleYear = '2015'
GROUP BY
    p.RegistrationState,
    p.VehicleMake;
```

Before we run the query for real, we will generate an estimated execution plan to figure out how many rows the optimizer thinks we will get back. You can see this in Figure 11-5.

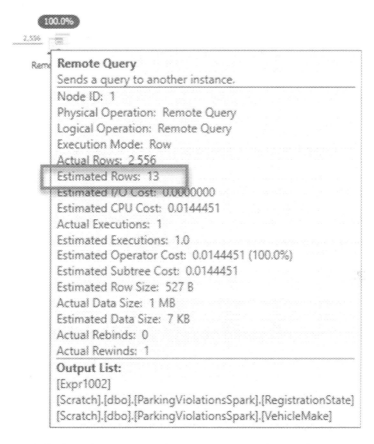

Figure 11-5. *With little information, the optimizer makes its best guess on row counts*

Expecting just 13 rows back, the optimizer decides to push down part of the operation to Spark and complete aggregation in SQL Server. Figure 11-6 shows the distributed request steps for this operation.

step_index	operation_type	location_type	row_count	command
0	RandomIDOperation	Head	-1	TEMP_ID_5
1	OnOperation	Compute	-1	CREATE TABLE [tempdb].[dbo].[TEMP_ID_5
2	OnOperation	Compute	-1	EXEC [tempdb].[sys].[sp_addextendedproperty
3	OnOperation	Compute	-1	UPDATE STATISTICS [tempdb].[dbo].[TEMP
4	OnOperation	Compute	-1	CREATE STATISTICS [partialagg1003] ON [t
5	MultiStreamOperation	Head	-1	NULL
6	ExternalGenericShuffleOperation	DMS	2557	External Shuffle
7	StreamingReturnOperation	DMS	2556	SELECT [T1_1].[RegistrationState] AS [Regis
8	OnOperation	Compute	-1	DROP TABLE [tempdb].[dbo].[TEMP_ID_5]

Figure 11-6. *A set of request steps without good statistics*

In step 7, the streaming operation return step, we aggregate the 2557 results coming back from Spark to get the final 2556 rows.

In Listing 11-6, we will create statistics on year, registration state, and make, which should give the optimizer a better idea of our data needs.

Listing 11-6. Create external statistics on the columns we would like to use

```
CREATE STATISTICS s_ParkingViolationsSpark_VY_RS_VM ON dbo.
ParkingViolationsSpark
(
    VehicleYear,
    RegistrationState,
    VehicleMake
) WITH FULLSCAN;
```

With this new information in hand, our remote query operation has an estimate of 61,570 rows, as we can see in Figure 11-7. This estimate is not great either, but it does give the optimizer an idea that we won't get back just a couple of rows.

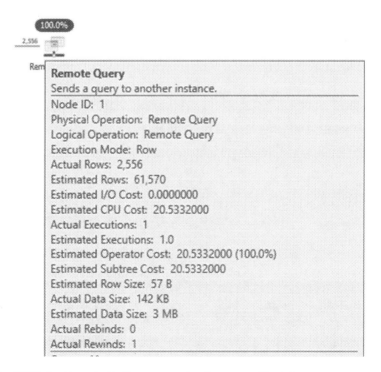

Figure 11-7. *With better statistics, we get a larger estimate*

With a smaller number of expected rows, the optimizer might have decided to avoid pushing down this operation, leading to streaming all of the data from Spark over to SQL Server rather than pushing down the operation. In this case, however, it did not change the final outcome.

Statistics provide the optimizer with additional information to make the best possible decision; execution plans, on the other hand, provide you with the information needed to tune queries.

Tuning Queries with Execution Plans

Reading execution plans is a critical part of query tuning, regardless of whether the query includes external tables. In this section, we will look at how external tables show up in query plans and the information we can glean from graphical execution plans as well as the plan XML.

Reviewing an Execution Plan

The first query we will use to generate an execution plan is in Listing 11-7. It joins the New York City parking violations data set from a remote SQL Server instance to three local tables.

Listing 11-7. A multi-table query which includes one external table

```
SELECT
    pv.RegistrationState,
    pv.VehicleMake,
    COUNT(1) AS NumberOfRows
FROM dbo.ParkingViolationsSQLControl pv
    INNER JOIN dbo.RegistrationState rs
        ON pv.RegistrationState = rs.RegistrationState
    INNER JOIN dbo.RegistrationRegion rr
        ON rs.RegistrationRegion = rr.RegistrationRegion
    INNER JOIN dbo.VehicleYear vy
        ON pv.VehicleYear = vy.VehicleYear
WHERE
    vy.VehicleYear IN ('2005', '2006', '2007')
```

```
    AND rr.RegistrationRegion = 'Midwest'
GROUP BY
    pv.RegistrationState,
    pv.VehicleMake;
GO
```

When running this query, end users are complaining about how slow it is: 11 seconds on my machine. If we execute the query and generate an execution plan, we can see why. Figure 11-8 shows the execution plan as seen from SentryOne Plan Explorer, a free and generally excellent tool for viewing execution plans.

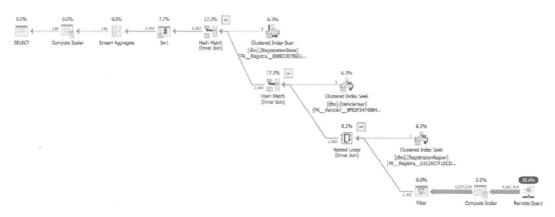

Figure 11-8. *The execution plan as seen from SentryOne Plan Explorer*

We immediately see the cause of the slowdown: our Remote Query operation—that is, retrieving data from an external table—is pulling back 4,237,519 rows, but then we filter down to the 2302 rows we actually need.

SentryOne Plan Explorer is great for figuring out the immediate cause of performance problems—enough so that it is my go-to choice for viewing execution plans and tuning queries—but it will not (as of the time of writing) provide us any additional information about our remote query. If we want to learn more about it, we will need to return to SQL Server Management Studio. Figure 11-9 shows some of the additional information which Management Studio surfaces when you mouse over the Remote Query operator.

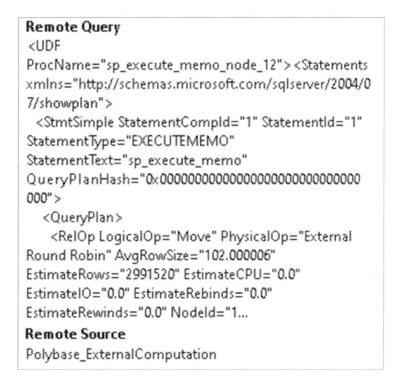

Remote Query
```
<UDF
ProcName="sp_execute_memo_node_12"><Statements
xmlns="http://schemas.microsoft.com/sqlserver/2004/0
7/showplan">
  <StmtSimple StatementCompId="1" StatementId="1"
StatementType="EXECUTEMEMO"
StatementText="sp_execute_memo"
QueryPlanHash="0x000000000000000000000000000000
000">
    <QueryPlan>
      <RelOp LogicalOp="Move" PhysicalOp="External
Round Robin" AvgRowSize="102.000006"
EstimateRows="2991520" EstimateCPU="0.0"
EstimateIO="0.0" EstimateRebinds="0.0"
EstimateRewinds="0.0" NodeId="1...
```
Remote Source
```
Polybase_ExternalComputation
```

Figure 11-9. *Additional properties available to remote queries*

For additional information, we can click the Remote Query operator and press F4 to display properties. The most important of these is the Remote Query property, which you can see in Figure 11-10. This includes some of the information that we can find in `sys.dm_exec_distributed_request_steps` but also includes more information as well.

Parallel	False
Physical Operation	Remote Query
Remote Query	<UDF ProcName="sp_execute_m
Remote Source	Polybase_ExternalComputation

Figure 11-10. *Remote query information in the execution plan*

Copy the text starting with `<UDF ProcName` and paste into a text editor of choice, and you'll see that the remote query is another block of XML. Alternatively, in the accompanying code repository, open up `04 - SQL Remote Query Operator.txt` to follow along.

Inside our block, we have a simple statement (StmtSimple) which contains an external query plan. It shows the three columns we want back, registration state, vehicle make, and vehicle year. To get these, we perform a select with an estimated 2,991,520 rows. In actuality, we know that we retrieved 4,237,519 rows, but either way, the query plan indicates that we want a large number of rows back. After these, we get into a filter operation which indicates why we have a problem. Figure 11-11 shows the filter predicate.

```
<Predicate>
  <ScalarOperator>
    <Logical Operation="AND">
      <ScalarOperator>
        <Compare CompareOp="GE">
          <ScalarOperator>
            <Identifier Table="ParkingViolationsSQLControl">
              <ColumnReference Database="Scratch" Schema="dbo" Table="ParkingViolationsSQLControl" Alias="pv" Column="VehicleYear" />
            </Identifier>
          </ScalarOperator>
          <ScalarOperator>
            <Const ConstValue="2005" />
          </ScalarOperator>
        </Compare>
      </ScalarOperator>
      <ScalarOperator>
        <Compare CompareOp="LE">
          <ScalarOperator>
            <Identifier Table="ParkingViolationsSQLControl">
              <ColumnReference Database="Scratch" Schema="dbo" Table="ParkingViolationsSQLControl" Alias="pv" Column="VehicleYear" />
            </Identifier>
          </ScalarOperator>
          <ScalarOperator>
            <Const ConstValue="2007" />
          </ScalarOperator>
        </Compare>
      </ScalarOperator>
    </Logical>
  </ScalarOperator>
</Predicate>
```

Figure 11-11. *Our predicate includes only vehicle year and not state*

Our query implies a predicate on vehicle state, but does not explicitly state it. We selected the "Midwest" registration region, which includes three states in this sample: Ohio, Indiana, and Wisconsin. Ideally, the optimizer would recognize this and push that filter down to the remote server, but we can see here that it does not.

Our practical conclusion here is to give the optimizer enough information to push down the filter on states. One option is to change AND rr.RegistrationRegion = 'Midwest' to AND pv.RegistrationState IN ('OH', 'WI', 'IN'). This option works if you already know what the states are and can modify your query to support it. If not, you can use dynamic SQL to generate the list of states and concatenate this list into your main query. This is more complicated to write and to maintain but will also allow the optimizer to return results much more quickly. Figure 11-12 shows what we wanted to see, predicates which include registration states.

```
<ScalarOperator>
  <Compare CompareOp="LE">
    <ScalarOperator>
      <Identifier Table="ParkingViolationsSQLControl">
        <ColumnReference Database="Scratch" Schema="dbo" Table="ParkingViolationsSQLControl" Alias="pv" Column="VehicleYear" />
      </Identifier>
    </ScalarOperator>
    <ScalarOperator>
      <Const ConstValue="2007" />
    </ScalarOperator>
  </Compare>
</ScalarOperator>
<ScalarOperator>
  <Logical Operation="OR">
    <ScalarOperator>
      <Compare CompareOp="EQ">
        <ScalarOperator>
          <Identifier Table="ParkingViolationsSQLControl">
            <ColumnReference Database="Scratch" Schema="dbo" Table="ParkingViolationsSQLControl" Alias="pv" Column="RegistrationState" />
          </Identifier>
        </ScalarOperator>
        <ScalarOperator>
          <Const ConstValue="IN" />
        </ScalarOperator>
      </Compare>
    </ScalarOperator>
```

Figure 11-12. *We now have registration state as an input filter*

Now that we have seen the internals for a PolyBase query against an external SQL Server, we can look at an example using MapReduce against a Hadoop cluster.

Reviewing MapReduce Queries

The file 05 - MapReduce Plan file is a saved execution plan of a simple query against Hadoop. Opening this plan in SQL Server Management Studio shows the result, like in Figure 11-13.

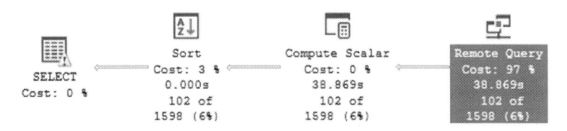

Figure 11-13. *Another execution plan, this time hitting a Hadoop cluster*

Just as in the SQL example, we can review the Remote Query properties to learn more about our operations. This one is a bit more complicated, but we can still read through it. This plan starts with a Project operation, which returns our results, vehicle year, and an aggregate operation. Drilling further through the execution, we can see in Figure 11-14 that the aggregate is a COUNT_BIG operation.

```
<GbAgg IsScalar="false" AggType="Local">
  <GroupBy>
    <ColumnReference Database="Scratch" Schema="dbo" Table="ParkingViolations" Alias="pv" Column="VehicleYear" />
  </GroupBy>
  <AggFunctions>
    <DefinedValue>
      <ColumnReference Column="partialagg1003" />
      <ScalarOperator>
        <Aggregate AggType="COUNT_BIG" Distinct="false">
          <ScalarOperator>
            <Const ConstValue="0" />
          </ScalarOperator>
        </Aggregate>
      </ScalarOperator>
    </DefinedValue>
  </AggFunctions>
</AggFunctions>
```

Figure 11-14. *Our partial aggregation is a count operation*

Included in the code samples are a few other execution plans hitting different data sources, such as Cosmos DB, Spark, and Azure Blob Storage. These are all fairly straightforward query plans to make it easier to follow along.

Conclusion

In this chapter, we looked at using statistics and execution plans for performance tuning when working with PolyBase. Statistics provide the database optimizer with expected cardinality, helping with decisions around predicate pushdown and join order. Then, we looked at execution plans, which give us information in conjunction with the DMVs we saw in Chapter 10.

In the next chapter, we will look at PolyBase in practice, where we put the lessons from the first 11 chapters into good use.

CHAPTER 12

PolyBase in Practice

In this final chapter, we will take what we have learned throughout the book and apply it to three separate scenarios. Each scenario will cover a practical business use case for PolyBase, starting with "cold storage" of data, then moving into replacing a classic Extract-Transform-Load (ETL) process with Extract-Load-Transform (ELT), and finally wrapping up with a pure data virtualization scenario.

Cold Storage

This first scenario will cover "cold storage" of data. Most environments have a few large tables which store a great deal of data. Most of the time, users only need to query the past year, but we need to maintain several years of data for regulatory or archival purposes. This pattern of keeping all of your data in one place certainly works, but it can drive up the cost of storage—needing to buy larger or more drives to store the data—as well as degrading performance as the database engine has to traverse deeper indexes and possibly scan large amounts of data to get expected results.

Another option is to shunt older data off to a separate location. We could take archival data from our main SQL table and put it into another table on the same SQL Server instance, which solves the performance degradation issue. With slower, less expensive disk for that archival data, the total cost of ownership can also be lower. Along these lines, we can also combine SQL Server with Hadoop or Azure Blob Storage and come up with a less expensive solution using PolyBase.

In this scenario, we will take advantage of PolyBase's ability to write data to Azure Blob Storage. We will start with all of our data on SQLWIN10 in a table called `dbo.FireIncidentsLocal`. This table contains calls to the Raleigh, North Carolina fire department over a ten-year period. Listing 12-1 groups rows by year so we can get an idea of the distribution of incidents.

© Kevin Feasel 2020
K. Feasel, *PolyBase Revealed*, https://doi.org/10.1007/978-1-4842-5461-5_12

Listing 12-1. Aggregate fire incidents by year

```
SELECT
    YEAR(fi.dispatch_date_time) AS DispatchYear,
    COUNT(1) AS NumberOfIncidents
FROM dbo.FireIncidentsLocal fi
GROUP BY
    YEAR(fi.dispatch_date_time)
ORDER BY
    DispatchYear ASC;
```

Figure 12-1 shows the results of this query.

	DispatchYear	NumberOfIncidents
1	*NULL*	1454
2	2007	13944
3	2008	14079
4	2009	13165
5	2010	13699
6	2011	14035
7	2012	13635
8	2013	13965
9	2014	14566
10	2015	15476
11	2016	16129
12	2017	18439
13	2018	15137
14	2019	15

Figure 12-1. *Incidents by year. Most of these rows are old*

For our purposes, we would like to archive any dispatches from before 2018, as end users do not typically look at this data. First, we will create an external data source for our Azure Blob Storage container. Listing 12-2 is an example of such an external data source.

Listing 12-2. Create an external data source for Blob Storage data

```
CREATE EXTERNAL DATA SOURCE AzureFireIncidentsBlob WITH
(
    TYPE = HADOOP,
    LOCATION = 'wasbs://visits@cspolybaseblob.blob.core.windows.net',
    CREDENTIAL = AzureStorageCredential
);
```

With this in place, our strategy will be to create one table per year. This way, if somebody does intend to query 2012 data, that person would not need to pull in all of the other years. It also will give us a pattern for shunting data from SQL Server into Azure Blob Storage periodically. Listing 12-3 gives us an example of one of the tables which will remain in SQL Server, holding dispatch data from 2019.

Listing 12-3. Creating fire incident data for 2019. The full script is available in the demo code repository

```
CREATE TABLE [dbo].[FireIncidents2019]
(
    [X] [float] NULL,
    [Y] [float] NULL,
    ...
    [Editor] [nvarchar](50) NULL
) ON [PRIMARY]

ALTER TABLE dbo.FireIncidents2019 ADD CONSTRAINT [CK_FireIncidents2019_
DispatchDateTime] CHECK
(
    dispatch_date_time >= '2019-01-01'
    AND dispatch_date_time < '2020-01-01'
);
```

In addition to creating the table, we will create a check constraint to ensure that we do not accidentally insert data from a different year into this table.

Next, we will need to create an external table for each year. To do this, we will use dynamic SQL; that way we don't need to create by hand 11 separate tables with identical schemas. Listing 12-4 takes us through the process.

Listing 12-4. Create a table for each year

```
DECLARE
    @year INT = 2008,
    @TableName SYSNAME,
    @sql NVARCHAR(MAX);

WHILE (@year < 2018)
BEGIN
    SET @sql = CONCAT(N'DROP EXTERNAL TABLE dbo.FireIncidents', @year);
    EXEC(@sql);
    set @year = @year + 1
END
GO

-- Keep older data in external tables on blob storage.
-- We'll break out by year and include every year
-- from 2017 back to 2008.
DECLARE
    @year INT = 2008,
    @TableName SYSNAME,
    @sql NVARCHAR(MAX);

WHILE (@year < 2018)
BEGIN
    SET @TableName = CONCAT(N'FireIncidents', @year);
    IF (OBJECT_ID(@TableName) IS NULL)
    BEGIN
        SET @sql = REPLACE(N'
    CREATE EXTERNAL TABLE [dbo].[FireIncidents$YEAR]
    (
        [X] [float] NULL,
        [Y] [float] NULL,
        ...
        [Editor] [nvarchar](50) NULL
    )
    WITH
```

```
(
    LOCATION = N"FireIncidents$YEAR/",
    DATA_SOURCE = AzureFireIncidentsBlob,
    FILE_FORMAT = OrcFileFormat,
    REJECT_TYPE = VALUE,
    REJECT_VALUE = 1
);', N'$YEAR', CAST(@year AS NVARCHAR(4)));

    EXEC(@sql);
END

SET @year = @year + 1;
END
GO
```

After running this script, we will have one external table for each year, each pointing to a different folder in Azure Blob Storage and expecting data in ORC format. Once I have the tables created, I can split out the data into each table using simple INSERT statements.

The last step is to replace our dbo.FireIncidentsLocal table with a view which UNION ALLs data from each separate table. In an explicit transaction, we will rename FireIncidentsLocal to FireIncidentsOld and create a new view. Listing 12-5 shows this switch.

Listing 12-5. Create a view to allow existing code to continue working

```
BEGIN TRANSACTION
EXEC sp_rename N'dbo.FireIncidentsLocal', N'FireIncidentsOld';
EXEC(N'
CREATE VIEW dbo.FireIncidentsLocal AS
    SELECT * FROM dbo.FireIncidents2008 WHERE dispatch_date_time >= "2008-
    01-01" AND dispatch_date_time < "2009-01-01"
    UNION ALL
    SELECT * FROM dbo.FireIncidents2009 WHERE dispatch_date_time >= "2009-
    01-01" AND dispatch_date_time < "2010-01-01"
    UNION ALL
    ...
    UNION ALL
```

```
SELECT * FROM dbo.FireIncidents2019 WHERE dispatch_date_time >= "2019-
01-01" AND dispatch_date_time < "2020-01-01"
UNION ALL
SELECT * FROM dbo.FireIncidentsNull WHERE dispatch_date_time IS NULL');
COMMIT
```

The WHERE clauses are critical here because even though we know each table has only one year's worth of data, the database engine has no way of guaranteeing that these conditions will hold. Suppose we run something like the code in Listing 12-6 but against a view which does not contain these WHERE clauses.

Listing 12-6. A simple query which should not hit Azure Blob Storage

```
SELECT
    fil.*
FROM dbo.FireIncidentsLocal fil
WHERE
    fil.dispatch_date_time >= '2018-01-01'
    AND fil.dispatch_date_time < '2019-01-31';
```

Without the explicit filters, we end up with an execution plan which looks like the one in Figure 12-2.

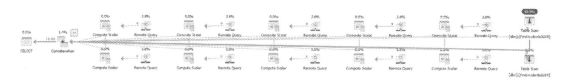

Figure 12-2. *Despite an explicit filter, we still hit every table*

We have to pull in data from every table even though all of our relevant data is stored directly in SQL Server. If we add in the WHERE clauses, we can take advantage of contradiction detection. Then, the execution plan looks like the one in Figure 12-3.

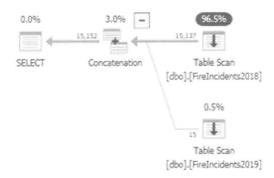

Figure 12-3. *We no longer hit any of the Azure Blob Storage tables*

This looks much better. We can also bring in data from Azure Blob Storage without changing the structure of our query. Listing 12-7 pulls data from both Azure Blob Storage and a local table to give us data from 2017 and 2018.

Listing 12-7. Query data from Azure Blob Storage

```
SELECT
    fil.*
FROM dbo.FireIncidentsLocal fil
WHERE
    fil.dispatch_date_time >= '2017-01-01'
    AND fil.dispatch_date_time < '2018-01-31';
```

This generates the execution plan in Figure 12-4.

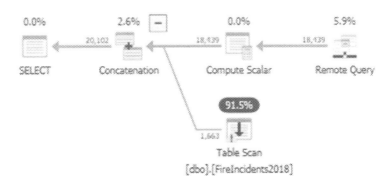

Figure 12-4. *Combining data from local and external tables*

This process lets us retain data off-site in an accessible manner. When we roll over years, we can create an external table, shift data to that external table, and replace the table reference in our `FireIncidentsLocal` view. This strategy also supports adding new years: create a new local table and add it to the view.

Alternate Approaches

There are a few alternative approaches to this strategy. For example, instead of creating a partitioned view, we could simply migrate old data off to Azure Blob Storage and have people directly query external data. This approach does require knowledge of the separate tables, but it also reduces the risk of accidentally hitting every Azure Blob Storage file on a poorly written query. It also works better in cases where you need the data for archival or auditing purposes but expect that people will rarely (if ever) actually look at it.

Another riff on this theme is to store everything in one folder, so instead of partitioning by year, we keep adding to the same external table. The downside to this strategy is that, with Azure Blob Storage, we will need to pull back all of the archival data and that might take a while. If we store the data in HDFS and use a Hadoop cluster to retrieve our data, this strategy makes much more sense, as we can have the Hadoop cluster build a MapReduce operation to retrieve our data.

Replacing ETL Jobs with ELT

Our next PolyBase pattern will replace a set of hypothetical Extract-Transform-Load (ETL) jobs with an Extract-Load-Transform (ELT) approach. Tools like SQL Server Integration Services (SSIS) are intended to retrieve data from a source system (Extract), reshape that data to fit a destination (Transform), and insert the data into the destination (Load). This pattern works well for data warehouses, but as data sets get larger, performing transformations in memory can get expensive. For example, merge joining two unordered data sets in SSIS requires extracting all of the data from both sources, sorting both in memory, and then joining the data together. This can slow down data loads considerably.

An alternative approach to data movement is ELT. In this approach, we first retrieve the data form the source system, and then we land the data in staging tables on our destination. Once we have landed the data, we perform all transformations on our powerful destination server. The ELT strategy also works in scenarios where we wish to defer transformation until a later time, such as landing raw data in a data lake.

Getting on the Bus

For this example, we will use a mock data set which includes school buses in a metropolitan area and expenditures associated with those buses. In the accompanying code for this chapter, there are a number of scripts which create a database named ForensicAccounting and then populate it with several tables. Listing 12-8 gives us an example of the VendorExpenseCategory table.

Listing 12-8. Create a table for expense categories by vendor

```
CREATE TABLE dbo.VendorExpenseCategory
(
    VendorID INT NOT NULL,
    ExpenseCategoryID TINYINT NOT NULL,
    CONSTRAINT [PK_VendorExpenseCategory] PRIMARY KEY CLUSTERED (VendorID,
    ExpenseCategoryID)
);
```

Listing 12-9 shows the LineItem table, which contains line item expenses for our mock transit authority.

Listing 12-9. Create a table containing expense information. Foreign keys have been removed from this script to save space

```
USE [ForensicAccounting]
GO
CREATE TABLE dbo.LineItem
(
    LineItemID INT IDENTITY(1,1) NOT NULL,
    BusID INT NOT NULL,
    VendorID INT NOT NULL,
    ExpenseCategoryID TINYINT NOT NULL,
    EmployeeID INT NOT NULL,
    LineItemDate DATE NOT NULL,
    Amount DECIMAL(13, 2) NOT NULL,
    CONSTRAINT [PK_LineItem] PRIMARY KEY CLUSTERED (LineItemID)
);
GO
```

After running each of the scripts, we will have a transactional database. Suppose we want to migrate this data to a data warehouse, integrate it with additional data sources, and report against that warehouse. In a traditional environment, we would take this ForensicAccounting database, create a series of SQL Server Integration Services packages, and move the data into a database on a separate server. This comes with benefits around auditing and ease of execution—running dtexec against a package is something you can easily automate in a SQL Agent job or scheduled task—but creating all of those packages does come at a development cost. It takes development time to create these packages, and any edit to the source or destination tables might require rebuilding packages and updating metadata. Integration Services is also not the easiest system to debug when things go wrong, so finding a simpler solution which does the job seems like it would be a win. That is where PolyBase steps in.

Note   If you do regularly create SQL Server Integration Services packages, I recommend looking into the Business Intelligence Markup Language, Biml. Biml allows you to write code in a combination of XML and C# to automate SQL Server Integration Services packages, as well as plenty more. You can find more information on Biml at `https://www.varigence.com`.

We can create external tables against this remote ForensicAccounting database from our data warehouse (conveniently located in the PolyBaseRevealed database), one external table per table in our source system. To separate these external tables from our warehouse facts and dimensions, we can create the external tables in a separate schema, such as ELT. Doing so is an indication to developers that this table is meant for data transit rather than direct customer interaction. Creating each ELT table follows the same pattern, so we will look at that pattern in Listing 12-10 using the Employee table as an example.

Listing 12-10.   Create an external table pointing back to the remote ForensicAccounting database

```
CREATE EXTERNAL TABLE ELT.Employee
(
    EmployeeID INT NOT NULL,
    FirstName NVARCHAR(50) NOT NULL,
```

```
    LastName NVARCHAR(50) NOT NULL
)
WITH
(
    LOCATION = 'ForensicAccounting.dbo.Employee',
    DATA_SOURCE = SQLCONTROL
);
```

As an external table, we do not create any constraints and ignore identity values; otherwise, we can use the same column definitions as in our source system. Because the data already exists in a remote SQL Server instance, we do not need to set a rejection threshold—our schemas match, so rejection should not be possible.

Tip   In a realistic data warehousing scenario with dozens of tables, scripting each table out manually can get tedious. It is possible, however, to write a dynamic SQL statement against the `sys.tables` and `sys.columns` system views in the ForensicAccounting database to generate a create statement per table. Doing so is left as an exercise for the reader.

With these external tables in hand, we can easily write T-SQL queries against these tables to reshape them as necessary in order to load dimensions. Listing 12-11 gives us a simple example of joining several external tables together to flatten out a many-to-many relationship.

Listing 12-11. Joining together three virtual tables

```
SELECT
    vec.VendorID,
    v.VendorName,
    vec.ExpenseCategoryID,
    ec.ExpenseCategory
FROM ELT.VendorExpenseCategory vec
    INNER JOIN ELT.Vendor v
        ON vec.VendorID = v.VendorID
    INNER JOIN ELT.ExpenseCategory ec
        ON vec.ExpenseCategoryID = ec.ExpenseCategoryID;
```

Our ETL process now becomes a virtual ELT process: we "land" the data on our local SQL Server instance and then transform it as we merge the results into our existing dimensions and facts.

Alternate Approaches

One alternative approach to the model we developed is to create a set of views on the source system which perform some of the transformations in advance. This could include joining tables together, concatenating columns, grouping and aggregating data, or any other transformations upfront. To do this, we can create a view on the remote ForensicAccounting database, and our external table would reference the view. This strategy makes sense in a few specific cases. First, if you are performing complex filters and aggregations on your data and can afford the load on your source server, creating a view can keep that processing on the source system side instead of bringing rows over to our PolyBaseRevealed database and aggregating on our destination server. Second, if you have a large number of source tables which reduce to a relatively small number of facts and dimensions through joins, it might make sense to create the views on the source system; that way, we need to create and manage a much smaller number of external tables.

An extension to the model we developed, meanwhile, is to use the ELT pattern across several source systems. Not all of the ELT tables need to come from the same source system, after all: we can pull data from a number of source systems and combine them together just as easily as we can from a single system. This leads into our third pattern: data virtualization.

Third-Party Applications and External Tables

One of the benefits of creating external tables to resources like Teradata or Cosmos DB is that we can treat those resources as though they were normal SQL Server tables. Some applications, such as Power BI, have a large number of connectors to different data sources, but not all third-party tools may integrate with all of your external data sources.

Suppose, for example, that Power BI were incapable of connecting to Cosmos DB directly, but we wanted to use data stored in it to populate a Power BI dashboard. In that case, we could create an external table which connects to Cosmos DB and then reference that external table in Power BI. Refer to Chapter 7 for more details on how to create the Volcano external table. Then, in Listing 12-12, we will create a stored procedure which retrieves data by volcano, including coordinates so we can get an accurate location of each volcano on our map.

Listing 12-12. Create a stored procedure which retrieves volcano data from Cosmos DB

```
CREATE OR ALTER PROCEDURE dbo.Volcano_GetVolcanoData
AS
BEGIN
    SELECT *
    INTO #Volcanoes
    FROM dbo.Volcano;

    SELECT
        _id,
        v.VolcanoName,
        v.Country,
        v.Region,
        v.Location_Type AS LocationType,
        STRING_AGG(v.Volcano_Coordinates, ',') AS Coordinates,
        v.Elevation,
        v.Type,
        v.Status,
        v.LastEruption
    FROM #Volcanoes v
    GROUP BY
        _id,
        v.VolcanoName,
        v.Country,
        v.Region,
        v.Location_Type,
        v.Elevation,
        v.Type,
        v.Status,
        v.LastEruption
```

```
ORDER BY
     v.Elevation ASC;
END
```

With this stored procedure in place, we can build a Power BI dashboard which calls the procedure. Figure 12-5 shows what we need to do to call this stored procedure.

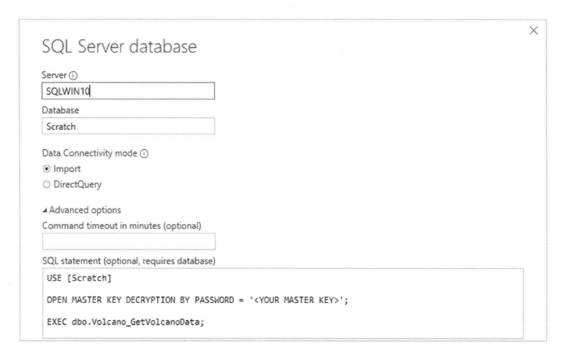

Figure 12-5. *Call a stored procedure which references an external table. If you have followed along with examples in the book, this database will be named PolyBaseRevealed instead of Scratch*

Note that we need an explicit call to use the database in the SQL statement box and then open the master key in Power BI. It is not sufficient to open the master key within the stored procedure itself; you need to open it before calling the procedure.

After loading this data set, we can perform whatever transformations we desire, integrate it with other data sources, and use visuals to tell a story to our users. In any scenario where hitting SQL Server is easier than hitting an external data source, PolyBase can simplify the process of displaying data.

PolyBase external tables can also feed data to features such as SQL Server Machine Learning Services. We might have some data stored in HDFS, other data in Azure Blob Storage, and yet more data in Excel spreadsheets on the network. We could create external tables to make the data accessible within SQL Server and reference these disparate data sources as though they were regular tables in our R and Python scripts.

Generalizing PolyBase Scenarios

Before we wrap up, I would like to provide some general advice on scenarios where PolyBase works well vs. cases where you would be well advised to pick a different technology.

In particular, PolyBase works great when you need to connect to heterogeneous, remote data sources. If you have one SQL Server instance which contains isolated data, PolyBase will not provide any benefit. Furthermore, the greater the number of independent data sources, the better PolyBase looks as an alternative. If you have two SQL Server instances, PolyBase V2 can be an option, but there are several other viable alternatives, replication, linked servers, and ETL with SQL Server Integration Services among them. As you add more sources, the value proposition for PolyBase improves.

Next, PolyBase works well in cases where you need to join data from these heterogeneous, remote sources together in one query. If you have general ledger data in Oracle, customer data in SQL Server, historical sales in Teradata, and product catalog data in Cosmos DB, a technology like PolyBase can simplify life considerably. Without PolyBase, the best alternative route might be to use a general-purpose language like C#, F#, or Java to connect to each of these data sources in turn, retrieve data, and join together data sets in memory; or, create an ETL process and migrate all of the data to a single source. Both of these are viable options, but in a world with PolyBase, this extra work has the potential to become unnecessary.

Another case where PolyBase works great is in high-latency data requests. Data virtualization is by necessity slower than having all of your data in one data source, as we need to take the costs of network transit and suboptimal filters into consideration. When data lives in multiple sources, complex filters across sources will not work, requiring us to pull more rows than we need and filter them in SQL Server. This is going to be slower than simply storing the data in SQL Server to begin with, where the optimizer has more tricks available to it. If your queries need to return in milliseconds, PolyBase will not be a good technology choice; similar to Apache Hadoop and Apache Spark, there is a startup cost to a PolyBase query as the control node needs to coordinate with worker nodes and assign tasks, as well as ensure that worker nodes are available and online. For larger data sets, we tend to amortize this time cost over the length of the query, but for speedy single-row lookups, PolyBase should not be your first choice.

Conclusion

In this chapter, we looked at several practical scenarios around data virtualization using PolyBase. Some of these scenarios can reduce costs. For example, storing archival data in Azure Blob Storage is usually less expensive than purchasing fast disks; and if your ETL processes run on virtual machines in Azure or AWS, using external tables and an ELT model might let you power those machines down and save some licensing and compute costs. Other scenarios, such as exposing external data as SQL Server tables to third-party products, can make your life easier, particularly with older products which were designed prior to the explosion in data storage technologies. These are by no means the only scenarios for which PolyBase is well suited; with your imagination and the skills you have picked up throughout the course of this book, you have what it takes to solve business and technical problems using data virtualization and PolyBase.

Index

A

Apache Hive integration
    database scoped credential, 221
    driver installation, 217, 218
    DSN, 218, 220
    external data source, 221, 222
    external table, 222, 223

Apache Spark integration
    database scoped credential, 210, 211
    driver installation, 206–208
    DSN
        options, 209, 210
        setup, 208, 209
    external data source, 211, 212

Azure blob storage, 152, 163, 233
    account, creation
        access key, 36, 37
        connection string, 38
        cspolybaseblob, 35
        resource group, 34
        zone redundant storage, 36
    concepts, 33
    credentials, 42, 43
    external data sources, 43, 44
    external file format, 45
        creation, 46, 47
        delimited files, 45, 46
        flat file compression, 46
    external tables (*see* External table,
        PolyBase data)

big data systems, 49
    creation, 48
    parameters, 48
    REJECT_VALUE setting, 49, 50
HADOOP, 44
querying external data, 51
    estimation based on population, 54
    quality checks, 52
    retrieving data, 53
    WHERE clause, 52
uploading data, 39, 40

Azure Databricks, 200

Azure Data Factory, 200

Azure portal, 36

Azure SQL Data Warehouse, 236
    CETAS statement, 248, 249
    client IP address, 238
    creation, 236
    CTAS
        results, 244
        status, 243, 244
        table creation, 243
    FIRST_ROW, 247, 248
    functionality, 249
    load data
        data loader login, 239
        external data source, 240
        external file, 240
        external table, 240–242
        scripts, 240

F, G

H